CliffsNotes®

Praxis II®: Education of Exceptional Students (0353, 0382, 0542, 0544) Test Prep

CliffsNotes®

Praxis II®: Education of Exceptional Students (0353, 0382, 0542, 0544) Test Prep

by

Judy L. Paris, M.Ed.

WILEY

Wiley Publishing, Inc.

About the Author

For more than 35 years, Judy has been professionally involved in the field of education as a teacher, special education director, superintendent, consultant, author, and mentor and currently serves as adjunct faculty at several universities. She holds degrees and certifications in special education, early childhood education, elementary education, and educational leadership/administration. It is because of her desire for all children to be allowed to learn through discovery, to be offered a variety of educational opportunities, and to experience the world around them that has led to her newest endeavor of developing a children's museum for her community.

Author's Acknowledgments

Preparing teachers for the future is my passionate mission—to ensure that all children are provided opportunities to learn surrounded by the educators who encourage, support, and guide them in enriching environments. A special thanks to all the teachers I have known who have impacted children every day by simply *caring*. But, truly unforgettable in their compassion and dedication are John, Jocelyn, Dale, Andrea, Dianne, Nancy, Ron, JoLayne, Pat, Cheri, Cindy, Lisa, Trudy, and Donna.

Thank you, Kelly, for the superb guide preparation, and thanks to Greg, for selection of this project.

Publisher's Acknowledgments

Editorial

Project Editor: Kelly D. Henthorne

Acquisitions Editor: Greg Tubach

Production

Proofreader: Toni Settle

Wiley Publishing, Inc. Composition Services

CliffsNotes® Praxis II®: Education of Exceptional Students (0353, 0382, 0542, 0544) Test Prep

Published by:
Wiley Publishing, Inc.
111 River Street
Hoboken, NJ 07030-5774
www.wiley.com

Copyright © 2008 Wiley, Hoboken, NJ

Published by Wiley, Hoboken, NJ
Published simultaneously in Canada

Library of Congress Cataloging-in-Publication data is available from the publisher upon request.

ISBN: 978-0-470-23844-8

WILEY

Table of Contents

PART I: REVIEW OF SPECIFIC EXCEPTIONAL STUDENTS TEST SECTIONS

PART II: PRACTICE TESTS WITH ANSWER EXPLANATIONS

Introduction

The time has arrived to take the final steps in acquiring teacher certification or licensure to become a professional in the field of the education of exceptional students. This career choice requires strong knowledge about special education regulations, instructional theories, techniques, and strategies as well as a general understanding of the characteristics and abilities of all types of exceptional students. Working with these students can be exciting, yet challenging.

Children enter educational institutions with individual strengths and specific needs. It is the educator's role to address both of these areas in a respectful and appropriate manner, which will help the exceptional students adjust to the environment, learn the concepts of the curriculum, and reach the goals they desire to become more independent and capable citizens.

Educators accept a wide range of responsibilities. They must work closely with other educators and parents to manage individualized education programs for students with exceptional needs. They must learn to be creative, flexible, and positive as they work in an array of educational activities and settings with students who possess a wide range of abilities.

Effective educators apply conceptual knowledge to classroom management, behavior interventions, curriculum design, and learning strategies. Educators should stay current on policies and instructional strategies as changes occur often. They may be part of the solution in resolving critical issues that impact exceptional student programs. Joining professional organizations, reading research studies, taking additional university courses, attending professional workshops, and subscribing to professional journals will help guide the educator in having a positive influence on students' futures.

Getting Started

Whether a recent college graduate or an experienced teacher, examinees who adequately prepare to take a Praxis II exam are taking a critical step toward meeting state certification requirements. The final score on these exams will reflect all that was learned from teacher preparation courses and from utilizing teaching practices in classrooms.

Examinees may need to take a Praxis II exam in a specific exceptional student area as well as in the core content area. This guide helps prepare the examinee to take four of the specific Praxis II exams, because it offers study information and practice exams with answer explanations for each of these Praxis II exams. Examinees may also want to review college texts, conduct Internet research, visit the library, and use other school resources to gather further study information for exam preparation.

Remember that the practice exams offered in this guide convey an idea about the format and types of questions on the Praxis II exams and should help examinees learn to pace testing time. The content and questions in the practice exams and on the actual exams may differ in subject matter and difficulty. After completing a practice exam, use the answers and detailed explanations for further study on these specific topics.

Format of the Exam

Each Praxis II exam identified in this guide is composed to help individuals evaluate general knowledge regarding exceptional students as well as some specific specialty areas in the field of special education. Examinees may be required to take more than one Education of Exceptional Students Praxis II exams, according to each state's certification or licensure requirements. Performance on these exams will be determined by what the examinee has gained from coursework, student teaching, or internship experiences.

Each of the exceptional student exams covered in this guide are slightly different in composition. Some of the exams are comprised of a set of *multiple-choice questions;* however, the number of questions varies. Some of the exams are comprised of *constructed-response questions,* which require more thoughtful and detailed narrative answers. All of the questions in the exams are based on a teaching situation, definition, concept, or topic that relates to exceptional students.

There are four general topics related to the education of exceptional students included in this study guide, each with an accompanying practice exam. The specific code and title of each exam are listed here.

#0353 Education of Exceptional Students: Core Content Knowledge

#0382 Education of Exceptional Students: Learning Disabilities

#0542 Education of Exceptional Students: Mild to Moderate Disabilities

#0544 Education of Exceptional Students: Severe to Profound Disabilities

Multiple-Choice Questions

Multiple-choice questions include a statement (*stem*) and four answer choices. The four answer choices that follow the stem are identified by letter selections "A," "B," "C," and "D." Only one of these four choices is the correct answer (*key*). The other three possibilities (*distractors*) may be closely related to the actual answer, but be prepared to select only the best possible answer.

The multiple-choice questions are not designed to trick examinees but instead to test absolute knowledge of the subject material regarding students with exceptional needs. These questions are factually written with all possible answers most likely related to the stem in some way. Think carefully when making final answer selections.

There are five sample multiple-choice questions included for each of the four main topic sections in this guide. These questions are intended for examinees to test general knowledge of the main topics, while also providing an example of the questions that may be included on the actual exam.

In both the practice test and the actual exam, some of the multiple-choice questions may be centered on a case history that resembles a classroom or school situation. Read the case history carefully and think about how these questions should be answered in reference to the information presented. Consider what an educator should do if placed in this particular circumstance, based on federal law and best practices.

Multiple-Choice Strategy

When answering discrete multiple-choice questions, strong reading skills are critical. It is important to read carefully and understand the basic premise of the question, while being confident in the knowledge of the content area being tested. These questions reflect the *best practices* that are reflected in teaching situations and information about students with exceptional needs.

Prior to taking the practice or actual exam, read and then reread each question. Think about the answer before looking at the list of presented possibilities. Check to see whether that answer is listed in the four choices, which will make finding the best answer an easier task. If the information is unknown, look at all of the options and try to use the process of elimination. Remove any choices that seem impossible or not probable, as that may help in selecting an answer from fewer choices.

The several types of *multiple-choice formats* are explained here.

- **Complete the Statement:** This type of question offers information and a partial sentence that must be finished by using one of the presented options. Select the option that best completes the sentence using the facts and data known about exceptional students.

- **Which of the Following:** This type of question asks a short question that must be answered by selecting one of the four options provided. It is a frequently used question type on multiple-choice exams. Read the question carefully and think about all of the options, choosing the one that BEST suits the question posed.

- **Least/Not/Except:** This type of question often requires that an examinee select an answer that is not correct, or less likely to be correct. These questions place a more negative slant on the outcome of an answer, so beware of selecting the appropriate response. It requires that examinees think very carefully about which of the three options are correct answers, so those may be eliminated to determine the incorrect answer, which is what this type of question seeks. Examinees may need to rephrase the question in a positive way in order to select the correct answers.

An example may read: Which of the following is NOT included on a transition plan for older students? Watch for questions that are worded as "Which is the LEAST likely," or "All of the following are _____ except...," or "Which choice is NOT a component of." These questions can be tricky, so beware!

The multiple-choice questions termed with "Least", "Not", or "Except" are included on the Praxis exams, but samples are **not** included in this guide, for fear that examinees may study incorrect information in preparing for the actual exam.

Case-History Strategy

On the practice test and the actual exam, some of the multiple-choice questions are based on a minimum 500-word case history that provides an actual educational situation. Think about how to answer the questions that follow in reference to the case presented and what a teacher should do based on federal law and best practices for exceptional students in that specific circumstance. Read each case carefully and consider all of the information when answering the related questions. Examinees may want to read the questions that follow the case history before reading the scenario to determine what will be asked.

Constructed-Response Questions

A constructed-response question is related to a situation or an educational scenario in which the examinee must construct a written answer. This response may be in the form of a narrative essay, or a series of short answers. Answers must be written in a test answer booklet provided at the testing center. These questions are scored using a preset and standardized grading rubric. Since the questions are not known prior to the exam, examinees must be careful regarding pacing and developing the responses that include all of the necessary information.

The following strategies or steps may be helpful to examinees on the actual Praxis II exams:

1. Read the questions prior to reading the case history.
2. Engage in reading the case history by taking notes and thinking about the questions.
3. Reread each question and review notes and ideas.
4. Outline the constructed response to the questions.
5. Review the case history and the outline for accuracy.
6. Think about the needed details and focus on the accuracy of the answer.
7. Develop a clear and concise narrative response specific to the case.
8. Review the response to be sure all points were answered.

It is very important for the examinee to write complete and concise answers. Simple answers may not receive full credit, so remember to include information for every portion of the question asked. Watch for questions that have more than one part and may require multiple answers.

The three Praxis II exams that include constructed-response questions in this study guide are

Education of Exceptional Students: Learning Disabilities (0382)

Education of Exceptional Students: Mild to Moderate Disabilities (0542)

Education of Exceptional Students: Severe to Profound Disabilities (0544)

Time Frame

The amount of time allowed for taking each Praxis II exam is based on the specific format of the test. For the four exams listed in this book, examinees are allotted 1 hour to answer between 33 and 60 multiple-choice questions and 1 hour to answer 5 constructed-response questions.

Examinees should learn to pace themselves prior to taking the actual test. They should think about the times given as they work on the sample questions and take the practice exams. When taking the actual Praxis II exam, examinees need time to read each question, to consider each answer, and then to review all of the final answers before submitting the test for a score. When writing a constructed-response answer, examinees need time to read the question, consider the formation of a narrative answer, take the time to write the answer, and finally review the answer by reading through it.

When addressing the multiple-choice questions, examinees must think about all the answer possibilities and select the most appropriate response. Examinees who may be unsure of the correct response for a multiple-choice question should answer every question on the exam. No penalty is assessed for guessing an answer on these exams. For the constructed-response questions, examinees should make every attempt to develop a thorough and thoughtful response in a narrative or essay format.

The specific exams, the number of questions, and the time limits are listed here.

Core Content Knowledge	60 Questions	1 hour
Learning Disabilities	33 Questions	1 hour
Mild to Moderate Disabilities	5 Questions	1 hour
Severe to Profound Disabilities	5 Questions	1 hour

Content of the Exam

Each of the specific subject area tests in this guide are comprised of *Content Categories,* and the actual Praxis II exams assess an examinee's understanding of the concepts related to these specific content areas.

The following list includes the broad topics, the number of questions, and the percentage of the final score dedicated to that section for each exam.

- Education of Exceptional Students: Core Content Knowledge
  - Understanding Exceptionalities — 15–18 — 25–30%
  - Legal and Societal Issues — 9–12 — 15–20%
  - Delivery of Services to Students with Disabilities — 30–36 — 50–60%
- Education of Exceptional Students: Learning Disabilities
  - Learner Characteristics; Historical & Professional Context; Definitions — 15 — 25%
  - Delivery of Services to Students — 15 — 25%
  - Problem Solving Exercises — 3 — 50%
- Education of Exceptional Students: Mild to Moderate Disabilities
  - Assessment — 1–2 — 25–42%
  - Curriculum and Instruction — 1–2 — 25–42%
  - Structuring and Managing the Learning Environment — 1–2 — 25–42%
- Education of Exceptional Students: Severe to Profound Disabilities
  - Assessment — 1–2 — 25–42%
  - Curriculum and Instruction — 1–2 — 25–42%
  - Structuring and Managing the Learning Environment — 1–2 — 25–42%

Frequently Asked Questions

Examinees generally have questions prior to taking a Praxis II exam. These questions are presented to help answer the most commonly posed questions. However, if you still need assistance, contact the Educational Testing Services at www.ets.org/praxis or call 800-772-9476.

Q. What is an Education of the Exceptional Student Praxis II exam?

A. The Praxis II exam(s) has been developed by the Educational Testing Service (ETS) to measure an individual's knowledge in specific topics related to the education of exceptional students. It includes general teaching practices that pertain specifically to students with exceptionalities. Many states require these examinations in order to complete the certification or licensure process for professional practice. There may be some professional organizations that also require the completion of a Praxis exam for membership.

Q. How should an examinee register for a Praxis II exam?

A. Most individuals find that registering online is quick and easy. Contact the Educational Testing Services on its website or at the telephone number listed previously. Registration may be completed any time prior to taking the test, but it is recommended that registration be completed 1 to 3 months ahead of the testing date.

Q. What if an examinee misses the registration for the test date preferred?

A. Late registration is allowed, but examinees must hurry to get the correct information and obtain a seat at the testing location. There may be a fee for late registration, so check the specific information about late registrations on the ETS website.

Q. Can the registration date be changed if needed?

A. Contact ETS as soon as possible if a conflict or problem arises with confirmed registration dates. ETS should be able to help with scheduling issues or changes to the existing registration; however, there may be a fee for changes.

Q. Which states require the various Education of Exceptional Students Praxis II exams for certification?

A. Some states use certification tests created in that state or those developed by a testing company and do not require the use of the Praxis II exams. Contact the specific state department of education to find out which exams are required in each state of interest. Ask about the scores that are considered as passing, since the acceptable scores differ in each state. If an examinee has already taken the exam in one state and is moving to another state, he should ask if the current score will be accepted. Most states will allow the transfer of a score as long as it meets the required passing score in that state and the completed exam is recent.

On the ETS website, (www.ets.org/praxis/states) examinees may access each state's requirements by clicking on the name of that state. However, it is highly recommended to speak with someone at the state department of education, since regulations sometimes change before websites do.

Q. How does an examinee know which exam should be taken?

A. Each state mandating Praxis II exams for certification or licensure differs on which particular test is required. Research the testing requirements by contacting the department of education in the particular state. The teacher certification office should have the information needed to select the correct exam or the combination of exams.

Q. What is considered a passing score for teacher certification?

A. The teacher certification office at the department of education in each state should provide the score considered acceptable for teacher certification. Contact this office in the specific state to find out which score is adequate.

Q. When can an examinee expect to receive the scores?

A. The ETS attempts a quick return of scores, so expect the scores to be delivered in 4 to 6 weeks, pending no major holidays. A list of dates is available on the ETS website, as well as an informational guide to interpret the score received.

Q. Are accommodations permissible for an individual with a disability?

A. Yes. Individuals may apply for accommodations if they have a disability or if the primary language is not English. Information on accommodations is available in the Praxis II test registration booklet, or on the ETS website.

Q. What should an examinee plan to bring to the exam site on the date of the test?

A. Examinees will need to consider the following items:

- Identification that includes name, a photo, and signature
- An alternative identification that includes the same (optional but recommended)
- Admission ticket (proof of registration)
- Several pencils (#2) and an eraser
- Ink pens (two or three, blue or black) for narrative answers required on some tests
- Watch (optional but recommended)
- Extra clothing (optional but recommended, as the temperature in the rooms vary)

Q. How can an examinee best prepare to take a Praxis II exam?

A. Using this study guide should help improve the chances of passing a Praxis II exam. Understanding the test format, taking the practice exams, and reviewing the contents of the study guide should reinforce an examinee's knowledge base. Use of the websites in the "Resources" section to seek additional information may also be helpful.

Using this Study Guide

CliffsNotes Praxis II: Education of Exceptional Students (0353, 0382, 0542, 0544) Test Prep includes several supports to help guide examinees.

1. **Introduction sections:** Included for each topic exam are general broadly stated questions about the subject and samples of test questions. Some also include a case history and associated multiple-choice questions or constructed-response questions.

2. **Content area information:** This comprehensive section is to be used for study purposes according to the content categories described on the exam. The headings should guide the examinee in selecting topics to study, as well as help find the areas determined as needing additional review and further study.

3. **Final thoughts and tips:** Test-taking strategies and techniques are provided on how to answer the various types of questions which include multiple-choice and constructed-response questions. Tips for test preparation to achieve exam success are also available.

4. **Resource section:** A list of specific websites, categorized by subject areas are found at the back of the book, as it includes information pertinent to all four exams.

5. **Practice exams:** A sample full-length test is provided for each of the four separate topics in the education of the exceptional student series. These tests are offered as a guide about the content and format of the actual Praxis II exams.

6. **Special Education components:** A detailed explanation on how to develop certain special education documents with examples.

PART I

REVIEW OF SPECIFIC EXCEPTIONAL STUDENTS TEST SECTIONS

Core Content Knowledge (0353)

Learning Disabilities (0382)

Mild to Moderate Disabilities (0542)

Severe to Profound Disabilities (0544)

Final Thoughts and Tips

Core Content Knowledge (0353)

Introduction

Children with exceptional needs differ from the norm and may be either above or below in their ability to perform and achieve. The term **exceptional children** includes all children who have disabilities and those children who are identified as **gifted** *or* **talented.** These exceptional children may require specialized services, programs, modifications, or accommodations to benefit from an education. When identifying exceptional children, it is important to review the 13 categories in federal law for students with disabilities as well as to include the separate category of *giftedness and special talents*.

The history of special education has been an ebb and flow of changes. These changes are due in part to legal actions, political situations, societal attitudes, medical technologies, instructional improvements, and the students themselves. These students may endure complications, experience hardships, and face barriers, but with adequate support, they will achieve academic success and experience positive accomplishments.

Most examinees have completed university studies or work in this field and may have discovered that the information regarding exceptional students is largely complex. Various influences impact student success including the type of exceptionality, the variety of program services, and the variations in curriculum design and instructional strategies. Pertinent information that includes current and contemporary practices about students with exceptional needs, as well as topics concerning special education is summarized in this study guide.

In preparing for the exam, review the basic concepts about exceptionalities: the characteristics, the causes, the prevalence factors, the various definitions, the facts about assessments, the placement steps, the program issues, as well as curriculum and instruction information. Since this guide is not comprehensive of the materials regarding exceptional students, examinees may need additional information, which may be found in college texts, on the Internet, or by speaking with practicing educators. Websites related to exceptional students and special education topics are provided in "Resources" at the back of the book.

This Praxis II exam (0353) is a knowledge-based assessment prepared for individuals who plan to teach in programs for exceptional students in grades preschool through 12. Examinees are allowed 1 hour to complete the 60 multiple-choice questions on the exam that focus on three content categories of core knowledge, which include *Understanding Exceptionalities* (15 to 18 questions, 25 to 30 percent), *Legal and Societal Issues* (9 to 12 questions, 15 to 20 percent), and *Delivery of Services to Students with Disabilities* (30 to 36 questions, 50 to 60 percent).

Two other Praxis II exams, titled Special Education: Knowledge-Based Core Principles (0351) and Special Education: Application of Core Principles across Categories of Disability (0352), are available and may be required for certification in some states. The study guide information for these exams can be found in *CliffsNotes Praxis II: Special Education (0351, 0352, 0690, 0371, 0381, 0321) Test Prep*, developed by the same author and published by Wiley Publishing, Inc.

Note: Only limited information is included in this guide about students who are deaf and/or blind since they are often supported by specialized professionals, and the information is not included on the Praxis II exams. There may, however, be some references to students who are deaf or blind since educators may need to serve students with multiple disabilities.

Content Clusters

This Core Content Knowledge Praxis II exam will consist of multiple-choice questions based on the three specific content categories. The following set of 10 questions, although written in narrative format, should assist examinees in assessing basic knowledge related to the primary topic of students with exceptionalities in preparation to take the core knowledge exam. Examinees may prefer to answer these questions by jotting notes, outlining, or writing in paragraph form to help in their further studies.

1. Explain the primary outcome of each of the following legal cases related to the education of exceptional students: *Rowley, Tatro, Honig, Oberti, Mills,* and *Brown*.

2. Identify the influences of each type of exceptional condition throughout an individual's lifespan.

3. List some of the causes of the various exceptional conditions in the federal law and identify the prevalence rates for each.

4. Describe the historical movements and trends that have affected the connections between exceptional students and the larger society over the past 50 years.

5. Detail the purpose and process of an IEP (individual education plan), an IFSP (individual family service plan), and an ITP (individual transition plan), including the roles of the professionals, students, parents, and community.

6. Define the use of assessments for exceptional students in the following processes: screening, diagnosis, placement, and programming.

7. Provide examples of classroom management techniques and the different ways to structure and maintain effective learning environments for students with varying types of exceptional needs.

8. Analyze the transition process for exceptional students including the formal steps, important components, professional roles, and community involvement.

9. State the responsibilities of teachers, parents, the related service providers, and outside agencies in program implementation for students with exceptional conditions.

10. Name the characteristics of students with exceptional conditions in each of the special education categories (include factors related to culture, gender, socioeconomic status, genetics, language, and cognition skills).

Preview Questions

This section includes five multiple-choice questions that pertain to topics about exceptional students. Examinees should use these questions to self-assess their recall of knowledge and to become familiar with the types of questions included on this Praxis II exam. Although practices may differ across states, consider your answer based on the terminology, policies, best practices, and the law according to IDEIA.

To practice for the Core Content Knowledge Praxis II exam, read each of the multiple-choice questions more than one time to fully understand the main idea. Read the four choices and think about each of the possibilities. Only one of the choices is correct based on the information given, but each of the others may have relevance to the topic. The answers to these questions are provided, and further information is found interspersed in the study guide that follows.

---

1. The case of *Timothy v. Rochester School District* required that without exception, children with disabilities must be

   A. accommodated on all assessments.
   B. placed in general education classes.
   C. expelled for severe discipline actions.
   D. provided a free and appropriate education.

---

2. In this federal law, funds were provided specifically for students considered economically disadvantaged, limited English proficient, or disabled if also identified as gifted or talented.

   A. Carl Perkins

   B. J. B. Hinckley

   C. Jacob K. Javits

   D. Rowley A. Garrett

3. An _____ is mandated for all children who are identified as disabled and require special education services.

   A. individual education plan

   B. inclusive environment project

   C. independent evaluation program

   D. integrated employment preparation

4. A primary factor in the diagnosis of mental retardation is the lack of appropriate

   A. motor planning skills.

   B. adaptive behavior skills.

   C. sensory integration ability.

   D. auditory processing ability.

5. The most restrictive model in the list of continuum of services considered in the *least restrictive environment* provision is

   A. self-contained.

   B. resource room.

   C. residential facility.

   D. general education class.

The correct answers are

1. D. The 1989 court case of *Timothy v. Rochester School District* required that children with disabilities must be provided a free and appropriate education without exception.

2. C. The law titled Jacob K. Javits Gifted and Talented Student Education Act–1988 (PL100-297) provided funds specifically for students considered economically disadvantaged, limited English proficient, or disabled if also identified as gifted or talented.

3. A. An IEP or an individual education plan is mandated for all children who are identified with a disability and require services from the special education program to benefit from an education.

4. B. The area of adaptive behavior skills is critical in the assessment to identify a student with mental retardation.

5. C. Of the choices given, the model that is the most restrictive is the residential facility. It promotes a segregated setting with limited access to the general education curriculum and programs.

Topic Overview

The education of exceptional students includes children with a wide range of abilities that span from one end of the curve to another, but it is difficult to assess the numbers as they constantly change. Approximately 5.5 million children are served with disabilities, and about 2.3 million are provided services as gifted or talented. These numbers are likely under represented. The reasons for these changing statistics include the definitions and procedures used for the identification of students, the numbers of students with multiple conditions, the range of culturally and linguistically diverse students, the movement of students across districts, and the manner in which states promote their programming.

Professional practices, trends, issues, and research all contribute to the richness of the education of exceptional students. The laws and organizations that pertain to exceptional students and the proper terminology used in special education is important to those who work in the field. Study the research-based instructional strategies and teaching methods and seek understanding of the interventions for exceptional students that support academic achievement.

Examinees may find that states differ in definitions, terminology, and practices, but this exam follows the required federally imposed provisions and best practices in the field. When examinees are ready to teach in a certain state, they should check with the school district or state department of education on the appropriate terminology and practices.

Note: The category of Gifted and Talented (G/T) is NOT a category in special education under the federal law; however, it is considered a category of exceptional students in the public schools, and these students do receive specialized services according to the particular state or district of residence. Therefore, the G/T students are represented throughout the core knowledge section of this study guide. When the terms *disability* or *students with disabilities* are used, they indicate reference to the categories defined in the federal special education law for specific disability conditions. When the terms *exceptional students* or *students with exceptional needs* are used, they refer to those disability categories in the federal special education law and include students identified as *gifted or talented*. In some states, G/T students may be served through the district or regional special education department.

Understanding Exceptionalities

Public schools are required to provide an essential menu of services for students who exhibit exceptional needs. These children may qualify for special education, as a gifted/talented student, or as a culturally or linguistically diverse student. In order to accommodate the varieties of exceptional needs that students possess, many professionals are involved in the programs to serve these children. Not all schools are able to provide all services, so they must be creative and flexible in the design and implementation of the programs for these children.

Understanding exceptional students is complex and requires a background in special education and knowledge of human development. A disability, or an exceptionality, involves not just the characteristics of the individual, but the attitude, the culture, the behavior, and the needs that each student emanates. Diversity is a critical element of working with exceptional students as every one is very different.

Human Development and Behavior

Educators working with exceptional students must be familiar with the typical patterns of growth and development in all domains of learning. Knowing these stages helps in understanding the delays children with exceptional conditions exhibit. Examinees may download a copy of a growth and development chart from the Internet or obtain one at the local health department to use for further study.

Following is a brief description of each area of development.

Social-Emotional Development and Behavior

The social-emotional area of development is a primary area of focus for students, as it is so important to have "a sense of self." When students have developed a set of learned skills in the social-emotional domain, they can build upon their self-concept, self-esteem, self-confidence, and self-competence. Social-emotional development has been influenced by the work of Maslow (Humanism), Skinner (Behaviorism), Erikson (Psychosocial), Bandura (Social Learning), Gardner (Multiple Intelligences), Kohlberg (Moral Reasoning), and Freud (Psychoanalytical).

Environment has tremendous impact on social-emotional development. Children have the opportunity to bond with early caregivers as they depend on them to ensure that basic needs are met. Through this process, parents, gender, siblings, and individual temperament are all factors in how well a student will develop in this domain. Children gain social skills through interactive experiences and by engaging in relationships and social situations.

Communication, language, and cognition are very important to the proper growth of this area. Communication impacts the child's ability to function with peers and affects the social-emotional status. When a child develops typically in the cognitive and language domains, she begins to understand, which develops emotional competence and expands upon social skills. Having positive social interactions and using effective communication skills allow the child to exhibit appropriate social behaviors.

Language Development and Behavior

Communication and language are of great importance throughout our lives, and it is from the everyday experiences that language becomes meaningful. Language affects reading, listening, writing, all academic subject areas and social relationships. Key components to a student's success in academic areas are significantly tied to communication, language, speech, and literacy.

Learning vocabulary, utilizing structures, and using correct patterns are important, but also knowing how to make word connections, use gestures, observe body movements, and figure out facial expressions are critical to using and understanding language. Bilingual and second language learners often demonstrate additional issues that cause delays in this area.

The following is a list of important terms related to the language domain.

- **Language:** The systematic use of sounds, signs, or written symbols for the purpose of communication or expression
- **Receptive language:** Ability to understand and comprehend information that is presented
- **Expressive language:** Ability to communicate thoughts, feelings, and ideas through words, gestures, sign systems, assistive devices, and so on
- **Articulation:** Using movements of the mouth area to make speech sounds
- **Pragmatics:** Knowledge of successful and appropriate language use, such as in conversation
- **Semantics:** The meaning that language communicates; it governs vocabulary development
- **Syntax:** A system of combining words into sentences with rules that govern how words work together in phrases, clauses, and sentences

Cognition

Mental skill development (cognition) focuses on thinking and reasoning with specific clusters that are important in all aspects of learning. These clusters of mental skills include remembering, using abstractions, paying attention, problem-solving, making decisions, labeling and naming, organizing ideas, conceptual development, knowledge and recognition, developing rules and generalizations, reflecting on judgments and evaluations, understanding cause-and-effect relationships, and drawing inferences and understanding perceptions. The cognitive domain, which affects all areas of development, is the most significant domain, and can transform, through maturity, practice, and normal aging.

Several theorists have influenced the perceptions about the cognitive domain. Some of the more familiar include Watson/Skinner (Behavioral), Piaget (Cognitive), Vygotsky (Socio-Cultural), and Gardner (Multiple Intelligences).

Physical Development

Physical development is the first area of growth and learning that a child experiences. Children are capable of collecting enormous amounts of information through the motor domain and storing the data in their brains for later use. Physical development includes skills related to gross motor, fine motor, sensory-integration, and perceptual motor development, which are described here.

- **Gross motor:** Large muscle movement such as in the torso, neck, arms, legs
- **Fine motor:** Small muscle movement of the hands, fingers, feet, toes, face
- **Sensory-integration:** Use of sensory information such as tactile, vestibular, and proprioceptive
- **Perceptual motor:** How muscles coordinate movements with the information received through the environment by the senses

The theories that impact this area of development are those of Gesell, Piaget, Ayres, and Kephart.

Adaptive Behavior

Adaptive behaviors are a composite of abilities based on a child's age and the cultural mores of the family. Adaptive behaviors are normally acquired during daily routines and activities in the early years, and acquisition often depends on the family involvement. Adaptive behaviors include self-help skills, such as feeding, dressing, and toileting. A child who can master these competencies will build upon his self-esteem and learn to function more independently.

Characteristics of Students with Disabilities

Students with disabilities exhibit their own very special qualities and unique characteristics. They should be considered individuals first, with traits specific to the disability second. The list that follows briefly explains the basic, stereotypical characteristics of each type of exceptionality with the more specific characteristics related to a certain disability listed in, "Types of Exceptionalities."

- **Medical/Physical:** Includes problems related to diseases, illnesses, trauma, genetics, fine and gross motor, sensory input, and sensory perception.
- **Educational:** Includes cognitive and meta-cognitive deficits, low academic achievement, poor memory, attention problems, hyperactivity, and perceptual disorders.
- **Social:** Includes affective behaviors, poor social skills, poor self-concept, poor motivation, and debilitating mood states.
- **Psychological:** Includes various behaviors, adaptive behavior deficits, disruptive behaviors, and withdrawal.

Types of Exceptionalities

The following is a list of disability categories included under federal law and a brief summary of the typical characteristics for the major conditions. (Not included on this list are the categories of Deaf-Blindness, Multiple Disabilities, and Developmental Delays.)

- **Autism:** Communication and language deficits, impaired social relationships often interacting with objects and people in unusual manners, exhibition of difficult behaviors, and demonstration of limited intellectual functioning and atypical reactions to sensory stimuli.
- **Emotional Disturbance/Behavioral Disorder:** Exhibits inappropriate internalizing and externalizing behaviors, atypical emotions, and disruptive behaviors and lacks the skills for developing positive relationships
- **Hearing Impairment:** Difficulties processing linguistic information and using spoken language to communicate, problems with social relationships, deficits in emotional maturity, and delays in academics
- **Mental Retardation:** Deficits in adaptive behaviors, problems with learning related to cognition, difficulties with memory, issues with problem solving, delays in social skills, difficulties generalizing skills, and attention problems
- **Orthopedic Impairment:** Physical problems such as cerebral palsy, muscular dystrophy, and spina bifida, possibly requiring adaptations with devices and equipment.
- **Other Health Impairment:** Conditions of medical problems with limited strength, vitality, and alertness, such as diabetes, epilepsy, attention deficits, and disease.
- **Specific Learning Disability:** Achievement is not commensurate with abilities and demonstrates difficulties with listening, reasoning, memory, attention, social skills, perception, and processing information, which may emerge with problems in reading, written language, math, and behavior.
- **Speech/Language Impairment:** Difficulties using expressive and receptive language, delays in pragmatics and problems with fluency, voice, and articulation.
- **Traumatic Brain Injury:** Difficulties in the areas of cognition, memory, attention, judgment, and problem solving, as well as physical and sensory changes, social, behavioral, or emotional problems.
- **Visual Impairment:** Problems with developing language concepts, impaired motor development and mobility, lack of social adjustment skills, and problematic relationship interactions

Characteristics of Gifted or Talented Students

Individuals in this exceptional student category possess a wide-range of levels, abilities, talents, and traits and include those students also affected by a cultural, a linguistic, or a disabling condition. Any individual may be considered G/T and require specialized assistance in school to benefit from an education. Some of the characteristics these students may demonstrate include high verbal abilities, intellectual curiosity, the ability to make sound decisions and solve difficult problems, perfectionism, intuitiveness, a need for mental stimulation, difficulty conforming, possessing early moral or existential conscience, and introversion.

Basic Concepts

To obtain appropriate services, children who differ from the norm, physically, intellectually, or behaviorally, must be identified under a category of special education or as an exceptional child. Children are eligible for services only if the condition has a major impact on learning and a special program is necessary to benefit from an education. Categories of exceptionalities are defined under federal law.

Definitions and Classifications

Although debates are prevalent regarding definitions of exceptionalities, children must be identified with a specific label through a comprehensive assessment process and determined eligible for services. Although federal law provides general categories for exceptionalities, each state may develop a precise label based on the interpretation of the law.

The following list includes the 12 disability categories suggested in federal law for students, 6 through 21 years, along with a summary of the definitions found in the federal law.

Autism: A syndrome related to neurological function that is evidenced by deficits in social interactions, communications, and patterns of behavior; associated with **pervasive developmental disorder** (PDD), more currently referred to as **autism spectrum disorders** (ASD); various disorders in this group are differentiated by age of onset and severity of symptoms.

Deaf-Blindness: Includes the combination of both auditory and visual disabilities that are the cause of severe communication deficits and other learning problems; individual may need a combination of supplementary assistance.

Emotional Disturbance/Behavioral Disorder: This category refers to conditions that exhibit two or more of the following: an inability to learn, an inability to maintain relationships, or the exhibition of inappropriate behaviors, pervasive moods, or a tendency to develop physical symptoms or fears.

Hearing Impairment: A condition that may adversely affect the educational performance of students and includes deafness and hard of hearing.

Mental Retardation: Defines an individual with significant subaverage general intellectual functioning concurrently with deficits in adaptive behavior manifesting during the developmental period and adversely affecting performance.

Multiple Disabilities: A combination of concomitant impairments (mental retardation–vision impairment, learning disability–physical impairment, traumatic brain injury–hearing impairment, and so on) that causes severe educational conditions that cannot be accommodated in special education programs for only one disability.

Orthopedic Impairment: A physical impairment, caused by such conditions as genetic anomalies, diseases, and trauma, which adversely affect a student's educational performance.

Other Health Impairment: Related to diseases or chronic health conditions a student with limited strength, vitality, or alertness that adversely affects educational performance.

Specific Learning Disability: This refers to a disorder in one or more of the basic psychological processes involved in understanding or in using language and may manifest itself in an imperfect ability to listen, think, speak, read, write, spell, or do math.

Speech/Language Impairment: Communication disorders that affect the educational performance in an adverse manner, including stuttering, impaired articulation, language impairments, or voice impairments.

Traumatic Brain Injury: An acquired injury to the brain caused by external physical force that results in total or partial functional disability or psychosocial impairments that adversely affects educational performance and does not include brain injuries that are congenital, generative, or birth induced.

Visual Impairment: Includes any impairment of vision (totally blind, functionally blind, and low vision) that, even with correction, adversely affects a student's educational performance.

Another category of exceptional students not included under IDEIA is:

Gifted/Talented (G/T): Although students who are identified as gifted or talented are not included in the special education law, they are considered students with exceptional needs under a federal definition and are provided services accordingly in most states. This category includes students with high performance or abilities in general intellect, specific academic aptitude, creative or productive thinking, leadership abilities, visual or performing arts achievements, and psychomotor abilities. In 1992 the federal definition promoted the identification of students to not be based solely on an IQ score but also on the student's performance.

Incidence/Prevalence

There has been some difficulty in determining the actual incidence/prevalence rates across the nation for specific categories of exceptional children as states differ in the established criteria required for students to be considered for these programs. Even school districts in the same state can establish varying levels of qualifications and accept certain components of definitions, as long as each district and state follow the basic premise of the federal laws regarding students with exceptional needs.

This section shows by division of categories for exceptional students the rates of incidence/prevalence based on those reported to the United States Department of Education (USDOE).

Autism (A): The most rapidly increasing category, this condition affects boys four times as often as girls. In the past 10 years, it is estimated that the numbers of children served has increased by more than four times the previous rates with 20 to 60 children per 10,000 being affected.

Communication Disorder: The second largest category, it is estimated that between 18 and 20 percent of children in special education programs receive communication-related services, although some estimate the numbers at 50 percent. The categories of mental retardation, learning disability, hearing impairment, autism, and others may include significant numbers of students who qualify for speech and language services. Speech and language impairments are more common among male students, with most of those served being in preschool and early elementary programs.

Emotional Disturbance/Behavioral Disorder (ED/BD): Estimates of 33 percent of the school population are regarded as having emotional and behavioral problems, with about 10 percent requiring specific assistance and about 3 percent identified with problems significant enough to require direct special education services. The differences in the definitions and identification requirements across the country cause the numbers to vary. As the fourth largest category, the majority of the children served are boys, but recent estimates show that just as many girls have ED/BD problems requiring special education.

Gifted/Talented (G/T): Students who fall in an intelligence range that is two standard deviations above the norm may fall in the population that is 3 to 5 percent of all school-age students. However, if the G/T category includes students also considered *highly talented,* the rates surge to 10 to 15 percent. Under the exceptional student categories, G/T ranks as the second largest group receiving services, although professionals believe this category is under identified and underserved.

Hearing Impairment (HI): In 2004, the USDOE reported that about 1.2 percent of the school-age children received special education services under the category of hearing impairment with about 0.1 percent of those students placed in residential schools. This category may be under reported because many deaf and hard of hearing children are also identified with other disabling conditions that may include learning disability, emotional disorder, mental retardation, vision impairment, or speech disorders. There seems to be an even division of children who are deaf and those who are hard of hearing.

Learning Disability (LD): This is the largest category served, estimated at about 3 million students each year, which represents about 50 percent of the school-age population. These numbers have multiplied greatly over the last few years, which may be a result of the definition changes and over representation of minority groups.

Mental Retardation (MR): The reported calculations may be difficult to assess accurately, due to the varying attitudes across the states to correctly identify and service those students who qualify under the mild mental retardation criteria. Additionally, some students with mild mental retardation may be provided regular education services and are not reported under this category. The current reporting numbers are about 10 percent of the special education population or 1 percent of the school-age population making this category the third largest.

On a historical basis, the federal numbers reflected for mental retardation were based on the intelligence quotient (IQ) scores, so it was estimated that about 3 percent of the school age population would be expected to be identified as mentally retarded. If the adaptive behavior function is also considered, these estimates fall between 0.8 and 1.3 percent of the population.

Other Health Impaired or Physical Disability (OHI): Together, these categories support about 8 to 9 percent of the special education population receiving services in schools. There is an estimate of about 20 percent of the total school-age population affected by chronic medical conditions, but who may not receive special education services since their condition does not adversely affect their educational performance.

Multiple Disabilities (MD) (mild, moderate, profound and severe): There is no specific definition to base this category, but most professionals consider students who perform in the lowest one percent of the school population may be severely multiply disabled. Children who are served in this category exhibit two or more conditions of disability, with one being a category of sensory impairment.

Traumatic Brain Injury (TBI): It has been reported that the most commonly acquired disability in children is a traumatic brain injury. Although injuries to the head are very common among children, very few receive special education services under this category of TBI. This may be due to the brain's recovery and natural ability to compensate or because the injuries occurring are primarily mild and have no adverse effects on educational performance. Most children with brain injuries are served under other categories in special education (MR, LD, ED/BD, and so on).

Vision Impairment (VI): A low incidence disability, vision impairment accounts for about 0.4 percent of children, and there are very few children served under this category alone. Most students labeled as VI receive services under other categories and may be categorized with a multiple disability.

Causation/Prevention

There are thousands of known causes for conditions of disability, and some may influence the development of several different disabilities, but sometimes the cause is unknown. Common causes related to a specific disability are listed here.

- **Autism:** Not a specific known cause, but may be related to neurobiological conditions, abnormal brain development, genetics, multiple biological causes, and environmental factors.
- **Emotional Disturbance/Behavioral Disorder:** Two major areas may contribute to these disorders: biological factors (brain disorders, genetics, temperament) and environmental factors (home, community, school).
- **Hearing Impairment:** Many causes, but the more common are genetic factors, illness, prematurity, disease, noise-induced.
- **Mental Retardation:** Causes classified as either biomedical, environmental, or unknown and that result from factors that occur in one of three stages: prenatal, perinatal, or postnatal.
- **Orthopedic Impairment:** Primarily related to illness, disease, trauma, accident, or injury.
- **Other Health Impairment:** Primarily related to illness, disease, trauma, accident, or injury.
- **Specific Learning Disability:** Cause is often unknown; however, the four most prevalent known causes are brain damage, heredity, biochemical imbalance, and environmental.
- **Speech/Language Impairment:** Many possible causes, most likely attributed to damage or dysfunction of a specific part of the body, environmental factors, cognitive impairments, hearing loss, brain injury, or disease.

- **Traumatic Brain Injury:** Primarily related to illness, disease, trauma, accident, or injury.
- **Visual Impairment:** Damages or changes in the optical, muscular, or nerve system, which may be related to diseases, trauma, malnutrition, or genetics.

Disability conditions may result from unknown causes, and some may remain lifelong problems. With the improvements available to the health of individuals, some disabilities are preventable through the following:

- Proper and early medical care
- Appropriate mother and child nutrition
- Advances in medical treatments
- Genetic counseling for families
- Testing such as a PKU or amniocentesis
- Environmental improvements
- Early intervention programs
- Parent training programs
- Elimination of childhood diseases, traumas, and accidents
- Availability of vaccinations and immunizations

Behaviors

The varieties of behaviors that children display are unlimited and may be specifically related to a type of disability or to a particular group of students. Managing these behaviors can be complex, so using methods and strategies that are particular to an exceptionality group may be beneficial. Those tips would be described in specific materials about certain conditions.

The following list provides terms and definitions related to behavior interventions.

- **Duration:** The measure of the length of time a student engages in a particular behavior.
- **Degree of severity:** The measure of how problematic or complicated a particular behavior is.
- **Extinction:** A reinforcement for a previously reinforced behavior is withheld, so the behavior will decrease until it no longer exists.
- **Frequency:** The amount of time (how often) that a behavior reoccurs.
- **Intensity:** The degree to which a behavior is repeated.
- **maintenance:** The extent that a previously learned behavior continues after the intervention to support it has been ended.

Multiple Exceptionalities

Multiple conditions can concomitantly exist in students. According to the federal law, a multiple disability is defined as the presence of more than one impairment that causes severe educational problems where the student cannot be completely serviced or accommodated in a program for just one condition. Some of the more complicated multiple combinations are deaf-blindness, gifted-learning disabled, and mental retardation–emotional disturbance. Many of these individuals with multiple exceptionalities require a multitude of services based on the student's specific and unique characteristics as well as the current functioning level.

Students with multiple exceptionalities or severe disabilities may demonstrate slow learning rates, poor generalization of skills, delays in language and physical development, deficits in adaptive behaviors, demonstration of inappropriate or challenging behaviors, and deficits in social-emotional development.

Life Span Influences

Attitudes and laws have changed since the mid-1950s in favor of more inclusive involvement in communities for adults with exceptional needs. These individuals live outside of institutions in independent housing, in group homes, and in assisted-care centers while working in integrated community settings.

There are still societal problems that individuals with exceptional needs face today. Unfortunately, it is the social-emotional areas that continue to have a negative impact on adults with exceptional needs. Many of these adults find it difficult to establish and maintain social friendships and work focused relationships.

These individuals are entitled to the same opportunities to participate in the living, working, and recreational activities of the community that other typical adults partake ("quality of life issues"). Planning and preparing for proper transitions and transition programs include instruction in self-advocacy, problem solving, self-care, employment skills, community development, behavior management, leisure activities, and independent living. It is the specific characteristics of the exceptional individual that affect the long-term goals and long-range plans as well as the adjustment into the local society across the life span.

Legal and Societal Issues

Litigation and legislation have been the key factors in identifying the services and programs for students with disabilities, as well as other groups with exceptional needs. Laws and regulations have been influenced by judicial decisions handed down as a result of legal cases.

Federal Laws

Special education programs have a long history dating as far back as the early 1950s, but the primary impetus for the development of the special education laws began during the peak of the civil rights movement. In 1954, the decision from the *Brown v. Board of Education* case caused a movement in the education field that has been unequaled. This influence then focused on children with disabilities, resulting in a series of laws to protect students with exceptional needs. The passage of the Education for All Handicapped Children Act (EAHCA, also EHA) in 1975 (PL94-142) is considered landmark legislation and signifies a remarkable change in how the needs of exceptional students were addressed in public school settings (free and appropriate public education). The current federal law for special education defines *children with disabilities* and the services they are entitled to receive.

Since EHA, the federal law has been amended and reauthorized five times.

> 1983—Amendments to the Education of the Handicapped Act
>
> 1986—Education for the Handicapped Act Amendments
>
> 1990—Individuals with Disabilities Education Act Amendments (PL101-476)
>
> 1997—Individuals with Disabilities Education Act (IDEA) (PL105-17)
>
> 2004—Individuals with Disabilities Education Improvement Act (IDEIA), also known as IDEA-2004 (PL108-446)

The advocacy actions surrounding the rights of individuals with disabilities and the collaborative efforts of professionals, parents, political figures, and community members were instrumental in making changes in the law. The federal special education law is designed for the provision of educational rights to children with disabilities and their parents in accessing services in public schools. States may individually and appropriately interpret this law, but all states must comply with the basic provisions if they accept federal funding to the schools.

The purpose of IDEIA is identified in four key statements:

1. To ensure all children with disabilities are guaranteed a free and appropriate public education (FAPE)
2. To assist all states in establishing early intervention services for infants and toddlers with disabilities

3. To ensure that educators and parents have the necessary tools to improve the education for all children with disabilities

4. To assess the effectiveness of the education for children with disabilities

IDEIA (Individuals with Disabilities Education Improvement Act)

Also known as IDEA-2004, IDEIA extends the right to an education for all students with disabilities in the public school system across the country, not including those identified as gifted or talented. There are six major principles:

1. Zero reject (**Child Find** system): No child with a disability may be excluded from a public education.

2. Protection in the evaluation process (**non-bias testing**): Nondiscriminatory identification and evaluation must be conducted, which includes procedures followed and tools utilized.

3. **Free and Appropriate Public Education (FAPE):** The education of students with disabilities must be at the public expense based on the development of an **IEP (Individualized Education Program**) that includes **related services.**

4. **Least Restrictive Environment (LRE):** Children with disabilities must be educated with non-disabled children to the maximum extent appropriate and a continuum of placement services must be imposed.

5. **Due Process Procedures (Procedural Safeguards):** Requires parent and student rights regarding assessment, placement, and service implementation of education program be instituted.

6. Parent and Student Participation (**Shared Decision-Making**): Parents and students (as appropriate) must be included in the special education process helping to make plans and decisions.

Other provisions stressed for students with disabilities include the following:

- Extension of services to children ages 5 and under
- Access and participation in the general education curriculum
- Participation in and accommodations for district and statewide high-stakes tests
- Related services and Assistive Technology (**AT**) to access and benefit from special education
- Federal funding to states to support special education programs
- Tuition reimbursement costs for private school placement

When IDEA-1997 was reauthorized to IDEIA (IDEA-2004), all of the major provisions and components were still intact, but some changes were added, and the impact they may have on school programs for exceptional children remains to be seen. The following were included:

- Paperwork reduction
- Short-term objectives and benchmarks eliminated from IEPs
- Implementation of comprehensive and multiyear (3-year) IEPs
- Focus on **highly qualified** teachers to align IDEA with NCLB

Specific under the federal special education law are two main sections that pertain to students with exceptional needs. Schools and states must utilize them to provide the most appropriate services to children with special needs. These components, Part B and Part C, are outlined here to demonstrate the similarities and the differences.

IDEIA-Part B focuses on the following:

- Students with disabilities ages 3 through age 21
- Educational programs in public schools settings
- Educators, staff, and other school professionals providing services
- Yearly evaluations and an annual review of a student's program
- Participation in transition services from Part C
- An IEP that describes the individual student's needs

IDEIA-Part C focuses on the following:

- Students with disabilities ages birth to 3 years
- Family and child services in natural environments, such as the home
- A service or case manager to coordinate the necessary services
- Evaluations two times per year with regular reviews
- Participation in the transition services to Part B
- An IFSP to describe the child's and family's needs

Students identified in public schools as gifted or talented (G/T) also need a form of special education; however, they are no longer included in the federal special education laws. Separate laws, funding, and requirements are established for this population and are further explained in the following section. Students who are G/T require modifications and accommodations to the general education curriculum, as well as for instructional activities. It is helpful for this population to be served by persons specially trained to support their unique needs.

Other Federal Laws

Section 504 (Rehabilitation Act of 1973): Extends civil rights to individuals with disabilities focused on prohibiting discrimination in education, employment, and other community settings; requiring compliance by any recipient of federal funds even though these requirements are not monetarily supported by the federal government.

ADA (Americans with Disabilities Act–1990): Based on Section 504, it extends civil rights to individuals with disabilities in private sector employment, public services, public accommodations, transportation, and telecommunications. These employment and public service entities must accommodate persons with disabilities in an appropriate and nondiscriminatory manner.

NCLB (No Child Left Behind-2001), the Reauthorization of the Elementary and Secondary Education Act): Primary goal is for *all* children to be proficient in *all* subject matter by 2014 and imposes a requirement that *all* teachers must be "highly qualified." There are four key principles:

- Stronger accountability through district and state testing for every student
- Increased flexibility to schools for use of federal funds
- Additional options for parents regarding the education of their child
- Focus on curriculum and instructional methods with scientifically researched and proven effects

FERPA (Family Educational Rights and Privacy Act): Although not a specific special education law, it affects schools, education programs, and those persons associated with students who have exceptional needs. This federal law protects the privacy of all students' educational records and applies to any and all schools receiving federal funds.

Gifted and Talented Children's Education Act-1978 (PL95-561): Allows for funding to support the exceptional needs of students in the areas of identification, education, and programming.

Education Consolidation Act-1982: Merged the federal Office of Gifted and Talented with other federal programs and states received block grants to determine which programs and students to support.

Jacob K. Javits Gifted and Talented Student Education Act-1988 (PL100-297): Federal funds provided specifically to students who are considered economically disadvantaged, who demonstrate limited English proficiency or have a disability while also identified as gifted or talented.

Legal Issues

There have been a multitude of issues raised related to special education programs, children with disabilities, and the services provided in school systems. These issues have often been taken through the judicial system to be resolved as they typify difficulty for parents and school personnel to debate and settle. These issues can be packed with emotional and philosophical ideals. The decisions made by the courts have proven to be critical indicators of the interpretations and changes that have occurred in the special education laws as they have been continually amended over the years.

The interpretations of the provisions that are outlined in IDEIA remain with the powers of the individual states. The interpretations and decisions that occur in one region of the United States may not be the same as those in another region. Decisions finalized at the Supreme Court level produce a different standard of expectations regarding compliance in all states. Some of the specific areas that are repeatedly tried in the courts include:

- Assessment and identification
- Free and appropriate education (FAPE) opportunities
- Least restrictive environment (LRE) definitions
- Related services and implementations
- Discipline
- Students' and parents' rights
- Medically related conditions

Although the law does not clearly define many of the provisions and requirements, schools should strive to define parameters and avoid the confrontational proceedings, as they are costly and time-consuming. There is a process for due process hearings, but in some states, filing a complaint or participating in mediation are viable options.

One of the most difficult rulings for districts and schools is the requirement to provide health-related services for medically fragile students. These services could include a one-on-one nurse and medical equipment necessary for a student with a disability and may impose a financial burden.

The following is a list of the more significant historical cases that have changed laws and procedures for services to children with disabilities. It is not inclusive of the many cases across the country but does provide the examinee with an idea of the types of issues that have been presented. Cases every year cause schools to change their perspective and plans for implementing services to exceptional students.

1954, *Brown v. Board of Education:* Based on the segregation of students according to race, it was tried at the Supreme Court who ordered that education must be on equal terms for *all* children.

1967, *Hobson v. Hansen*: Determined the tracking system for regular and special education students based on intelligence scores was discriminatorily unconstitutional for some populations of students and could not be used.

1972, *Mills v. Board of Education*: Determined that financial problems cannot be a reason for the lack of appropriate programs to children with disabilities.

1972, *Pennsylvania Association for Retarded Citizens v. the Commonwealth of Pennsylvania:* Established the right for all children with mental retardation to a free public education.

1979, *Armstrong v. Kline*: Ordered schools to provide extended school year services for students with disabilities who may regress over long periods without attending formal school programs.

1979, *Larry P. v. Riles:* Ruled that IQ tests could not be used as the primary or sole basis of placing students in special programs.

1982, *Board of Education of the Hudson School District v. Rowley:* Upheld that each child with a disability has the right to an individualized program and supportive services deemed appropriate and necessary.

1983, *Abrahamson v. Hershman:* Ruled that the training and education for a student with multiple disabilities required in private residential placement would be supported through district funds.

1984, *Department of Education v. Katherine D.*: Ruled homebound instruction for a student with multiple health problems did not comply with the LRE and required the student be placed in a class with non-disabled children and receive the necessary related medical services.

1984, *Irving Independent School District v. Tatro*: Forced the school to provide non-physician required medical services to allow a physically impaired student to attend school.

1988, *Honig v. Doe:* Ruled that students with disabilities may not be excluded for misbehavior that is disability-related, but services could cease if the behavior was not related to the disability.

1989, *Timothy v. Rochester School District:* Upheld that all children with disabilities must be provided a free and appropriate public education without exception.

1993, *Zobrest v. Catalina School District:* Determined that a student in a parochial school should be provided the assistance of a related service pertaining to the disability and that these findings did not violate the constitution of the separation of church and state.

1993, *Oberti v. Board of Education:* Ruled to support a family preference to educate a child with mental retardation in the general education classroom.

1998, *Foley v. Special School District of St. Louis County:* Affirmed that public schools are not obligated to provide special education services if parents choose to place their child in a private school.

1999, *Cedar Rapids v. Garrett F.:* Ruled that medical services necessary to a student with a disability to access and benefit from special education must be provided by the school as long as the service does not require a physician.

Issues of Family, School, Community

Families, schools, and communities may positively or negatively contribute to student achievement and life outcomes. In the early years, it is the family who has the most powerful influences on a child and after the school becomes a partner, collaboration of these two entities is critical for continued success. The attitudes of community members are also important, but they are an essential ingredient in the development of a transition plan for a high school student and the transition into adulthood. Combined efforts of these three will impact exceptional individuals throughout their lifetimes.

Advocacy

Advocacy is defined as the process of supporting the abilities of and promoting the causes for persons with exceptional needs. Advocacy by parents, educators and community members for exceptional individuals has an impact on the laws, the programs, and the delivery of services. Whether those changes happen because of amended laws, court cases, or awareness rallies, the influence on those with exceptional needs can be overwhelming.

Advocacy instruction should be a part of the educational program for students with exceptional needs, especially as a component of a transition plan for students 16 years and older. Through instruction on advocacy issues and self-advocacy actions, individuals with exceptional needs are better able to understand their rights and their capabilities, as well as develop a more positive self-concept and be involved in meeting their own needs.

When students transition into the community as adults, they may face barriers, such as discrimination, problems with employment, and issues about living conditions. Joining an advocacy group for persons with exceptional needs helps them to protect their rights, allows them to access information, and supports them in maintaining their dignity. When a person with exceptional needs joins in advocacy efforts, it provides an opportunity to meet others with the same conditions and together pursue positive outcomes.

Parent Partnerships and Roles

Parents of children with exceptional needs play demanding roles, as they must meet the child's basic needs, take on additional expenses, understand complicated issues, and support programs. Considering parents and family members as equal partners in a child's education and creating partnerships through respect and dignity will result in explicit outcomes for the child. Parents and other family members can be positive influences in improving a child's performance.

One of the six principles of IDEIA is that parents should be included in **shared-decision making** regarding their child. Involving parents as a team member is a critical aspect of developing proper IEP goals, providing support and consistency to the child, accessing additional resources and providing opportunities for additional learning situations. Educators who demonstrate devotion to the child and are considerate of the parents will gain the trust and the commitment necessary to support the child. Improving the lines of communication and respecting culturally and linguistically diverse families are critical elements in encouraging parent partnerships.

Professionals must practice active listening when working with families and promote communication efforts. There are many methods of providing home-school communication that effectively involve parents on a regular basis. Here are several types:

- Parent-teacher conferences
- Telephone calls or e-mails
- Written messages
- Class newsletters or websites
- Parent group meetings
- Parent classroom volunteers
- Family homework activities
- Class activities with family spectators

Public Attitudes

How others react to an individual with exceptional needs affects her life in school and later as an adult. In spite of advocacy efforts, there remain problems with the lack of overall acceptance of individuals who are different. Because exceptional individuals exhibit unique characteristics and diverse abilities, they face problems from the ignorance of others and with discrimination, teasing, and cruelty. **Handicapism** is a term used to describe this phenomenon of the biased reactions to those with disabilities. However, public attitudes toward exceptional individuals are far less negative and more accepting, tolerant, and respectful today than in previous decades.

Educators must prepare exceptional students for community life by effectively guiding and supporting them to use their realistic potential, to reach reasonable academic and behavioral performance, to improve their self-esteem, and to develop independence. Teachers must also provide awareness to the community about individuals with exceptional abilities so the public is better informed and better able to allow effective integration for these individuals.

Cultural and Community Influences

Communities and the cultures represented have great influence on the development and progress of exceptional individuals. Society establishes rules about how people should function, and in the past, individuals with disabilities were not completely approved as members of society due to their lower and differently functioning abilities. Since attitudes have changed more individuals with exceptional needs have become positive contributors to established communities. A community that embraces these individuals in work environments, local businesses, and neighborhood living situations has a positive influence that will be reflected in the performance of those individuals.

Addressing cultural and community influence begins with transition services. Educators must collaborate with agencies to find opportunities for students to prepare for the adult world. Awareness and acceptance are two critical factors in sustaining positive situations for individuals with exceptional needs.

Interagency Agreements

Primary responsibility for the transition of services to students with disabilities from a secondary school into the community lies within the school. Because **transition** means moving from one major service program to another, it is critical that schools collaborate with and work through the community agencies available to individuals with disabilities. Although these differ among communities and across states, this list may include potential employers, postsecondary education facilities, residential care and housing providers, vocational training or rehabilitation centers, and so on.

Collaboration, communication, and consideration of the individual student's needs are all very important to the implementation of an effective transition plan (ITP). The involvement of agencies in student assessment, planning, and consultation is critical to supporting the student and the family in this end of service/beginning of service process. When school and community entities voluntarily cooperate and involve the student and the family, they demonstrate a valid cohesion in the delivery of much-needed services.

Historical Movements and Trends

The history of individuals with exceptional needs spans centuries. Even before federal laws mandated services, dedicated adults and teachers educated exceptional children in homes and in schools. Yet, some children were institutionalized and prior to 1970, schools could deny enrollment to children with exceptional needs.

After schools began allowing educational access to these unique children, they were served through the practice of segregation. Although students with mild learning problems remained in the general education classes and were considered "slow learners," other children with more severe needs were placed in schools or other facilities that specialized in certain conditions. The recommended practice of inclusion did not occur until recently, and the issue of placement for children with exceptional needs is an on-going and debated topic.

Community-Based Placement

After students transition into adult services in a community setting, variables will influence the individual's success. Community placements should be based on the the individual's preferences and the services and resources available. There are three main areas of community-based placements: residential, employment, recreation. Although there are pros and cons to consider in each area, final decisions should be made with the knowledge of the individual's needs, abilities, supports, and future plans.

Inclusion

The basic premise of **inclusion,** which began in the 1990s is that it is a philosophy, not a place or a program. It surmises that students with exceptional needs should be placed in classrooms along with students who are non-disabled so they may receive the general education curriculum instruction with supportive services. The inclusion practice was encouraged by professionals who worked with exceptional children, to avoid placements in segregated settings.

Students with varying disabilities and unique exceptional needs are diverse learners and often require adaptations, modifications, and accommodations to meet their needs. The methods and strategies these students need require special consideration and additional time to implement, which may cause difficulty for a general education teacher. It is important that the special education teachers support and assist the general education teachers for inclusion to work.

Application of Technology

A requirement of IDEIA is the provision of technology as a related service for students to access and benefit from special education. This requirement may be met in two ways. One is through the implementation of technology in classrooms for all students. Basic computer programs, use of video tools, amplification devices, or dual auditory/visual modalities to aid in instruction are highly effective instructional strategies and techniques for exceptional students. The second way is through **assistive technology** (AT), the more individually directed use of technology. AT includes specific devices, equipment, and services, based on an assessment of the student with the disability. It may also incorporate other advances in technology, such as cochlear implants for the deaf or basic computer systems or auditory/visual modalities for all disability conditions.

Transition

Adults with exceptionalities face daily challenges that encompass under-employment, job dissatisfaction, dependent living arrangements, social skills deficits, lack of work skills, and isolation from leisure activities. These barriers prevent some of them from being independent or successful. It is for these reasons that federal special education law mandates guidelines for school personnel to assist and prepare students for the future in the adult community.

Under the special education law, a transition plan must begin at age 16 for a student with a disability. The transition plan must outline the activities and resources needed to support the student's movement from school to adulthood. The process of transition requires that the team, which may consist of school personnel, the student, the community, and agency personnel assist the student in preparing for post-school activities. If able, the student should be involved in the creation and development of this plan, since consideration of the student's ideas, interests, and preferences is important to the outcomes. The areas to be incorporated are listed here:

- Postsecondary education
- Integrated or supported employment
- Vocational training
- Continuing and adult education
- Adult services
- Independent living
- Community participation
- Recreation and leisure activities

State laws are in effect regarding the **majority age,** which is the legal age that a student becomes an adult. When a student reaches majority age, parents may not be included in educational programming, unless invited by the student or if decided by a court proceeding.

Another formal transition period mentioned in the law occurs when a child moves from Part C services (early intervention) to the Part B services (early childhood–school age). Prior to the child's third birthday, an IEP should be developed based on the assessments conducted and the services implemented under the IFSP. The Part C personnel, the Part B professionals, and the parents must convene to discuss the student's present needs, create an educational program, and make an appropriate placement.

Accountability

Two distinct laws require accountability of programs for students with disabilities: IDEIA and NCLB (refer to section "Federal Laws"). For the exceptionality of gifted/talented, there are also supportive laws, however, the accountability requirement is identified under NCLB.

Under IDEIA, one of the four major purposes is "to assess, and ensure the effectiveness of efforts to educate children with disabilities." State and federal reporting requirements are set to analyze the efficacy of school programs across the country regarding this population. Under this law is the inclusion of the term "highly qualified special educators", which attempts to align IDEIA with NCLB. A highly qualified special education teacher must be certified as a special education teacher or pass the state special education teacher licensing exam. There may be additional requirements based on the state of residency or employment.

Under NCLB, the term "highly qualified" teacher has districts and states scrambling to organize and identify educators who are certified to teach children of all abilities, in all programs, in the public schools. The requirement for the Praxis II exam is an example of an accountability feature for certain states. A highly qualified teacher is considered a teacher, who is competently trained in the subject area he will teach. Included in this law is the requirement that every educator who teaches a core academic subject be certified as **highly qualified** by the end of the school year 2006.

In addition to the teacher requirements, both of these laws require that states demonstrate a system and verify the results for student achievement and academic success. Individual states and many districts are implementing **high-stakes** testing, expecting that all students will meet this requirement. Under NCLB, annual school **report cards** allow parents to choose a school for their child based on the school's **annual progress.** IDEIA has always had a system of accountability for students and programs through the IEP process and state reporting at the end of each school year.

Delivery of Services

The education of exceptional students spans as diverse a field as the students who are served in the programs. These students, whether identified with a disability or giftedness, differ from the norm, and it is those very differences that set them apart from their peers that will impact their success. Educators must ensure that exceptional students benefit from an education.

Students with disabilities must be provided an individualized program consistent with IDEIA, according to the premise that services be a free and appropriate public education in the least restrictive environment. Students who are gifted or talented are also supported by federal laws, state policies, district guidelines, educational procedures, and best practices but are not included in the specific special education mandates at the federal level.

Background Knowledge

Educating students with exceptionalities is more acceptable and more possible than ever before. The numbers of exceptional students has multiplied over the years, and they are significantly dispersed in the general school population. Research shows that when exceptional students are educated with typical students, both groups benefit academically and socially. Educators must determine the most suitable ways to educate and support these students in inclusive environments so they may lead productive and independent lives.

A student's team makes difficult decisions when designing and implementing a program specifically for the exceptional student. Imperative in delivering the appropriate services to exceptional students is the consideration of several essential elements: the student's abilities and assessed needs, the learning environment, the recommended strategies, the professionals involved, the parent partnership, and the available resources. The delivery of services may include the assessments, the curriculum components, the instructional strategies and methods, and the management of the environment.

Conceptual Approaches

Theories related to learning are vastly important to educators, although different theories work best for certain students in particular situations. The conceptual approaches selected to support an individual's needs must be based on research, theoretical information, and the specific student. When educators formalize their own personal philosophy about how students learn, and apply that to the selection of one or more theories specific to the children served, needs will be met, and academic achievement will soar.

In this section are descriptions of several theories related to learning and academic achievement: Cognitive, Constructionist, Psychodynamic, Behavioral, Sociological, Ecological, Therapeutic, and Medical.

Cognitive

Cognitive theorists believe that an individual constructs the acquisition of new information and skills based on prior knowledge. Stemming from the work of Gestalt and Piaget, this theory examines the internal mental processes that include problem solving, memory, and language while focusing on how people understand, analyze, and solve problems.

Instruction must be delivered at the student's academic level (stage of development) in a managed environment while allowing the student to develop the necessary skills and learn to generalize them. The instructional application of the cognitive theory includes the strategies of addressing styles of learning, encouraging metacognition, teaching learning strategies, using peer tutoring, providing scaffolded instruction, analyzing behavioral temperaments, and understanding the social context of learning. Employing motivational activities should enhance and encourage learning.

Constructionist

Learning is an active process in which the learner must be involved. This reinforces learning so it may be effective and successful. Piaget's ideas of experiential learning where individuals are engaged in actively creating things and constructing mental models are based on this theory. Students may be involved in experimentation and hands-on learning while the teacher is the facilitator of the educational experiences. Constructionist theory examples include the **inquiry-based learning** most often used in science and math instruction.

Psychodynamic

The psychodynamic theory is the study of human **behavior** based on **motivation** and **drives,** and the functional significance of **emotions.** According to Brucke, Jung, and Freud, an individual's personality and her reactions to situations are the result of interactions within her mind, genetic constitution, emotional state, and environment. These interactions affect behavior and the individual's mental state, and internal forces can affect a person's behavior. This approach is based on the premise that human behaviors and relationships are shaped by both conscious and unconscious influences.

Behavioral

The behavioral theory emphasizes a systematic approach to learning and instruction. Based on the work of Skinner, it incorporates the ABC model of instruction, which stands for **a**ntecedent or stimulus, target behavior or response, and consequences or reinforcement. Examples of this theory include the development of an **individual education plan** (IEP) and the use of **functional behavior assessments** and **behavior intervention plans** (FBA, BIP). These processes demonstrate measurable learning behaviors that can be observed, measured, and documented.

Skinner believed that learning is a function of the changes in behaviors and the responses to those events; therefore, the key components of the behavioral theory promote the effectiveness of explicit teaching and direct instruction. This specific type of instruction focuses on the tasks to be learned, the skills to be developed, and the use of the environmental setting. Educators can assess a student's learning by examining the presented task and how well the student performs to the response, known as **operant conditioning.**

Sociological

Bandura based the social (sociological) learning theory on student observation in order to gain knowledge. Because individuals may learn from watching others, educators should provide modeling and demonstrations that allow students to learn through observation.

Ecological

This theory is based on the study of how humans may develop within their specific environments. From the influences of home, school, and the community along with the interaction among these factors, the learning and development of an individual are impacted. This theory focuses on how social experiences and culture affect an individual's development and future success. The **family systems theory** is a classic example of the ecological influences and how academic success is related to these experiences.

Therapeutic

A collaborative approach, the therapeutic theory utilizes the expertise of specific related service providers such as the speech-language pathologist, the occupational therapist, the physical therapist, and medical personnel, as appropriate. It focuses on the specific needs of the exceptional student across all educational settings, and therapy may be conducted and interventions implemented through a rich array of reach-in and pull-out models.

Medical

Students with exceptional conditions often have medically related issues. Conditions are due to genetic causes, diseases, illnesses, accidents, and other etiologies. Through the medical field, educators may gain information about a student's diagnosis, treatment, and prognosis, while sharing opinions about the delivery of services. Clinical therapy and support from medical practitioners such as physicians, public health professionals, and mental health professionals aid the educational team in making appropriate decisions. Medical theory does not apply specifically to school programs, but the factors of medical issues should be considered in developing an individual's educational program.

Placement and Program Issues

According to the law, students with disabilities should be placed in the environments with non-disabled peers to the maximum extent possible as long as their needs are met. The inclusive programs allow students to access an education in a more natural environment and prepare to participate as adults in community settings. The setting selection is made by the IEP team based on a comprehensive assessment and should be the primary placement for all services provided.

Program issues include debates regarding inclusion, addressing cultural and linguistic diversity, involving parents as partners, utilizing assistive technology, encouraging integrated therapies, participating in high-stakes testing and aligning with No Child Left Behind (NCLB) requirements.

Early Intervention

From the research on brain development and human growth, as well as the professional knowledge of early learning and interventions, the field of early childhood education has received credibility regarding its importance to children with exceptional needs. Young children are entitled to individualized programs of instruction that focus on their exceptional needs according to IDEIA, Part B, and Part C provisions. States are encouraged to establish statewide interagency programs for early interventions services for children under the age of 3 but are mandated to implement services for children in early childhood settings ages 3 through 5 years. Categories for identification and placement of these children differ among the states, but the federal label used is **developmental delay.**

Additional information may be found in the Wiley Publishing, Inc. study guide, *CliffsTestPrep Praxis II: Special Education (0351, 0352, 0690, 0371, 0381, 0321),* specifically the "Preschool/Early Childhood" section.

IEP Team

An individual education plan is a requirement of IDEIA and is used to manage a student's school program. Participants of the IEP team may include the parents, the student, a regular education teacher, a special education teacher, a school representative, the evaluator, therapists, community agency personnel, and others with knowledge or expertise that pertains to the student's needs. As the team members work together, they enhance the educational programs to exceptional students, since they all contribute expertise to implement and support an appropriate program. This approach is called **collaborative teaming,** and it usually focuses on the successful programs of inclusion models.

If collaborative teaming is to be effective, the members should determine their shared goals, apply voluntary participation procedures, use proper on-going communications, practice team decision-making, share the responsibilities, schedule planning time together, and pool resources. Team members may work collaboratively in several different ways: **coordination, consultation,** and **co-teaching.**

> **Coordination** is a simple form of collaboration that includes communication and cooperation so student services are ensured delivery. Professionals may not directly share their expertise, information, or ideas with one another, but they do provide updates on the progress of the student.
>
> **Consultation** is the process in which professionals work with one another by directly communicating and sharing expertise to improve services to students. Teachers and other professionals share strategies and methods to help the student access the educational program.
>
> **Co-teaching** is an effective tool for inclusion settings. When two or more teachers work together to plan activities, deliver instruction, and assess students, additional supports are provided to all students in the classroom, thereby improving achievement.

Three team models exist in schools and are critical to the effectiveness and implementation of the special education process.

> **Multidisciplinary Team:** Described as professionals with defined roles, working independently of one another. This is not an encouraged practice as it promotes fragmentation of student programs. These team members often conduct separate assessments, deliver services independent of others, and work with the families apart from of other professionals. This team may exhibit a lack of communication or understanding of the student's needs.
>
> **Interdisciplinary Team:** Members conduct independent assessments, but unlike the multidisciplinary team, this team works to promote communication and collaboration. This team uses more formal communication efforts by meeting together to share information and develop a plan of interventions and strategies to enhance student educational success. Team members implement their portion of the program, while remaining in contact with other members.

Transdisciplinary Team: Highly recommended, this team model demonstrates coordination and involvement; however, due to schedules and the numbers of professionals involved, it may be difficult to achieve this team status. This team delivers services in an integrated approach across disciplines, to include assessment, sharing information, program development, and implementing interventions, while including the family at all stages. Members work together sharing roles and responsibilities unlike other teams, who work in isolation.

Continuum of Services

Under IDEIA, the provision that relates to a range of placement and service options for students with special needs is called the **continuum of services,** and it must be available in each district. It includes discussion of where students will receive special education services, what the necessary related services are, and how they will access their education.

This continuum of services options is discussed by the IEP team who decides what will best meet the social and educational needs of the student. The general education setting is the first recommended placement (and **least restrictive environment** for all students) to be considered. Many students with disabilities are successful when appropriate services, accommodations and supports are implemented in the general education environment. Usually, the more restrictive options are available to the more severely disabled, but the process must be reflected in the final decision.

Least Restrictive Environment

The **least restrictive environment** (LRE) is a provision of the federal special education law that pertains to the educational placement of students with disabilities. It is described as the setting for service delivery that most closely resembles a regular school program while meeting the student's exceptional needs. After the student's educational needs are determined and the goals and related services are outlined, the IEP team considers the most appropriate environment according to the options which include:

- General education classroom (inclusive model)
- General education classroom (consultative model)
- Co-teaching setting (collaborative model)
- Resource room (pull-in model, integrated model)
- Self-contained program (separate, segregated model)
- Separate school (private setting)
- Residential facility
- Homebound placement
- Hospital setting

Each student with a disability has the right to be educated with non-disabled peers to the maximum extent appropriate. Special classes, segregated programs, and separate schools are to be the chosen placement only when the severity of the condition prohibits the education of a student with a disability in a more typical setting. A **natural environment** is recommended under the law for a student with a disability, as it is the setting that would typically be selected if the child did not have the disability.

Related Services

According to IDEIA, students with disabilities must be provided additional services in order to access and benefit from special education. These services are called **related services** and are a component of the IEP. Decisions to include specific related services are based on the comprehensive assessment of a student. How the services are provided and where they are conducted is at the discretion of the professionals who implement the services. Related services may include transportation, speech therapy, physical therapy, occupational therapy, counseling, behavior coach, or a paraprofessional.

Accommodations

Accommodations, modifications, and adaptations are terms that have been used in the special education field interchangeably when referring to the supports to a student in the instructional program, the educational environment, and the general curriculum. Some professionals use these three terms as one in the same, and others believe they are quite different. The following definitions reflect the opinion and experience of the author and other respected resources.

> **Accommodations:** Instructional supports or services necessary to access instruction or the learning environment and to demonstrate individual knowledge. These supports and services may not change the curriculum or the subjects covered, but may reduce the barriers caused by a deficit or disability, providing an "equal opportunity" to students with exceptional needs.
>
> Examples of accommodations most often used in general education settings may include an amplification system, a Braille writer, preferential seating, additional time for completing tasks, using books on tape, access to a note taker, or delivering an oral rather than written report.
>
> **Modifications:** Include actual changes made to the curriculum, to the environment, or to the expectations of an instructional task in order to meet the student's specific needs. These changes are often imposed when the task is above the student's ability level, so they reduce the expectations or content to support the severity or type of disability.
>
> Examples of modifications that are used in school settings include selecting a limited number of math problems, completing half of the spelling words, exempting some learners from certain tasks, and providing a different task with the same concept.
>
> **Adaptations:** Most widely used in reference to facilities and equipment and may be reflected under the requirements of Section 504. Adaptation supports may make changes in *how* the student accesses the environment or in instructional delivery but may be confused with accommodations and modifications.
>
> Examples of common adaptations in schools include wheelchair accessibility, use of head gear on computers, access to specialized furniture, or posting a daily picture chart.

Accommodations, modifications, and adaptations should be consistently applied and used to support an individual's program. Accommodations utilized during the regular school day are also allowed in testing situations; however, modifications may not be allowed on tests, as they alter the validity and reliability.

Accommodations and modifications are most useful when implemented in inclusion models to help address individual student needs. Training and monitoring the general education staff in the selection of and the use of accommodations and modifications is recommended. Accommodations and modifications may be used across a broad range of general topic areas: accessing the general education curriculum, conducting instruction and activities, implementing strategies, providing therapy, and participating in extracurricular activities.

Due Process

Due process is allowable under IDEIA and emphasizes certain rights for children with disabilities and their parents (**procedural safeguards**). It ensures that schools follow the procedures set forth in the law for assessment, identification, placement, instructional services, and related or supplementary services. If parents believe that a **free and appropriate public education** is not being provided to their child with a disability, they may file for a **due process hearing.** Many states encourage parents to resolve their issues in a preliminary process called the **complaint process or mediation** in which solutions are discussed with the school team or an appointed mediator prior to requesting a legal due process hearing. The right to reasonable legal fees may be awarded to the prevailing party depending on the outcome of the decision.

Integrating Best Practices/Research/Literature

The most critical tool in the success of students with exceptional needs is the quality of instruction provided, which depends solely on the educators who deliver it. Students with disabilities require intensive, specialized, and systematic instruction and interventions that are the result of scientific research, a base of best practices, and professional knowledge. For educators to address issues related to prevention, factors related to remediation, and support disability compensation, they must be knowledgeable about an enormous amount of information and know when and how to apply it.

Issues and trends are on-going concerns, but fads and cures come and go. The key to knowledge is deciphering the best practices and scientifically based knowledge that best suits the population being served. Professional literature, published journals, and related organizations allow educators to seek new information in the fast paced field of exceptional students.

Empirical research studies are based on realistic school situations and actual students with disabilities. These scientific studies provide information about students that are similar to current school situations and, therefore, may indicate the outcomes that may be expected. Studies on exceptional students include information on brain development, gifted/talented, poverty and achievement levels, cultural diversity, advocacy, and behaviors. Scientific research is valuable to a classroom teacher as it provides content regarding instructional strategies, interventions, motivation, behaviors, enhancing skill development, early intervention, transitions, and vocational training.

Curriculum and Instruction

Curriculum design for exceptional students is an important factor in their education. Curriculum and instructional program choices can be difficult as they must consider the special characteristics of each student. The need for special materials, distinctive methods, and individualized adaptations, modifications and accommodations of the general curriculum are all necessary to address their very unique needs and all levels of abilities.

Exceptional students need systematic direct instruction, proven procedures, and effective strategies that allow them to organize, comprehend, and remember educational information and acquire skills. The general education curriculum may be appropriate for some exceptional students with accommodations, while others will need a more intense and specialized instructional program and supplementary materials to gain appropriate skills and academic knowledge.

Different curriculum types are available for students with disabilities.

- **Behavioral-based curriculum:** Demonstrates student interactions in the environment in order to instruct students in functional and age appropriate skills
- **Cognitive-developmental curriculum:** Provides age appropriate activities that are discovery-based and interactive, such as DAP
- **Life skills curriculum:** Uses functional skills training to support transition into the community
- **Social skills curriculum:** Improves social skills areas such as engaging in personal interactions, following directions, handling situations, increasing self-competence, and utilizing appropriate behaviors
- **Functional curriculum:** Helps develop knowledge and skills to support independence in school, community, employment, personal, social, and daily living situations

IEP/IFSP/ITP Process

Mandated under IDEIA is the development and implementation of plans designed to manage educational programs for students with disabilities: an **individual education plan,** an **individual family service plan,** and an **individual transition plan.** These plans are created according to a systematic team-decision process based on the results of a comprehensive, non-discriminatory, and individualized assessment conducted on the student. Each written plan should reflect the characteristics of the disability, establish realistic, measurable goals, and ensure an appropriate program according to the strengths and needs of the student.

These three plans, each developed and implemented by specific personnel, are constructed for particular age groups at specific times in the special education process. An IEP supports services for school-aged children 3 through 21 and an IFSP is prepared for families and children ages birth through 3, enrolled in state intervention programs. An ITP is an additional component of an IEP for students ages 16 through 21.

Individual Education Plan-IEP

The primary purpose of an IEP is to guide the instruction of a student with a disability in the least restrictive environment and measure program accountability. It requires team work and planning to determine the correct type of program for each student. Seven components must be included in an IEP:

1. Statement of present levels of educational performance pertaining to disability
2. Statement of measurable annual goals and may include objectives
3. Description of the method to measure progress
4. Statement of related services, supplementary aids, and services
5. Explanation of the extent of involvement in general education programs
6. Statement of accommodations and participation in state and district testing
7. Description of the date, frequency, location, and duration of services

Specifically discussed under these seven components are the requirements of the least restrictive environment, assistive technology, related services, the scope and sequence of the curriculum, the methods and strategies for instruction, participation in high-stakes testing, and regularly scheduled progress reports.

Individual Family Service Plan-IFSP

The primary purpose of an IFSP is support for the entire family of an infant who exhibits a developmental delay. Resources and needs are assessed to design a plan with specific outcomes for the child and the family. The plan outlines family goals, identifies the service providers, and establishes the specific services. Family members are considered team members who provide input about their child's development and share goals to support the program. A service coordinator assists the family during the implementation of the services, and each six months, the family has the option to accept or decline continued services.

Components of an IFSP are similar yet differ from an IEP. The present levels of educational performance provide an overall statement of functioning across all developmental abilities, creating general goals primary to the family's needs and the child's needs, with progress reviewed every six months.

Transition services are required under an IFSP as a child moves from early intervention to a public preschool program. A re-evaluation of the family needs and the child's progress helps to identify the current educational needs that must be addressed in the pending IEP. The law does allow an IFSP be used for preschool-aged children or an IEP for children aged 2 transitioning within a year to a preschool program.

Individual Transition Plan-ITP

To become a successful contributing adult, a student with a disability needs assistance and training prior to graduation. **An individual transition plan** is required, in addition to an **individual education plan,** for all students, ages 16 and over. The student's needs, interests, and preferences must be addressed through non-bias assessment instruments and procedures. The student, the parents, the teachers, and appropriate community partners are involved in the process, and throughout program development, resource identification, and service implementation. The areas addressed include employment, continued education, daily living, health, leisure, communication, and self-determination/advocacy.

Instructional Implementation

Instruction for exceptional students must be more individualized than that for a typical child. Because exceptional learners are so diverse, the instruction delivered must include specific activities, curricular materials, resources, equipment, specific classroom personnel, tutoring, and the use of technology. Integrating all of these features into a general education classroom requires the support of the special education teachers.

Instructional variables related to learning and student achievement make a difference in the success of the program and the outcomes for the student. When preparing to implement instruction, teachers should do the following:

- Focus on learning time
- Ensure high rates of success for students
- Provide easy access to materials and supplies
- Impart a quality educational environment

- Plan and maintain motivation
- Participate in teacher training programs

Enrichment and remediation are important for special needs learners. **Enrichment** extends the lesson for those capable of more, which may help students with learning disabilities, autism, deafness, blindness, orthopedic impairments, and emotional disabilities. **Remediation** is important for its use of various strategies to teach and reinforce skills to those needing more practice. Although this technique may apply to all students, it is particularly helpful to those with mental retardation, deafness, speech-language problems, other health impaired, and traumatic brain injury.

Gifted/Talented

Recommended for students who are gifted or talented is a **differentiated** curriculum that is responsive to the needs of these students, based on their individual strengths, and allows them opportunities to use their exceptional abilities, talents, and skills. It should reflect an interdisciplinary focus so the many aspects of academic subjects, and student interests are covered. Some G/T students may need **acceleration** of this curriculum which is a modification of the pace allowed for the student to proceed. Some strategies for acceleration include: self-paced instruction, compacting or telescoping the curriculum, mentoring programs, tiered lessons, summer programs, special focus courses, ability grouping, advanced placement courses, extracurricular programs and skipping grade levels.

Teaching Strategies and Methods

Individualization is the key to the selection of instructional strategies and teaching methods for exceptional learners. Since students with disabilities are ensured an appropriate education through the IEP format, the chosen strategies and methods should flow from that content and the team decisions regarding the student's needs. For other exceptional learners, an assessment drives instruction, as the results should deliver a realistic view of the student's present levels of educational performance.

The strategies and methods chosen for each student must support the learner in the areas of strengths and needs, encourage independence, and focus on the generalization of skills and knowledge. Most strategies used with exceptional learners are an outcome of empirical research. However, strategies work with certain groups of students, and some are more beneficial to particular subject areas.

Due to the diversity of exceptional students, teachers must know how to use a multitude of different instructional programs and materials. Many marketed curricula options available are specifically designed for special learners. But, these published materials cannot address all the unique needs of students. When educators select methods, strategies, or curriculum, they must know which will meet the educational goals appropriate for a classroom of diverse students.

There are two distinct methods of providing instruction and these are used for various student groups depending on the functioning level and the subject area:

> **Explicit instruction:** The teacher provides the information and content to support the learning process.
>
> **Implicit instruction:** The focus is on the student as an active and involved learner who constructs knowledge by using previously learned information.

Following are some of the terms related to instructional strategies and teaching methods:

> **ability grouping:** Placement of students in educational activities according to performance and academic achievement levels.
>
> **accommodation:** An adjustment that enables a student to participate in educational activities.
>
> **active student response:** A measure of the engagement of the learner in tasks and activities.
>
> **adaptation:** A change made to the environment or curriculum.
>
> **authentic learning:** Instruction using real-world projects and activities to allow students to discover and explore in a more relevant manner.
>
> **chained response:** The breaking down of a task into component parts so a student finishes the task by starting with the first step in the sequence and performing each component progressively until the task is completed.

chaining: A technique in which student performance is reinforced so the student will continue to perform more complex tasks in the sequence.

choral responding: Oral response of students (in unison) to a question or problem presented by the teacher.

chunking: A strategy that allows a student to remember and organize large amounts of information.

Cloze procedure: The use of semantic and syntactic clues to aid in completing sentences.

concept generalization: The ability for students to demonstrate concept knowledge by applying the information to other settings without prompts from teacher.

content enhancements: Techniques used to aid in the organization and delivery of curriculum such as guided notes, graphic organizers, mnemonics, and visual displays.

contingent teaching: A strategy for helping a student and eventually fading out the support as he gains mastery.

cooperative learning: Classroom is divided into groups to work together to complete a task or participate in an activity.

cues and prompts: Provides assistance to ensure adequate support of instruction.

diagnostic-prescriptive method: Individualizing instruction to develop strengths and remediate weaknesses.

differentiated instruction: To address the varying abilities, strengths, and needs of learners and their styles of learning by imposing a choice of learning activity, tasks that suit the learning style, student groupings, authentic lessons, and problem-based activities.

direct instruction: A systematic approach of teaching with specific goals, active learner engagement, and positive reinforcement for student performance (synonymous with explicit instruction).

direct measurement: Checking on student achievement during a period for a specific opportunity to perform and recording the response.

facilitated groups: Students engage in active learning with lessons designed and overseen by the teacher but managed by the students.

fluency building: A measure that encourages practice of skills to improve the accuracy and rate of use.

generalization: The ability to use skills learned across various settings.

graphic organizer: A visual-spatial organization of information to help students understand presented concepts.

guided practice: Providing opportunities to gain knowledge by offering cues, prompts, or added sequential information.

learning centers: Specific areas or activities that enhance the curricular content and allow independent or small group instruction.

learning strategy: An approach that teaches students how to learn and remember particular content.

mediated scaffolding: A procedure that provides cues and prompts, while gradually removing them so students can perform and respond independently.

mnemonics: A strategy that enhances memory through key words, acronyms, or acrostics.

modeling: A method that helps make connections between the material to be learned and the process to learn it by acting out sequences while students observe and then imitate the task.

modification: Changing the content, material, or delivery of instruction.

multiple intelligence strategies: The nine areas of learning that are addressed in classroom instruction: linguistic, logical-mathematical, spatial, bodily-kinesthetic, musical, interpersonal, intrapersonal, naturalistic, and existential.

naturalistic teaching: Procedures that involve activities interesting to students with naturally occurring consequences.

peer tutoring: Under the guidance of a teacher, a non-disabled student with competencies in a particular area works with a student with a disability who needs assistance to enhance an area of study.

precision teaching: An approach that identifies the skills to be taught and uses direct daily measure of the student's performance to acquire the skills.

prompting: A technique in which a visual, auditory, or tactile cue is presented to facilitate the completion of a task or to perform a behavior.

remediation: A program technique to teach students to overcome an exceptionality through training and education.

repetition: Continual work on a specific skill or content concept to help build rote memory skills.

response cards: A method that allows all students to answer simultaneously by using signs, cards, or items held up to demonstrate responses.

scaffolding: Applying stages to learning content and tasks by first observing the student to see what she can do and then helping her understand the how and why until she can perform herself (direct instruction, tutoring, modeling, independence).

skill drill: Repetition and practice of new skills until the learner performs without cues and prompts.

strategic instruction: A planned, sequential instruction to show similarities and differences between acquired and new knowledge.

systematic feedback: Providing positive reinforcement and confirmation to improve learning.

task analysis: A strategy in which the goals are broken into smaller steps and sequenced while keeping the learner's pace in focus.

time trial: A procedure that improves fluency of new skills through time limits.

transfer of stimulus control: Providing instructional prompts to aid in correct responses.

universal design: The concept that everything in the environment, in learning and in products, should be accessible to everyone.

Study Skills

The use of appropriate study skills promotes student achievement, so providing exceptional students with extensive instruction in acquiring these skills has value. Students should be assessed in study skill areas so the most appropriate strategies for study skills instruction are implemented. Topics for study skills instruction include reading, listening, note taking, outlining, report writing, oral presentation, graphic aids, test taking, library use, time management, and behavior self-management. For students in secondary settings, a higher level of study skills are necessary and may consist of maintaining a schedule, learning to ask questions, skimming for information, outlining a chapter, using mnemonics, and paraphrasing.

Social Skills

Social skills development is critical for most exceptional students. An assessment in this area should identify those who lack the ability to perform in a social situation, are unable to maintain behaviors in various settings, have difficulty developing relationships, or those who find it hard to participate in activities with others. In general, students in the following exceptionality areas need focused instruction on social skills: autism, emotional disabilities, gifted-talented, hearing and vision impairments, learning disabilities, and mental retardation.

Self-Management

Self-management is a term that spans all exceptionality groups. It is the ability of the individual to maintain control of one's self and to generalize skills learned across various settings. For a child with mental retardation it may mean that he is capable of using functional life skills in a group home. For a student with emotional disabilities, it may mean that she is able to control her behaviors during a basketball game.

Instructional Components

Instructional formats vary according to the individuals, the environment, and the instructional content. Formats may include facilitated groups, cooperative learning situations, peer tutoring, one-to-one instruction, small groups, large groups, segregated settings, and inclusive settings. Choosing the one that is best for each student requires careful thought and planning and knowledge of the student and the educational materials. Some of the other components that affect instructional periods and academic gain for exceptional students are described here: groupings, functional needs, ESL programs, literacy acquisition, self-care/daily living skills, and vocational skills.

Small Groups

Teachers of exceptional students utilize various groupings at different times during the day, but an effective method of working with these students is in small group settings. Although there are advantages to one-to-one instruction, such as minimal distractions and an intensive instructional period, as well as to large group instruction, such as learning from others, and being cost-effective, the small group instruction period offers significant advantages to exceptional students.

Small group instruction helps students learn to generalize skills more quickly, allows for social interactions, permits more flexible involvement with the teacher, and helps students learn from other peers. Small groups may be established through the general education class programs, in resource rooms, in pull-out models, and in self-contained classes.

Functional Needs

Training students with exceptional needs in the competencies necessary for everyday living in selected environments and then being able to generalize those skills is a critical component of the integrated curriculum for moderately to severely impaired students. Learning functional skills reduces the dependence on others and allows the individual a chance to participate in less restrictive environments. These skills include dressing, toileting, eating, using simple sight words, managing self in a familiar environment, making independent choices, and handling small purchases. In most instances, using realistic objects in authentic settings to teach functional skills is most effective.

Functional training terms follow:

- **functional academics:** Focuses on basic educational concepts that may be useful in daily life, such as basic reading using survival sight words, basic math involving money and time, and basic writing like name, address, and telephone number.
- **functional curriculum:** Emphasizes the skills necessary to perform adequately in the community and is most often used with students who have mental retardation, autism, and other moderate to severe conditions.
- **functional skills:** The independent living skills considered important for self-care, social circumstances, employment, vocational situations, and recreational activities.
- **functional language:** The skills used to make a basic need or desire known.
- **functional literacy:** The level of communication and language that a person needs to live independently in the community.

ESL

Students who are described under the term *English as a Second Language* face barriers with language and culture in addition to their exceptional needs. Laws require that schools address issues of diversity and ensure that both the educators and the curriculum are responsive to the cultural heritage, ethnic backgrounds, and linguistic differences. For students with disabilities, rights related to diversity are reflected in the law and pertain to assessments and programming.

Self-Care Skills and Daily Living Skills

Self-care skills or daily living skills are an area of weakness exhibited by adults with disabilities. Student educational programs should be designed to daily integrate these skill areas so students have the opportunity to practice and generalize these skills. Instruction in the areas of personal hygiene, housekeeping, social skills, daily tasks, and social communications will prepare students to function appropriately in their communities. Students who retain these skills become more independent across various settings. Use of direct instruction, modeling, and utilizing environmental cues are effective strategies in learning these skills.

Vocational Skills

The selection of vocational skills training imposed depends on the type and characteristics of the individual's exceptionality. A thorough assessment of abilities and vocational needs should be conducted as a component of the transition plan described under federal law. Collaboration of school educators and outside agency personnel will enhance the student's program and help determine additional resources for vocational skills training.

Exceptional students should be trained to gain the proper skills for a productive life of independent living, access and maintenance of employment, enjoyment of leisure activities, utilization of routine living skills, and joining community events. To aid students with disabilities in learning these skills, they require structured learning experiences in integrated settings. **Community-based instruction** is one highly recommended method that includes hands-on, interactive opportunities in vocational and life skills training. **Supported employment** is another recommended method that is used with students who have more severe conditions.

Assistive Technology

Federal regulations state that assistive technology is any item, piece of equipment, or product system, whether acquired commercially off the shelf, modified, or customized, which is used to increase, maintain, or improve the functional capabilities of children with disabilities. Students must be assessed in the area of **assistive technology** in order for the proper program and device to be selected and training is necessary for the student, parents, and staff.

Assistive technology may consist of high- or low-tech devices used to remove barriers or help solve everyday problems for individuals with disabilities. The devices can aid individuals with writing, reading, communicating, listening, doing math, organizing, and remembering. These devices may be environmental controls, voice-activated, augmentative communication systems, or switch controlled. They may include simple tools such as a reaching device, or more complicated devices like audio instruction.

Following are some of the terms related to assistive technology:

augmentative and alternative communication (AAC): A set of strategies that aid a student to meet communication needs through symbols and other transmission devices

augmentative technology: Supports students with disabilities who have oral language problems

facilitated communication: A type of communication in which a person provides assistance to a student by pointing to symbols or letters

instructional technology: Provides drill and practice for students who have problems in the basic skill areas and with motivation issues

oral reading software: For use with students who exhibit reading problems

voice recognition system: Replaces the keyboard and the input device

voice synthesizer: Converts text from a computer into sound

word processing software: To support students with written expression deficits

Assessment

Schools are required to utilize non-bias, multifactored methods of assessing students for the purpose of determining a disability or exceptionality and what, if any, special services may be needed. Tests must be administered in the student's native language and free from any racial, culture, or language discrimination. Identification, placement, and program decisions may not be based solely on one test. Further information about the assessment process for special education is found in the provision under IDEIA called the **protection in evaluation procedures.**

The primary purpose of an assessment is to determine the specific needs of the student (discover the present levels of educational performance) and to identify the instructional strategies and methods that would provide the most benefit to the academic achievement of the student. The assessment results may lead the development of an educational plan and decisions that will support the student in accessing an education. Additional purposes are as follows:

- To determine the nature of the problem
- To decide the need for related services
- To target skills or identify content areas
- To ascertain which factors support learning
- To manage the data related to instruction

Gifted/Talented

Each state develops identification procedures for students who exhibit gifted or talented tendencies. Both quantitative and qualitative approaches to assessment for gifted and talented students are essential for accurate identification. Using a quantitative approach may include any number of standardized or teacher-gathered measurements. These may include past student performances, family history, standard achievement or intelligence quotient tests, teacher reports, teacher, parent or student recommendations, and current classroom achievements. The qualitative measures include portfolios, interventions, and observations.

Assessment Process

The steps in the assessment process are as follows:

Pre-referral: The initial step of the special education procedures, it also begins the assessment process. An informal step in the process, it helps the teacher to more specifically identify a student's problem areas. A student exhibiting problems in the general education classroom is provided interventions to determine any benefit from them. These concerns may be discussed with the school assistance team for more ideas and support. If the student makes adequate progress, the referral for special education is concluded. If the expected progress does not occur, the process moves to the second step.

Screening: Professionals provide a quick and simple test that covers basic skills and gathers additional information that may detect a student who is in need of a more comprehensive evaluation and possible support of special education services.

Referral: Professionals use information from a variety of sources, conduct an observation to study classroom performance and behaviors and then refer for further evaluations.

Evaluation and identification: This step necessitates a comprehensive evaluation by professionals to determine the student's disability and possible eligibility for special education services. Timelines are imposed and requirements for the types of measurement tools used must align with federal law. A **multifactored assessment,** conducted by a team, is an evaluation of a student using a variety of test instruments and procedures.

Instructional program planning: Assessment information is essential for program planning in order to create goals, determine placement, and make plans for instructional delivery. The team meets to share results of the evaluations and make critical decisions about the student and the services.

Placement: After the team designs the instructional program (IEP), decisions about the LRE and specifications about the services are made, and the program is implemented.

Review and evaluation: Monitoring the progress of a student according to the IEP is required in order to develop regular progress reports and adjust the IEP. A review of the student's achievements and progress is conducted using various approaches, such as formal, informal, or alternate measurements.

Procedures and Materials

Appropriate assessment procedures are required under the law and must be implemented for each evaluation and for every student. A variety of assessment tools and strategies must be administered in the student's primary language and be free from racial or cultural bias, because they are used with diverse groups of students. The assessment tools used must be appropriate for each student so relevant functional, developmental and academic information may be collected to help determine the educational needs of the student.

Several types of measurement tools may be used throughout the assessment process, whether during a comprehensive evaluation or for an evaluation of student progress. Following are some of the assessment types that may be administered.

- **Achievement test:** A formal tool used to measure student knowledge or proficiency in a subject or topic area.
- **Active student response:** This is a frequency-based measure used to determine a student's participation rate during an instructional period.

- **Anecdotal record:** An informal measurement of teacher notes based on observation of student work and performance, often used in parent conferences.

- **Aptitude test:** A formal measure of standardized or norm-referenced tests that evaluate a student's ability to acquire skills or gain knowledge.

- **Authentic assessment:** An informal method of determining a student's comprehension and performance of a skill, particularly used in classroom assessments of specific criteria.

- **Behavior assessment:** A variety of behavior evaluation tools are available to track student behaviors and to document progress on a behavior intervention plan or on the use of self-management techniques.

- **Criterion-referenced test:** A formal measure that evaluates a student on specified information, most often used to check a student's knowledge on subject areas by answering specific questions and does not compare one student to another.

- **Curriculum-based measure:** Evaluates student progress and performance of skills based on the curriculum and lessons presented, helping teachers determine how to assist the student and share with parents.

- **Ecological-based assessment:** Involves the use of an informal observation of the student interacting with the environment during a regular schedule.

- **Functional Behavior Assessment (FBA):** The process of gathering information about problem behaviors of an individual student and used to evaluate the need for behavior intervention and a behavior plan.

- **Intelligence test (IQ test):** A norm-referenced test used to assess a student's learning abilities or intellectual capacity as it measures cognitive behaviors.

- **Norm-referenced test:** Formal tool referred to as a standardized test is used when comparing a student to other peers in the same age group, primarily helpful in developing curriculum and identifying interventions needed.

- **Observation:** Teachers or professionals watch a student in several settings and take notes regarding performance and behaviors, particularly helpful in developing behavior plans and for use in comprehensive assessments.

- **Performance assessment:** An informal measure used by teachers to assess a student's ability to complete a task specific to a topic or subject area, such as a mathematic equation or an oral report.

- **Portfolio assessment:** An informal method of gathering information based on completed products (art work or compositions) over a period of time. Particularly helpful for evaluating progress and sharing information with parents.

- **Standards-based assessment:** Formal evaluation and either a criterion-referenced or norm-referenced test, it measures progress toward meeting goals or standards as previously established by district or state.

- **Summative evaluation:** Informal procedure is used to assess student achievement and teacher instruction.

Instructional Decisions

A comprehensive evaluation assesses all aspects of a student's growth and development. The results are used to help a team make quality decisions about the student's overall educational program. Scores and wide-ranging results should be translated into educational terms and a statement of present levels of educational performance. The team can construct a set of measurable goals that reflect the student's educational strengths and needs. Following these steps is the identification of the materials, methods, and strategies best suited for the student.

Certain assessments guide instructional decisions and are helpful in gathering additional information for periodic progress reports and for consideration at the IEP annual review. Some of these assessment options include systematic observations, criterion-referenced tests, curriculum-based assessments, functional behavior assessments, anecdotal records, rating scales, interviews, and alternative assessments.

Preparation of Reports

Report writing is a professional skill, and examiners must conform to the criteria required in preparing an assessment report. A written report must indicate the exceptionality, identify the pertinent characteristics, and explain how the exceptionality affects learning, as well as suggest methods and interventions for instruction. A review of the student's past performance, a summary of the health and developmental history, student behaviors and family influences, as well as the types of assessments conducted, and the related scores should be described in the final report.

The oral presentation of the assessment findings should be provided at a team meeting. The examiner, or a person qualified, will review the scores and collected data in order to interpret the results for other team members. Each separate participating examiner should present assessment information that will aid the team in making appropriate educational decisions about the student. After the results have been shared, the team may proceed with the development of the student's program (IEP).

Structuring and Managing the Environment

Effective instruction is the foundation for successful classroom management. A positive environment is bound to increase appropriate behaviors, encourage student-teacher interactions, and reinforce individual education programs. Management of the environment builds upon academic success.

Organizing a classroom requires established expectations and set criteria for several areas: the class tone, classroom rules, engaging the learners, organizing the instruction, and using accommodations. Including students in creating specific guidelines may help them accept the limitations and perform appropriately in the environment.

Classroom Organization and Management

Organizing and managing a classroom for diverse and exceptional learners is a tremendous task. Classroom management is especially essential in inclusion models, as there are many types of learners. In order to maintain classroom management, student behaviors must be under control, whether imposed by the teacher or self-regulated by the student. Educators must understand how behaviors impact learning and the influences that the classroom environment has on positive behavior management.

Procedures are a key component for classroom management. Students need to know the expectations so learning becomes their primary focus. A reduction in disruptive and inappropriate behaviors should result if these procedures are established: classroom rules, homework processes, transitions, discipline techniques, work guidelines, dismissal procedures, and so on.

Helpful in classrooms for exceptional students are effective learning strategies implemented so all learners may participate at their rate and level. Using a multimodal approach involves the use of teaching methods and strategies that are visual, auditory, tactile, and kinesthetic, as they address all styles of learning.

Some strategies for classroom management may include: removal of visual and auditory distractions, providing clear directions, modeling or demonstrating new tasks, providing access to materials, and delivering feedback and reinforcements.

Behavior Management Strategies

Behavior management is a designed program that integrates the needs of the individual student with the environment. Setting standard guidelines for behavior in a classroom with a system of rewards and consequences helps outline the expectations for students. An assessment of the student's academic skills and behaviors, along with an examination of how they impact the student's learning will provide a foundation for individual expectations. For those having problems managing behaviors, other strategies may be necessary followed by establishing **incentives.**

Students in special education are provided behavior management tools according to their Functional Behavior Assessment (FBA) and Behavior Intervention Plan (BIP).

General strategies to help individualize behavior management techniques are as follows:

- Make the environment comfortable and safe.
- Involve students in creating rules.
- Avoid power struggles and confrontations.
- Implement and track behavior plans.
- Develop expectations for appropriate behaviors.
- Use immediate feedback and consistent reinforcements.

The following terms will be helpful in the study of behavior interventions and management with exceptional students.

acting out behavior: Inappropriate behavior (aggressive or disruptive) considered more damaging and serious than other behaviors.

Applied Behavior Analysis (ABA): Method of behavior scrutiny to determine how and why a student responds to certain events, situations, or the environment and allows for a training component of rewards and reinforcements to help the student learn the target behavior.

alternative school placement: Public school option that may be utilized when a student cannot function in the traditional public school system due to uncontrolled behaviors or due to a disruption that caused a suspension or expulsion.

antecedent: Stimulus used in behavior management and behavior modification that occurs prior to the behavior and establishes the reason for the behavior.

behavior intervention: Strategies or actions used to extinguish, change, or redirect an inappropriate behavior; three types are positive reinforcement, negative reinforcement, and aversive intervention.

behavior rating scales: An evaluation tool that lists specific observable behaviors to assess the severity, frequency, and type of exhibited behaviors completed by staff, parents, or student.

consequences: Stimulus that follows a behavior action used in behavior management or behavior modification to increase or decrease the behavior.

contingency contract: Written agreement between the student and the teacher that outlines the expected performance and the consequences or reinforcers used.

discrete trial training: Strategy in which the function or task is broken down into steps that are rewarded immediately in a trial-by-trial basis.

manifestation determination: Team review of the relationship between a student's inappropriate behavior and the disability, required under IDEIA when a student violates a code of conduct.

modeling: Use of imitation to set in place the desired behaviors.

negative reinforcement: Used in behavior modification in which the student is motivated to use a desired behavior in order to avoid a negative consequence.

perseveration: When a behavior continues repeatedly beyond the typical endpoint and the student demonstrates difficulty switching tasks.

positive reinforcement: Used in behavior modification in which the student is motivated to use a desired behavior because of the reward to be obtained.

response generalization: Application of a learned behavior or skill to another setting.

target behavior: The behavior selected for intervention, most often to be extinguished or changed, although it may be a positive behavior that should be used in other school situations.

Professional Roles and Responsibilities

The roles and responsibilities of teachers cover a broad expanse. When educators and other professionals share their expertise and respect one another's roles, the delivery of services to exceptional students is enhanced.

The inclusion movement changed how services to exceptional students are implemented and improved the interactions of educators. They share their expertise, their skills, their perspectives, and their ideas to enrich services and programs. Both the special education teacher and the general education teacher have important team roles working in inclusive settings.

The primary **role of the special education teacher** is to manage the IEP team, implement the IEP, provide accommodations to general education, and support the student and other teachers.

The basic **role of the general education** teacher is to instruct students in the general education curriculum according to district standards and state requirements, while implementing accommodations, modifications, or adaptations for exceptional students.

Specific duties of a special education teacher include the following:

- Conduct assessments.
- Plan for specifically designed instruction.
- Implement instruction and accommodations.
- Monitor student progress.
- Collaborate, consult, and confer with team members.
- Schedule and run IEP meetings.
- Conduct transition assessments and create ITP.
- Train staff and students in advocacy.
- Communicate with parents.
- Facilitate programs and activities.
- Supervise paraprofessionals.
- Manage behavior assessments and plans.
- Participate in staff development and workshops.
- Join professional organizations and attend conferences.
- Read research, articles, and journals about current trends.

In a segregated setting, a resource room, or an inclusive model, the roles of a special education teacher remain similar. Whether working with students who have disabilities or students with other exceptional needs, educators need to maintain a schedule and remain organized, using school resources to meet deadlines and complete tasks.

Paraprofessionals

As the numbers of identified exceptional students increase, the expansion of programs and services is possible with paraprofessionals. This position related to exceptional student programs has become an essential staff position that encompasses a wide range of duties and responsibilities. They may work with a wide variety of students, many types of exceptional conditions, and in various settings. Under the supervision of a certified teacher, a paraprofessional helps the teacher by providing more direct services and additional instructional opportunities on a regular basis. Establishing clear guidelines and outlining the roles and responsibilities of the paraprofessional are essential to ensure a successful working relationship and positive delivery of services to students. The traits most preferred in paraprofessionals include flexibility, dependability, motivation, tolerance, patience, cooperativeness, resourcefulness, and positiveness.

Documentation Management

Special education and regular education follow requirements for the completion of specific paperwork and management of these documents. Access to student information is protected, under IDEIA and FERPA, so storing student documents and records must meet the requirements of these laws. Parents have certain rights regarding access to their child's files.

Organization is a critical step in maintaining proper files and documents so record retrieval is simplified. Keep valuable written information about students prepared for meetings, progress reports, and annual reviews. The IEP and BIP are often used documents for classroom teachers, as goals and interventions are reviewed regularly, so easy access is important.

Some student records, which teachers may access, are stored in school offices. Special education offices may keep medical records, assessment results, psychological information, behavioral information, therapy summaries, progress notes, communications, meeting notes, and parent information on file. Records and files about special education students may not be destroyed without permission from the special education office as there are laws that regulate the destruction of such confidential records in each state.

Confidentiality

Confidentiality is a legal and professional practice that does not allow personnel to disclose information about an exceptional student without the express written consent of the parents or guardian. This information includes, but is not limited to, the diagnosis, the educational program, the behaviors, the medical information, the family history, the assessments, and classroom performance, unless the information is shared with another staff member who works directly with the student. However, should a student become a danger to himself or others, or if the student has committed a crime and the authorities are called, school personnel may provide certain information to protect the student.

Communication with Families

Under federal law, professionals working with exceptional students are encouraged to include parents and families as partners in the education process and during the implementation of special programs. This partnership should be based on reciprocal respect and dignity.

Research shows that parent involvement can be a positive influence on their child's education, which helps the child perform at a more successful level. Involving parents is a meaningful component to an education program as they can help develop goals, provide constant support to the child, access additional resources, and add opportunities for more learning situations.

Examples of providing home-school communication include the following: parent-teacher conferences, regular telephone or e-mail contact, written messages or daily log, newsletters, and group meetings.

Introduction

Students identified with learning disabilities cause quite a challenge for schools, educators, and parents. A learning disability seems to be steeped in mystery. It is not visible or easy to recognize, and at times, students seem to be more obstinate than exceptional. But, it is a complex condition for an individual to manage, as there is no one remedy, method, or piece of equipment that makes this disability more acceptable. Students diagnosed with learning disabilities do not fit easily into general education classrooms, even though their intelligence levels are considered average to above average, yet that is often the very best placement for them.

Aiding these students in school settings requires trained professionals who understand the many varieties of learning disabilities and who realize how to work with parents and general education staff to provide the most appropriate education. Each student presents with different, unique qualities and separate, individual needs. These are students who experience failure every day and who, at certain times, do understand the comprehensiveness of their own disability. Some believe they are different, stupid, and worthless. Some think they cannot learn and will not amount to much as adults. They need consistent and quality support to reach their individual potentials.

Educators with backgrounds in learning disabilities have an important job in the schools. They first must recognize the different characteristics of each of these students, discover each student's personality, and determine the many expectations for success for each student, while then imparting all of this information to those adults who are involved with the student. Students with learning disabilities, although the highest numbers of exceptional students in the schools, are the least understood and may receive fewer services.

The Praxis II exam, 0382, titled the Education of Exceptional Students: Learning Disabilities is a knowledge-based exam used for the purpose of granting certification to individuals who plan to teach students with learning disabilities at any grade level, preschool through 12. This 1-hour exam is comprised of 30 multiple-choice questions and 3 constructed-response questions, based on a narrative case study. Two content categories are identified in this exam: Learner Characteristics; Historical and Professional Context: Definitions (15 questions, 25 percent) and Delivery of Services (15 questions, 25 percent). The final section is called Problem Solving Exercises and contains three questions, which are 50 percent of the exam.

For recent college graduates or those taking jobs in states requiring this exam, studying for the Praxis II exam is critical to obtaining certification. The following study information, sample questions, and practice test should be helpful in preparing for this examination. Some of the information about specific learning disabilities, their causes, the educational practices, and instructional methods may have been delivered in detail during college coursework so use this study guide as review and determine the areas to which more study should be devoted. If additional information is needed, refer to texts on those topics, search the Internet, or speak with practitioners. Suggested websites are provided in the "Resources" section.

Since the category of *learning disabilities* is covered under the federal law, IDEIA, coursework should have included a review about the education of students with disabilities, as well as special education procedures and practices. More about this law may be found in "Core Content Knowledge." In preparing for this exam (0382), seek facts about learning disabilities; information about services; development and implementation of an IEP, an IFSP, and an ITP; classroom strategies and methods; family involvement; assessments; educator roles; curriculum; instruction; and program issues in school environments. Check the questions in the next two sections for recall of information and then refer to content found in the study guide, reading through these sample questions again before taking the practice test at the end of the book.

Another Praxis II exam, titled Special Education: Teaching Students with Learning Disabilities (0381), is also available and required for certification in certain states. The study information for this exam may be found in another guide developed by the same author and published by Wiley, Inc., called *CliffsTestPrep Praxis II: Special Education (0351, 0352, 0690, 0371, 0381, 0321)*. This other study guide also contains a section on core knowledge and one on the application of core knowledge, which may be required for certification as well.

Content Clusters

The Content Categories mentioned in the Introduction for this Praxis II cover a wide range of information about students with learning disabilities. The content covered includes details and descriptions of learner characteristics, historical information, and service delivery options. These categories have been summarized here into questions and grouped as content clusters. Some of the clusters are based on information from more than one content category.

This set of 10 questions is provided so examinees may evaluate their basic knowledge related to the subject of exceptional students with *learning disabilities*. Examinees should study the concepts and content for each of the broad topic questions as part of test preparation, especially those questions found to be difficult. By carefully reviewing these topics, examinees may prepare for the Learning Disabilities, Praxis II (0382) exam. Examinees may want to write out their answers and then check these responses according to the content provided in the study guide.

1. Describe the different philosophies related to the instruction of students with learning disabilities.

2. Identify the various influences that may impact a person with a learning disability across his life span.

3. Clarify the various aspects of classroom management (social competence, behavior modifications, and physical environment) as related to students with learning disabilities.

4. Illustrate the specific interventions utilized in the areas of oral language, remedial reading, written language, mathematics, and study skills instruction.

5. Explain the various professional resources and organizations available for special educators and how each of these is found to be beneficial to educators.

6. Outline the historical development of public school programs for students with learning disabilities.

7. Describe the effects of a learning disability on a student's cognitive function, academic performance, and social-emotional development.

8. Expound upon the various accommodations and modifications proven to be beneficial in the instruction of students with learning disabilities who are placed in general education classrooms.

9. Identify the current research on *learning disabilities* and the issues related to the instruction of students with these conditions.

10. List an assortment of technology instruments and methods that will enhance and benefit students with learning disabilities in their educational programs.

Preview Questions

Five multiple-choice questions and a constructed-response question that is related to a case study are provided so examinees may assess themselves regarding the content and types of questions included on this Praxis II exam. The answers to these questions are given, but further information about these answers can be found interspersed in the study guide section that follows.

When taking the actual Praxis II exam, read each question more than one time to determine the main concept of the stem. Think about each of the possible answers, knowing that only one is correct based on the information given. Choose the answer that is most appropriate after rereading the question and inserting the various possibilities. The answer will not always be the most obvious, but it should be the best fit for the concept.

All of the questions and answers are based on federal law and best practices for exceptional students with learning disabilities who are placed in school settings. Knowing that certain practices may vary in different states, consider the possible selections for an answer and determine which would be reflective of the law or primary best educational practices.

Multiple-Choice Questions

Read each of the following questions and select the best answer.

1. Many students identified with learning disabilities in the area of mathematics experience difficulties with

   A. principles and concepts.
   B. calculations and reasoning.
   C. formulas and word problems.
   D. examinations and homework.

2. The very simple definition for the term "learning disability" is

   A. an intellectual inability to perform.
   B. a neurological disorder of language.
   C. the physical problems affecting the brain.
   D. a language disability in math and reading.

3. The three main concepts of the cognitive psychology theory are

   A. knowing, thinking, and learning.
   B. learning, concepts, and readiness.
   C. thinking, identifying, and speaking.
   D. knowing, behavior, and processing.

4. When a student with a learning disability takes a statewide assessment an accommodation that may be appropriate is to

   A. give no score.
   B. extend the time.
   C. provide someone to read.
   D. accept answers for half the questions.

5. Students with learning disabilities often demonstrate the need for more well-structured transition periods between instructional activities, as disorganized transitions will result in

   A. a lack of active learning.
   B. the reduction of engaged learning.
   C. an increase of attending behaviors.
   D. the appearance of disruptive behaviors.

The correct answers are as follows:

1. **B.** Calculations and reasoning are the two specific areas in which students with learning disabilities are most likely to demonstrate delays. These two areas are assessed when determining whether a student has a disability in mathematics.

2. **B.** A learning disability has been specifically defined as a condition related to neurological processes, most particularly related to language. Students with learning disabilities are not to be considered intellectually delayed. A student with a learning disability may have a physical disability, but it is not part of the definition.

3. **A.** The cognitive psychology theory relates to the mental processes, and, therefore, the terms knowing, thinking, and learning are correct.

4. **B.** An accommodation is a support that does not alter the instruction or test. Extending more time is the best answer, as it does not change the content of the exam or the outcome.

5. **D.** Because transition periods are not structured, students often engage in inappropriate and disruptive behaviors during this interim time. Students with learning disabilities particularly need structure when moving from one task or activity to another.

Constructed-Response Questions

The following are samples of the *constructed-response* questions that are included in this Praxis II exam. On the actual exam, the answers for constructed-response questions should be written either as a short-answer narrative or an essay, depending on what is being asked. These answers will be scored by the examination readers using a standard rubric (scoring guide). More about this kind of question is found in the introductory portion of this study guide booklet.

A middle school student who is identified with a learning disability and an attention deficit disorder has received services for exceptional students since the third grade. This student has been primarily served in general education classrooms and has achieved adequately with supports. These supports have addressed the student's problematic areas of attention and hyperactivity, in addition to the identified mathematics delays. The state assessment is approaching, and the student's performance may impact the placement in high school programs. During the development of the student's IEP in the fall, the team considered specific testing accommodations.

In order to assist this student with the overall exam, the team implemented two assessment accommodations. One is in the area of *timing* and one in the area of *presentation*. Based on this scenario, identify an appropriate specific accommodation in each of these two areas and explain why these interventions would be helpful to this particular student.

Timing: The student should be allowed frequent breaks during the testing periods. This accommodation is appropriate because this student demonstrates hyperactivity and may need to have the exam broken down into smaller periods of time. Providing breaks would not alter the overall content or intent of the exam but would support the student and address the exceptional conditions the student faces.

Presentation: The student should be allowed repeated directions by the proctor or the teacher giving the test. This accommodation is most appropriate since this student appears to have difficulty with attending and may miss some of the information if given only one time. Test directions are very important during an exam, and, therefore, repeating these directions to the student may aid in the final outcome of this student's performance, while not altering the exam content, materials, or presentation.

Topic Overview

The condition of a learning disability and its unique characteristics has perplexed professionals and parents alike. For centuries, individuals with learning problems did not receive the support they needed to be successful in their lives. It was not until the 1960s that students with learning disabilities began to get the attention they deserved. The emergence of this area under the law, however, took the work of many professionals and informed parents who advocated for these exceptional individuals.

Definitions are continually debated, as are the methods and services for students with learning disabilities. But educators who work with these students know best that addressing their individual needs and providing adequate supports will help them become productive citizens, utilizing their strengths and talents throughout their adult years.

Many different types of learning disabilities make each student identified with this condition an exceptional individual. Learning disabilities prevent an individual from learning in the same manner and at the same rate as her same age peers. These students, therefore, must have access to unique learning strategies, varying instructional methods, and appropriate accommodations to the general education curriculum in order to gain benefit and demonstrate adequate educational performance.

This portion of the study guide is divided into two sections (Learner Characteristics and Delivery of Services), which are a reflection of the Education of Exceptional Students: Learning Disabilities Praxis II test. A great amount of information is available about exceptional students with learning disabilities, but this guide gives only an overview of those topics covered on the exam. For additional information about these exceptional students, refer to texts, the library, or websites about specific subjects (see the "Resources" listing at the back of this book).

Learner Characteristics; Historical and Professional Context: Definitions

Learning disabilities know no boundaries. Learning disabilities affect people of all ages, cultures, languages, and all countries and continue throughout the span of a lifetime. Since the 1970s, it is estimated that the numbers of students identified with learning disabilities has increased threefold. These individuals struggle to learn in school, and they often experience failure on a daily basis.

Learning problems and **learning differences** are common among all children in the general education population, but those are not considered exceptional under federal law. Children with *learning disabilities* are representative of a smaller group who actually possess neurological disorders and require special education services. However, students with learning disabilities have talents and capabilities that are often misunderstood, under valued, and go unrecognized.

The term **learning disability** emerged in the 1960s; prior to that, many professionals referred to these individuals with learning issues according to the focus of their own discipline. These terms included those developed by physicians and psychologists regarding the condition as *brain damage*, *neurological impairments*, *perceptual handicaps,* and *minimal brain dysfunction.* The latter term was used in the education system until Samuel Kirk coined the term that is used today: *learning disabilities*. Professionals from these various fields, as well as advocacy groups, still affect the focus and studies about individuals with learning disabilities, so it is expected that definitions and terms may change in the future.

Should examinees desire more general information about learning disabilities or need to access more about the historical and professional aspects of students with learning disabilities, they can research the following organizations and check the websites offered in the "Resources" section.

- The Council for Learning Disabilities (CLD)
- The Division for Learning Disabilities (DLD-CEC)
- The Learning Disabilities Association of America (LDA)
- The National Center for Learning Disabilities (NCLD)

Historical Information

The history of learning disabilities is fairly new, with the term only being coined in 1963. Prior to this time, students with learning disabilities faced a variety of problems in school settings.

This simplified timeline should provide an accurate picture of the historical overview.

- 1800s to 1930: Scientific studies focused on abnormal behavior and brain function.
- 1920s to 1930s: Samuel Orton (neurological specialist) created the developmental theory and remedial reading strategies for dyslexic children.
- 1930s to 1940s: Alfred Strauss studied children with mental retardation and brain injury and found relationships of these disorders to learning.
- 1940s: Laura Lehtinen developed systematic and direct teaching methods similar to those used today.
- 1930s to 1960s: Research of brain dysfunction was conducted by studying children with learning problems.
- 1950s to 1960s: Schools provided programs for children with mental retardation, sensory impairments, physical disabilities, and behavior disorders, but those with learning problems did not fit into any of the established categories and, therefore, did not receive needed services.

- 1960 to 1980: An overall increase in school programs, theories, assessment techniques, and teaching strategies related to children with learning disabilities occurs.

- 1960s: Marianne Frostig developed materials designed to improve visual-perceptual performance and schools focused on cooperative and work-study programs. Samuel Kirk published a test called the Illinois Test of Psycholinguistic Abilities (ITPA) to identify students with learning disabilities.

- 1963: The term, *learning disability*, was coined by Samuel Kirk.

- 1966: The national task force identified characteristics of the condition known as **minimal brain dysfunction.**

- Late 1960s: Schools provided programs only for elementary students with learning disabilities as it was thought that given an early focus and directed efforts on intervention and instruction, the student's learning disability would not continue past the sixth grade. It took years for this concept to change, but secondary programs for students with learning disabilities did not begin until the late 1970s.

- 1968: The Council for Exceptional Children, CEC, developed a Division for Learning Disabilities.

- 1969: Congress passed the Children with Learning Disabilities Act.

- 1970s: Newell Kephardt used physical exercise to aid children with problems in learning and found them to be beneficial.

- 1980s and 1990s: A focus on transition planning to help students with learning disabilities prepare for adult life. Don Hammell and Steve Larsen showed that perceptual approaches were seldom effective in teaching academic skills, but direct instruction does make a difference.

Once the first federal laws for special education was passed in 1975; children with learning disabilities were included in the description, and although limited, began to receive support. It has taken many years since for the definitions to evolve and for the appropriate services to be set in motion.

Philosophies and Theories

Several philosophic viewpoints have developed over the years regarding students with learning disabilities. These thoughts are based on research and the developmental stages of learning.

Three primary areas of psychology have produced the theories most prominent today: developmental, behavioral, and cognitive. Because of these theories, educators more clearly understand the multitude of learning disabilities and the impact these conditions have on children. These theories support professionals to better implement the proper assessments, utilize the appropriate instructional practices, and deliver individualized services.

Developmental Theory: Associated with Jean Piaget's theory on the maturational stages of development (sensorimotor stage, preoperational stage, concrete operations stage, and formal operations stage), this theory reflects that a student's cognitive skills follow a sequence of development as the child matures. One key point of this theory is that children should not be required to perform a task at a stage of development that is beyond their maturation, their readiness, or their ability, before they are ready to do so. This work is confirmed by the work of Lev Vygotsky who called "the zone of proximal development" the range between what a child is capable of doing independently and a task that needs assistance.

Behavioral Theory: This philosophy has its roots in the work of B.F. Skinner and includes the use of observable and measurable behavior. The behavioral theory promotes a systematic focus on assessment and instruction for students with learning disabilities. The area of instruction endorses explicit teaching and direct instruction to support students with disabilities in classrooms, and both have proven to be effective for students with learning disabilities. The behavioral theory supports the development and use of an IEP and a functional behavior assessment and plan.

Cognitive Theory: This theory emphasizes the mental abilities in order to understand how children think and learn. Students need to learn the concepts and problem-solving skills in all content areas as they move along the general education curriculum; however, for students with learning disabilities, learning these concepts and skills can be a challenge as it requires skills in many areas. From the cognitive theory, several instructional strategies for students with learning disabilities emerged. These include scaffolded instruction, learning strategies, graphic organizers, concept maps, and peer tutoring.

Current Research and Issues

Research is on-going in the realm of learning disabilities, especially with regards to the brain and how it relates to behaviors and learning. The knowledge gained about the function and the structure of the brain is important and has only recently come to the forefront. The advances in medical technology have allowed further and more in-depth studies, but there is much to learn about the neurological basis for learning disabilities. Research also continues on the appropriate and most beneficial practices and methods of instruction to use with students who are identified with learning disabilities.

The current issues associated with the services and programs for students with learning disabilities include the numbers of children being identified, the cost to schools, the special education departments to service these children, and the possible misidentification of children as learning disabled. Other critical issues that impact the services and the programs are inclusion practices, the cultural and linguistically diverse students, the neurological impact of ADD/ADHD, the students with nonverbal learning disabilities, and computer technology. Issues that affect the students more specifically include the focus on standards-based education, the state-required high-stakes testing, and assistive technology.

Professional Information

Educators should rely on professional organizations, publications, and professional development to gain the most accurate and up-to-date information about educating students with learning disabilities. Research is constantly being conducted, and educators should seek the empirical research studies that best align with their students' needs, as it seems to be the most reliable regarding classroom practices, learning strategies, and assessment of students with learning disabilities in order to improve the educational environment. Educators may find useful the continued studies on brain development, technology in education, policy issues, instructional methods, and transition practices.

Educators should join professional organizations and subscribe to professional journals that are appropriate for the specific ages and types of disabilities for the children in their classes. They will learn about techniques, practices, and studies related to students with learning disabilities. Educators, as well as parents may influence laws and impact changes in practices, so being knowledgeable about current trends and issues is valuable. Those that are most valuable for educators in the field of learning disabilities focus on brain development and its relationship to learning, medical progress and neurological information, technology in education, policy issues, genetic influences, instructional strategies, and transition practices.

Some of the most notable professional organizations include

- Learning Disabilities Association
- National Center for Learning Disabilities
- Coordinated Campaign for Learning Disabilities (CCLD)
- Council for Exceptional Children-Division for Learning Disabilities

Treatments and Therapies

In order to properly treat individuals with learning disabilities, an assessment must occur that recognizes the possible cause of the disability and the specific characteristics of the disability. Knowing the individual's strengths and needs helps the team determine the best possible course of action in delivering the appropriate services and setting measurable and attainable goals.

Students with learning disabilities demonstrate poor academic achievement, and because there are so many ways this disability can surface, educators need a selection of methods and strategies to use with numerous students. Learning disabilities can be addressed through a variety of interventions and combinations of techniques.

A learning disability cannot be cured as the processing difficulty is generally considered a lifelong neurological disorder. However, academic skills can be addressed and improved with targeted interventions. Some interventions are provided to accommodate the individual's disability, and some are designed to improve a weak area.

Interventions may include the following:

- Mastery model of specialized instruction
- Direct instruction methods
- Environmental adjustments
- Accommodations and modifications
- Special equipment or devices
- Peer tutoring
- Paraprofessional assistance
- Special education services
- Medications
- Related services

Many professionals believe that if a young student receives early intervention and remediation it can impressively reduce the chances of being labeled as learning disabled later. Children who attend preschool and early childhood programs or receive early intervention services may learn the strategies necessary to meet their academic needs and not need further assistance through special education programs.

Definitions

A wide range of definitions have been created to describe a learning disability, because there are various philosophical views about the exactness of the **specific learning disabilities.** This debate about the most appropriate terminology and definition for individuals with learning disabilities may continue, and educators must be cognizant of the pending changes.

The definitions that are most commonly used in school settings are formed either under the federal law, Individuals with Disabilities Education Improvement Act (IDEIA), or are gleaned from the National Joint Committee on Learning Disabilities (NJCLD), a government committee. Certain factors are repeated throughout in these definitions:

- Difficulty with academics and learning tasks.
- Discrepancy between potential and achievement.
- Uneven growth patterns and psychological processing deficits.
- Cause may be due to a central nervous system dysfunction.
- Possess perceptual problems.
- May have minimal brain dysfunction or brain injury.
- Problems exist across a person's life span.
- Exclusionary of other causes.

Federal

Under federal law, IDEIA, a definition for learning disabilities is provided based on a combination of several acceptable state definitions. The first definition emerged in 1975 when special education was first mandated (PL94-142, Education for All Handicapped Children). Over the years, the definition was amended under the revisions and reauthorizations of this law. The most recent reauthorization was approved in 2004 as the Individuals with Disabilities Education Improvement Act (IDEIA). A student may now be eligible without the evidence of a severe discrepancy between achievement and ability. The following is the most current rendition of the definition in the law:

> ". . . a disorder in one or more of the basic psychological processes involved in understanding or in using language, spoken or written, which disorder may manifest itself in imperfect ability to listen, think, speak, read, write, spell or to do mathematical calculations . . . includes such conditions as perceptual disabilities, brain injury, minimal brain dysfunction, dyslexia, and developmental aphasia . . . does not include a learning problem that is primarily the result of visual, hearing, or motor disabilities, of mental retardation, of emotional disturbance or of environmental, cultural or economic disadvantage."

The federal law includes an operational definition in the regulations for children with learning disabilities. This includes two main components to determine eligibility for a student with a learning disability.

1. The student does not achieve at the proper age and ability levels in one or more specific areas when provided with appropriate learning experiences.
2. The student has a severe discrepancy between achievement and intellectual ability in one or more of these seven areas (oral expression, listening comprehension, written expression, basic reading skills, reading comprehension, mathematics calculation, and mathematics reasoning).

Organizations

The National Joint Committee for Learning Disabilities (NJCLD) is an organization well known for its work in the field. It identifies that a learning disability is basically a discrepancy between a child's apparent capacity to learn and the child's level of achievement. It has defined learning disability as

> ". . . a heterogeneous group of disorders manifested by significant difficulties in the acquisition and use of listening, speaking, reading, writing, reasoning or mathematical abilities. These disorders are intrinsic to the individual and presumed to be due to Central Nervous System Dysfunction. Even though a learning disability may occur concomitantly with other handicapping conditions (for example, sensory impairment, mental retardation, social and emotional disturbance) or environmental influences (for example, cultural differences, insufficient/inappropriate instruction, psychogenic factors) it is not the direct result of those conditions or influences."

The Interagency Committee on Learning Disabilities (ICLD) was commissioned by Congress to develop a definition for the condition of a learning disability. This government committee developed a three-component definition that includes social skills deficits, which the federal definition does not include. The three elements are

1. difficulties in listening, speaking, reading, writing, reasoning, mathematics, or social skills.
2. can occur concomitantly with other conditions (socioenvironmental influences and attention deficit disorders).
3. are intrinsic to the individual and are presumed to be caused by central nervous system dysfunction.

Definition Summary

The federal definition is just a guideline for individual states to use in creating their own definition for a learning disability and the criteria for eligibility under this category. Because national organizations advocate for definition changes, states may be more accurate in their use of the information.

The three criteria most often used to determine whether a student has a learning disability include

- There must be a severe discrepancy between the student's intellectual ability and the student's academic achievement levels.
- The difficulties that the student is exhibiting may not be the result of other known learning problems, such as hearing problems, vision problems, educational disadvantage, among others listed in federal law.
- The student requires special education services directly related to the specific type of learning disability in order to access the general education programs and be successful in school.

In the most recent federal special education law, IDEIA-2004, a "response-to" model has been suggested for the identification of students with learning disabilities. It states that

> "when determining whether a child has a specific learning disability . . . a local educational agency shall not be required to take into consideration whether a child has a severe discrepancy between achievement and intellectual ability . . . (and) a local educational agency may use a process that determines if the child responds to scientific, research-based intervention as a part of the evaluation procedures."

Types

Individuals with a learning disability more often have average and above average intelligence but have deficits in certain academic areas. There are many different types and forms of learning disabilities and individuals may be diagnosed with more than one form or type of a learning disability because the academic areas that are reflected in the disability use the same brain functions. These include reading, writing, using mathematics, listening, and speaking. An individual's memory and social skills may also be affected. Specific areas that may be influenced may include abstract reasoning, auditory processing, language comprehension, memory deficits, spatial organization, and visual processing.

Following are helpful terms regarding the types of learning disabilities:

- **Dyslexia:** A disability of language in which the individual has problems understanding written words (reading).
- **Dyscalculia:** A disability in the area of mathematics in which the individual has trouble solving arithmetic problems, understanding math concepts, or remembering facts.
- **Dysgraphia:** A writing disability in which the individual has problems with writing.
- **Dyspraxia:** A form of the disability in which the brain messages are not processed well. This may cause problems with speech or motor control.
- **Auditory and Visual Processing Disorders:** Sensory disabilities that show up as difficulty using language or processing information about objects, even though the student has normal hearing and vision.
- **Nonverbal Learning Disability:** A neurological disorder that originates in the right hemisphere of the brain and may cause problems with visual-spatial, organizational, evaluative, intuitive, and holistic processing functions, as well as interpersonal skills. These individuals have problems with social relationships, poor self concept, poor social perceptions, a lack of social judgment, and difficulty perceiving other's emotions.
- **Specific Learning Disability:** A neurological disorder pertaining to the ability to understand or use language, spoken or written, expressive or receptive, and that may manifest through an inability to listen, think, speak, write, spell, or do math calculations.

Basic Concepts

A learning disability is considered a cognitive disability, as it is a neurological disorder that pertains to thinking and reasoning. It is suspected that when neurobiological abnormalities or atypical brain function exists there are problems specifically with how the brain processes information. Students with learning disabilities have typical intellectual capacity and often are found to have average or above average intellectual ability, but they do not process the information in the same manner or at the same time as typical same-aged peers.

A learning disability is a condition that may affect any family. It is a problem that may arise and be recognized during any stage of life, and in each stage there is a different set of characteristics and expectations. Therefore, the individual may present differently, and the disability emerges uniquely depending on the age. The majority of children who are determined to have a learning disability are generally diagnosed between the ages of 6 and 12 years.

A learning disability is a complex disorder appearing in school-age children that manifests as difficulty in reading, writing, spelling, reasoning, memory, and/or organizing information. Children with learning disabilities must learn to acknowledge their strengths, accept their weaknesses, and obtain personal strategies that will aid in academic success. Learning disability conditions can exist throughout a lifetime and affect adults in the areas of work, daily routines, family life, relationships, social situations, and leisure time.

Identification Criteria

There does not seem to be a uniform classification system for students with learning problems in every state. However, discrepancy formulas are most often used to determine a student's achievement gap. In spite of having average or above average intelligence, the primary characteristic that pertains to student identification is the demonstration of achievement deficits. As the students become older, the deficit gaps grow larger due to the academic requirements and expectations, and these problems then continue into adulthood.

Children as young as 3 may begin to exhibit delays in areas that indicate a potential for a learning problem. These include delays in gross motor and fine motor (actual motor skills, perceptual-motor skills, sensory integration, tactile/kinesthetic processing), auditory processing (phonological awareness, auditory discrimination auditory memory, auditory sequencing and sound blending), visual processing (visual discrimination, visual memory, visual closure), and problems with attention (hyperactivity, inattentiveness, impulsivity). A primary precursor to possible learning problems is the evidence of delays in language and communication skill development, which includes the acquisition or use of speech.

Some professionals believe that there is currently an over-identification of students with learning disabilities. This may be one way that educators believe students who have learning problems may get the assistance they need while not being identified with some other stigmatizing label. Students fail general education courses for a variety of reasons, and although students may not be truly learning disabled, some are identified under this category so their individual learning style may be addressed on a more individualized basis.

Incidence/Prevalence

The category of learning disabilities is the largest of all special education categories for school-age children with about 6 percent of the school population or 51 percent of the disability population being identified as **LD (Learning Disabled).** The numbers appear to have tripled since the mid 1970s with about 5 of every 100 children being identified. There is concern about the numbers of children in this category and questions about the over-identification of students and the misdiagnosis of low-achieving students. Some professionals believe these numbers may be due to the "newness" of the category while others think that societal, social, and cultural changes contribute to the increased numbers.

The overall prevalence for people with learning disabilities is estimated in the broad range of 3 to 30 percent of the total population. Most children are identified by the third grade due to the higher academic expectations of reading and writing. About 50 percent of those identified have problems in the area of mathematics.

It is also estimated that about 10 to 20 percent of the school population are identified with ADHD (Attention Deficit Hyperactivity Disorder). About 80 percent of those with ADHD also have known learning difficulties, and about 20 to 25 percent are specifically labeled as LD.

It has been determined that early intervention (EI) and early childhood education (ECE) provided to children who have the potential for learning problems or disabilities and to those children who deviate from developmental norms is quite beneficial. EI has been found to be a preventive measure that will reduce the possibilities of school failure. Additionally, studies have shown that providing EI or ECE services may accelerate cognitive and social development, reduce behavior problems, involve families who become more aware, understanding, and accepting, as well as aid society's resources in not needing to deliver services when these children are older.

Risk Factors

Although definitive answers about the causes of learning disabilities are lacking, there are certain risk factors that impact individuals in the area of learning. These risk factors can indeed cause an individual to develop a learning disability and include poverty, genetics, and environmental setting.

Factors surrounding the state of poverty, which contributes to a lack of adequate health care and nutrition, are found to be risk factors for children in later developing learning disabilities. Because their basic needs are not being met, there is improper nurturing, a lack of adequate food, and limited emotional support, it may cause these children to develop at slower rates. This contributes to overall learning problems and for some a specific learning disability.

Children with family members who have learning disabilities and children who lack pre-reading skills are most at-risk for developing learning disabilities. There seems to be a genetic predisposition to the pattern of acquiring a learning disability.

Another factor related to the acquisition of a learning disability is the lack of a supportive environment. Through research, professionals have determined that enriched environments that emphasize language development, phonemic awareness, and cognitive development will reduce the potential for learning disabilities in young children. These studies have shown that when young children, who are at-risk for learning problems, are provided with early intervention and early childhood programs, they will perform at and above grade level by middle school and are less likely to develop a learning disability.

Etiologies

There is much speculation as to the causes of various learning disabilities. A learning disability is a disorder that interferes with the learning process of an individual with typical intellectual abilities, but its cause is not always known. Possible etiologies may include, but are not limited to, neurological disorders or traumatic brain injury, genetic or heredity factors, biochemical influences, nutritional deficiencies, and environmental impacts.

Neurological Disorders or Traumatic Brain Injury

The central nervous system, comprised of the brain and the spinal cord, have a relationship to learning. Should this area become injured or damaged, the process of learning does not function appropriately, and a child may emerge with a learning disability.

Genetics/Hereditary

Evidence of learning disabilities exists among family members, and scientists believe that it is this inheritance in the brain dysfunction or structural brain differences that lead to a learning disability. Another genetic factor is having a chromosomal abnormality.

Biochemical Imbalances

Chemical imbalances in the brain caused by organic factors or imposed elements can affect learning. Toxins affect the health of newborns and may cause a learning disorder.

Environmental

Learning disabilities may be caused by traumas after birth, such as head injuries, malnutrition, and toxins, as these influences may disrupt the process of proper brain development in young children, affecting their learning. Some professionals believe that the family environment also influences development and, therefore, a child may develop a learning disability.

Influence during Life Span

A learning disability is a lifelong disability, and immense challenges are presented for these students after graduation from high school. It is, therefore, important for students to learn specific strategies that will aid them in monitoring and supporting themselves. These strategies support the areas of self-determination, self-maturity, advocacy, and understanding one's own strengths and weaknesses. Self-determination is an important factor toward being successful as it is the ability to make informed decisions that is critical to self-sufficiency and independence. By supporting students and planning for their futures, they will face far fewer barriers and lead positive and contributing lives.

Even with early interventions and learned strategies, many adults with learning disabilities struggle and may need to seek continued support systems. They must contend with issues about employment, independent living, positive self-esteem, and enjoying a social life. Specifically, they need to possess consumer skills (such as knowing the terms and procedures of banking, establishing credit, applying for loans, budgeting, understanding insurance, and purchasing large ticket items such as a house or car), participate in daily life activities (such as cooking, cleaning, using maps, and public transportation), and utilize appropriate work skills (like working with others, following directions, and maintaining organization).

Individuals with learning disabilities continue to change throughout their adult period, and their problems may become even more complex. Studies have shown that there are high numbers of adults with learning disabilities who are not employed and remain illiterate. It is necessary for society to find ways to support these individuals; otherwise, they remain on welfare or public assistance, or they commit crimes and may go to prison.

Research indicates that adults with learning disabilities demonstrate consistent difficulties and face negative effects throughout their lifetimes. Adults with learning disabilities seek isolation from family and community as they experience shame, memory problems, fear, or ridicule, and many become depressed. Several factors have influence on the outcomes: the environment, social life, employment, and biological needs. Adult success is based on the individual's ability to overcome limitations, focus on talents, and possess the determination and perseverance to grasp concepts and complete tasks.

Characteristics of Individuals with Learning Disabilities

For individuals with learning disabilities, problems manifest in different ways at the various ages of life, and new traits may even emerge during different stages. The characteristics exhibited by individuals with learning disabilities are very complex, since there are so many different types and combinations of learning disabilities. The problems a student faces are exhibited by behavioral and academic problems and may change as the student faces increased expectations in higher grade levels and various social or academic situations.

Research estimates that just as many girls as boys are affected by learning disabilities; however, the traits may differ. Since boys are more obvious in their outward behaviors and academic problems, it may appear that they run a higher risk of the tendency toward developing learning disabilities. However, it may be that the characteristics of learning disabilities recognized in girls are much different. Girls tend to have more language, social and cognitive issues, and academic achievement problems in math and reading. Girls seem less belligerent and less aggressive in school so they may go undetected and unidentified for several years. Their problems then magnify when the girls become adolescents and sometimes into adulthood. Boys seem to be impacted more by the biological causes, the environmental-cultural situations, and expectation pressures.

Cognitive Functions

Cognitive functions of students with learning disabilities are exacerbated by their problems in understanding how to learn and study. They lack organizational and study skills, as well as self-motivation to learn. They often do not recognize their own personal learning style or how to approach academic and learning tasks (**metacognitive skills**). These problems promote frustration, produce nonactive learners, and increase the behavior problems exhibited in the classroom.

In general, students with learning disabilities have significant cognitive and perceptual processing problems. They may demonstrate difficulty in one of the following areas:

- Reasoning
- Memory
- Attention
- Listening
- Language
- Perception/processing of visual and auditory information

Due to the cognitive or processing problems (visual or auditory information and interpreting presented stimuli), these students are faced with limitations on academic achievement and lack of performance issues that are related to reading, written language, and mathematics skills. They also have issues with social skills, attention deficits (attention span, poor concentration), and behavior problems (distractibility, hyperactivity).

To review the meaning of *learning disability,* it is assumed that a student will possess intelligence scores within the normal range, while performing below the expected academic achievement levels. This list indicates some of the most common characteristics of students with learning disabilities:

- Demonstrate language problems, such as listening and speaking
- Learn differently and at a different pace than peers
- Possess disorders of attention and memory

- Demonstrate poor perceptual abilities
- May be disorganized and a non-active learner
- Have poor motor ability
- Show difficulty in learning to read, is an underachiever in math, or has difficulty with written language
- May be deficient in using systematic approaches to new tasks
- Demonstrate emotional immaturity
- Lack motivation
- Have social skills deficits or poor peer relationships
- Have difficulty transferring and generalizing skills and knowledge to other settings or tasks
- Exhibit learned helplessness
- Exhibit behavior problems

Other characteristics and problems with learning styles may be evident in children with learning disabilities, as this list is not comprehensive. Additionally, children with learning disabilities may have complications related to other diagnosed disorders such as the condition of ADD or ADHD (attention deficit or attention deficit hyperactivity disorder) or types of autism. These characteristics are specific to displays of distractibility, hyperactivity, inattentiveness, poor problem solving skills, and poor social skills. See "Associated Conditions."

Affect on Academics

The affect a learning disability may have on a student's academic performance and achievement includes a wide range of problems (literally hundreds) too numerous to outline in detail. Identifying every characteristic that affects learning in these individuals would surely result in a missed trait since every student is unique and can be impacted in such varying ways.

Students who are diagnosed with learning disabilities generally have the same abilities in learning and behavior as do their peers, although their skills develop more slowly due to their different rates of learning. In the elementary years, the discrepancy between ability and achievement is the most noticeable for those who have emerging learning problems. These issues arise as academic problems in reading, written language, and mathematics.

Reading is the most common and has the most devastating effect on young children. When children have problems with reading, they become less motivated, use inappropriate behaviors, and develop a lack of self-confidence. These reading problems are most often related to comprehension, fluency, and vocabulary development. Mathematics is another critical academic area, and students may have specific problems with math calculations or math reasoning.

Under the federal definition, there are six key academic areas identified as possible concerns for an individual to develop a learning disability. This list summarizes the areas of academics most impacted by a learning disability:

- **Reading:** Problems decoding words, basic word-recognition skills, and reading comprehension
- **Writing:** Lacks skills that require written expression tasks, spelling, and handwriting
- **Mathematics:** Difficulties with quantitative processing, arithmetic, time, space, and calculation of facts
- **Oral language:** Issues identified in a variety of language disorders, such as difficulties with language development, listening, speaking, and learning vocabulary
- **Phonological awareness:** Possesses poor skills in recognizing the sounds of language (phonemes)
- **Motor skills:** Demonstrates problems with gross motor skills and fine motor coordination, therefore showing awkwardness, clumsiness, and little coordination

A comprehensive assessment conducted by a team of professionals and adults familiar with the student will help to identify the specific learning disability and develop the most appropriate individualized education program. Addressing academic problems early in a child's school career will help to create a more independent individual who understands and deals with her own learning problems for the remainder of her life.

Effect on Social/Emotional Development

A great majority of students with learning disabilities also possess problems with social and emotional development, which include behavior problems. According to research studies, about two-thirds of those diagnosed with learning disabilities also have deficits in the social skills areas. Social skills are defined as being unable to adequately act and talk in social situations and having complications with establishing and maintaining social relationships and friendships.

When a student has problems with social skills, he becomes lonely, frustrated, unmotivated, and isolated. The student may have feelings of rejection, poor social competence, poor self-image or concept, and paranoia. These problems then may be exhibited in erratic and inappropriate behaviors in the classroom and other social situations. Behaviors may include outbursts, vulgar language usage, fighting, arguing, defiance, and acts of juvenile delinquency.

Social and emotional problems can become more intense and complicated when students experience repeated failure in school. Students may begin to compare themselves to their peers and become more aware of their lack of achievement as they get older. These problems magnify in the middle school and high school years as the academic and behavior expectations rise, demands on abilities increase, and the curriculum becomes more challenging. Students may start to worry about their own futures and need increased supports during these periods.

When professionals plan programs for students with learning disabilities, the area of social-emotional development should be addressed and encompassed in the intervention strategies to alleviate the students' social and emotional problems.

Associated Conditions

Research shows there is a high incidence rate of children with learning disabilities who also possess co-conditions such as ADD, ADHD, or Giftedness. Students who have learning disabilities already have problems with academic tasks, daily routines, and social situations, and the characteristics of ADD/ADHD compound these problems. They may exhibit difficulties with completing tasks, distractions, attention, or understanding directions, which adds to being confused or disorganized or they may get into trouble for their behaviors and have problems maintaining relationships.

ADD and ADHD are two quite similar terms for the same condition. ADD is used most often in the education field, while ADHD is used by physicians and psychologists. These terms both name the same chronic neurological condition in which a student exhibits problems controlling his behavior in a school or a social setting. ADD means **attention deficit disorder,** and ADHD refers to **attention deficit hyperactivity disorder.** When a student has ADD or ADHD, he may demonstrate inattentiveness, impulsivity, and/or hyperactivity.

In order to obtain a diagnosis of ADD/ADHD, three criteria must be met: severity, early onset, and duration. A diagnosis is made based on an evaluation that is conducted through an observation of the student's behaviors, by a medical practitioner, or a psychologist. These professionals specialize in knowing the symptoms of this type of condition as the symptoms may change depending on the age group of the children. The observations of students' behaviors may be conducted by teachers, parents, and other adults who use rating scales that are then reviewed and interpreted by the evaluator.

ADD is not a separate category of special education according to the law, but children with this condition may be served as exceptional children under existing categories. It is the decision of the team reflected in the evaluations conducted on how the student shall be categorized. A student may qualify under IDEIA as Other Health Impaired, Learning Disabled, Emotionally Disturbed, or may receive services under the Section 504 mandate.

Students with learning disabilities have average and above average intelligence, and some may also be considered gifted and talented (G/T). Those considered gifted may demonstrate the following characteristics: creativity, spontaneity, imagination, enthusiasm, emotionality, and inquisitiveness. These characteristics are also sometimes reflective of children diagnosed with learning disabilities. G/T children may also be inattentive, disruptive, frustrated, and not complete their work. Like those with learning disabilities, children who are G/T need a variety of activities, unique instructional methods, and specific strategies to meet their needs. When these two conditions co-exist in the same child, it takes a strong team to manage the child's educational program. The child's learning disability, giftedness, and talents must be addressed while the child's strengths are emphasized.

Two other known neurodevelopmental conditions that are related to learning disabilities are forms of autism called Asperger's syndrome and nonverbal learning disorders (NVLD). These conditions affect a student's language development, communication usage, and social skills.

Delivery of Services

Students with learning disabilities have average to above average intelligence but are plagued with not being able to achieve at the same academic level as their same-aged peers. Five major areas of learning affect students with learning disabilities: reading, written language, oral language, mathematics, and behavior (social-emotional).

Assessments should have a primary focus on these five areas to determine a student's strengths and needs and to help in planning the individualized instruction. The delivery of educational services must pertain to the student's unique learning style: auditory, visual, or kinesthetic-tactile, and specific strategies and accommodations should be implemented to address the student's needs.

It is imperative that students with learning disabilities become active participants in their own learning, be able to generalize skills to future life situations, learn to self-regulate their behaviors, be more responsible for their learning, and use effective educational tools to become better organized. They may develop these abilities if the delivery of services meets the intent of the law: to provide an individualized and appropriate education to students with disabilities.

Assessments

A learning disability must be identified through an assessment process and a portion of that consists of an evaluation most likely conducted by a school psychologist. This process includes the administration of certain measurements, the collection of pertinent information, and an observation of the student in various settings. The assessment consists of a battery of intelligence tests, academic achievement tests, school performance indicators, social interactions, and an aptitude test. Other types of assessments may include tests on perception, cognition, memory, attention, language abilities, and assistive technology. The resulting information is used to determine whether a student is achieving at her potential.

This process of assessment is mandated under federal law, and its primary purpose is to gather information about the present educational levels of a student to assist the team with decisions related to educational program planning. For a student suspected of a learning disability, the assessment should determine the eligibility based on learning problems and provide an array of information to plan the instruction and determine the interventions.

Even though federal law provides a definition of learning disability, states establish their own criteria for the eligibility of students with learning disabilities. Discrepancy formulas are often used to qualify the disability and create an appropriate educational program. The discrepancy formulas are the unexpected differences or the disparity between achievement and general ability. However, the results of an IQ test do not always determine the interventions or relate well to the actual classroom performance of some students. A specific learning disability does not include academic learning problems that may be the result of mental retardation, emotional disabilities, sensory impairments, or the lack of opportunity to learn due to environmental, cultural, or economic conditions.

Procedures and Materials

Assessment procedures for students with disabilities follow the law and must be appropriate for the student, non-biased, conducted by trained professionals, and delivered in the student's native language. The assessment of a student with a learning disability should be comprehensive and include information about past performance, developmental milestones, medical history, behaviors across settings, and a description of the family. Various procedures to gather information may be used such as case histories, parent interviews, school records, rating scales, observation, formal assessments, and informal inventories.

Specific tests assess many academic domains that are necessary to identify the areas of student difficulties. Some of the more common types of achievements tests are the Woodcock-Johnson III (WJII), the Wide Range Achievement Test III (WRAT III), and the Stanford Achievement Test—10th edition.

Other assessment measures pertain to a particular academic area, such as reading (Gray's Diagnostic Reading Tests, Stanford Diagnostic Reading Assessment, Comprehensive Test of Phonological Processing), mathematics (Stanford Diagnostic Mathematics Test, Sequential Assessment of Mathematics Inventory), and social-emotional behaviors (Adaptive Behavior Scale-AAMR, Scales of Independent Behavior, Vineland Social-Emotional Behavior Scales).

Informal Assessments

Informal assessments help professionals gather pertinent information about a student in the natural environment. These informal measures may be used to support a more formal assessment or used for continued and on-going progress checks and may include checklists, rating scales, and interviews. Other informal assessments are anecdotal records, event sampling, and running records.

Alternate informal assessments may include the following:

- **Portfolio assessment:** Collected samples of student work during a specific period of time, used to assess the student's achievement level and progress.
- **Dynamic assessment:** Teacher determines a student's ability to learn in a certain situation rather than documenting what the student has actually learned.
- **Diagnostic teaching assessment:** Teacher collects information about a student to use in assessment throughout the period of instruction.
- **Direct daily measurement:** Classroom form of daily assessment of a student's performance on the skills that are taught each day and instruction for particular students may be modified as needed.

Formal Assessments

Formal assessments are used to evaluate students on standardized instruments. These administrations are conducted in structured settings with certain requirements imposed for both the examiner and examinee. Formal assessments include standardized achievement tests, norm-referenced tests, curriculum-based assessments, and criterion-referenced assessments. Formal assessments provide a student's team with quality information to use in the development of an individualized program but should also include informal assessment results.

- **Observation:** Required as a component of a formal assessment. Information is gathered by identifying the learning behaviors of a student and how those behaviors affect the student's learning. Information is collected about a student's participation in class, tasks completed, and social interactions.
- **Standardized tests:** Intelligence and achievement tests that are standardized offer information about the discrepancy between intellectual ability and achievement, which is necessary when working with students who have learning disabilities. Standardized tests are norm referenced so the student's score may be compared to other students of the same age. Tests that are used to evaluate a student's overall academic achievement include Iowa Tests of Basic Skills, the Woodcock-Johnson Tests of Achievement, and the Wide Range Achievement Test-3.
- **Curriculum-based measurement:** Recommended in the assessment of a student with a possible learning disability is the use of a curriculum-based measurement tool (CBM) as it is a more direct and regular assessment addressing the student's learning patterns and growth, while providing information to educators helpful in program development. A CBM is important as it measures a student's performance, checks the learning patterns and progress, and provides feedback to the teacher regarding effective instruction.

Formal and Informal for Planning Instruction

Both formal and informal assessments are useful during the IEP team's process of program planning for a student. The assessment information collected is useful in creating the instructional goals, making decisions about the placement, and identifying resources and strategies that will support the student's educational program.

The main purpose of an assessment for a student with a learning disability is to determine the specific needs of the student while identifying the types of instructional strategies and methods for learning most beneficial to the success of the individual. In creating the IEP based on the assessments, a student's present levels of performance will determine the proper goals, interventions, accommodations, and related services.

Assessments for **oral language** may be selected from informal measures (rating scales, language samples, or measures of listening) or formal tools (auditory discrimination tests, oral language tests, listening tests, speech articulation tests, phonological awareness exams, or word-finding tests).

Reading assessments are plentiful, and reading can be evaluated through informal measures such as reading inventories, miscue analysis, and portfolios or through formal measures such as surveys, diagnostic tests, and comprehensive reading batteries. An informal reading inventory (IRI) can determine a student's reading level: independent, instructional, or frustration. The formal reading tests can provide overall achievement level and information on strengths and weaknesses in reading.

Written expression assessments may be formal (academic achievement battery) or informal (curriculum-based assessments). Spelling is best conducted regularly on an informal basis.

Formal assessments for **mathematics** can include standardized survey tests (group or individualized), achievement tests, and diagnostic mathematics tests. Informal assessments, an alternative of determining math performance and abilities, may consist of inventories, error analysis, or curriculum-based measurements.

Curriculum and Instruction

Curriculum for students with learning disabilities previously tended to address academic topics in a remedial sense and did not focus on the functional skills needed. Current instructional programs have changed from methods of remediation to delivering instructional approaches that focus on core curriculum used in general education programs and the functional skills needed for a lifetime. The focus of instruction is on language, social-emotional skills, and cognitive-metacognitive skills as the students proceed through the general education curriculum. This realignment of instruction offers a more accurate academic focus for students with learning disabilities and may be monitored through data collection and developed through data-based decision making.

Students with learning disabilities demonstrate differences in how they collect and organize information. They have limited background knowledge on academic topics and are not efficient in approaching learning activities. They need research-based procedures, direct instruction, and strategies that teach them to organize, comprehend, and remember information. Many proven instructional practices and methods are effective with students who have learning disabilities, but when choosing, an educator should look for structured instruction, opportunities for practice, comprehensiveness, and how it fosters independence. Educators interested in selecting curriculum, instruction, and interventions can find research results through professional organizations that will aid them in selecting scientifically validated materials.

Educators who select curriculum or determine the proper instructional methods must focus on the specific students with learning disabilities and not those students with learning differences, learning problems, or learning difficulties. These terms pertain to all students across the general population, and although they do need some adaptations to the curriculum, they are not included in the special education programming. Learning disabilities pertains to a smaller group of the school population, who have been identified for special education services due to their neurological disorders and need specific instructional methods and curriculum to be successful.

Task Analysis

The purpose of task analysis is to help a student learn a specific skill through the process of sequential steps. A task or skill is broken down into a planned, organized, and logical sequence. The student is instructed on each step in the sequence, and as each step is achieved, the next step is taken toward attainment of the larger target skill. When a teacher creates a task analysis of a skill, there are several components to remember: the task or behavioral objective, the logical sequence of the steps, the informal evaluation of the student's performance, and the delivery of instruction of the sequential steps.

Placement Decisions/Delivering Instruction

The majority of students with learning disabilities are placed in inclusive general education settings, and when proper services and supports are implemented, they perform well. Individuals who exhibit learning disabilities are intellectually capable of achieving in the general education programs after specific strategies, methods, accommodations, and modifications are developed. The IEP team is required to evaluate and address each student's overall educational needs prior to making a final decision for placement. The IEP team is challenged with determining the proper placement for services as the ultimate goal is for the student to gain independence as an adult, so the team must base its decisions about placement on the individual student's strengths and needs while planning for the future.

Modifications

Modifications are changes made to the existing curriculum so the individual needs of a student may be met. Should the expectations of a certain class or curriculum be above a student's ability level, then the educator may choose to impose a modification, which may be complex or simple, but pertains to the student's performance. These modifications should be identified on the IEP, although for most students with a learning disability, **accommodations** are implemented as they do not change the curriculum. Some modifications include provide different materials, require a different task to be completed, remove some of the expected skills, or exempt the student from an assignment.

Accommodations

When appropriate accommodations created by the IEP team are followed consistently by all staff, students with learning disabilities perform adequately in general education classrooms. An **accommodation** is an adjustment followed in the general education program so the student may gain benefit from the instruction. Many types of accommodations exist and should be selected, designed, and implemented based on varying student needs. Accommodations are generally used to improve organizational and time management skills, increase attention and memory, develop listening skills, and adapt the subject area curriculum.

Accommodations may range from simple to complex and include instructional supports such as note-taking, test taking, and technology. The team must be innovative and specifically assess the student's needs so the resulting accommodations deliver the most benefit to the educational situation.

Students with learning disabilities may need accommodations for one or more of the following broad categories:

- Abstract reasoning deficit
- Auditory processing problems
- Dysgraphia
- Dyslexia
- Dyspraxia
- Language/communication delays
- Mathematics deficits
- Memory and retrieval deficits
- Organizational problems
- Processing and reasoning deficits
- Social skill development
- Study skill needs
- Visual processing deficits
- Writing and spelling skills deficits

Oral Language

Oral language, a component of the primary language system, consists of listening and speaking and is the first language system to develop (reading and writing are in the secondary language system). Encouraging early experiences in literacy enriched environments influences the success of oral language development as children learn language structures, increase vocabulary, and practice the use of sentence structures. Children acquire words by listening to stories, reciting poetry and rhymes, and singing songs, as well as becoming aware of print, words, and sounds within their natural setting.

Oral language disorders may consist of poor phonological awareness, delayed speech or poor articulation, disorders of grammar or syntax, deficiencies in learning vocabulary, and poor understanding of oral language and its uses. **Developmental aphasia** is a severe problem with the acquisition of oral language and may be described either as receptive or expressive language disorders. **Dysnomia** is a specific expressive disorder with problems involving word retrieval, word expression, or memory. To naturally stimulate language in young children, educators and parents should use the techniques of **expansion, parallel talk,** and **self-talk.**

When instructing students in the oral language area, the purpose is to help them build a speaking vocabulary, learn the proper language patterns, formulate spontaneous sentences, and practice the overall oral language skills. Specifically, students with learning disabilities require direct and specific instruction in listening and speaking.

Listening skills consist of the phonological awareness of language sounds, an understanding of words, an ability to build a listening vocabulary, an understanding of sentences, listening comprehension, critical listening, and an ability to listen to stories.

Strategies for teaching listening skills may include the following:

- Promote phonological awareness activities (clap rhythms, recite nursery rhymes).
- Help understand words and concepts.
- Build a listening vocabulary.
- Facilitate understanding of sentences and linguistic elements.
- Teach listening comprehension (follow directions or find the main idea).
- Allow listening to stories.
- Produce oral questions (instruct on who, what, when, where, why, how).
- Teach sentence structures and patterns.
- Instruct on homonyms, synonyms, and antonyms.

When selecting activities to instruct in the area of speaking, the stages of speaking must be considered. Children pass through five major stages in developing speaking skills: babbling, jargon, single-word usage, two- and three-word sentences and language acquisition. However, children who experience learning disabilities or language disorders seldom pass through these stages at the same time as their same aged peers and may skip steps in the stages that result in further complications.

Strategies for teaching speaking skills may include the following:

- Build a speaking vocabulary.
- Production of speech sounds.
- Teach linguistic patterns.
- Formulate sentences.
- Practice oral language skills.
- Engage in parallel talk.
- Utilize self-talk.

Reading

Reading is the foundation for all school-based learning and is critical to success in life. However, the majority of students with learning disabilities have problems with reading. Reading is divided into two distinct components: word recognition and reading comprehension. The essential elements for learning to read successfully are phonemic awareness, phonics, fluency, vocabulary, and text comprehension.

Students who are identified with problems in the area of reading demonstrate difficulties with decoding or recognizing words as well as with comprehending words. They may lose their place while reading or show a lack of fluency in reading. **Dyslexia** is a type of reading disability considered a congenital neurological condition.

Strategies to improve the various areas of reading follow.

- **Phonics:** Play word and rhyming games, analyze phoneme elements.
- **Word recognition:** Use remedial reading lessons.
- **Fluency:** Repeat readings, use predictable books, recognize sight words.
- **Vocabulary:** Teach content, find words to study, create word webs.
- **Reading comprehension:** Use basal readers, build vocabulary, use graphic organizers.

Two different approaches may lead to success in areas of reading:

- **Implicit:** A whole-language focus on the relationships of oral language, reading, and writing.
- **Explicit:** An emphasis on teaching skills by direct instruction in phonics, word identification, and decoding skills.

Additional reading information, includes the following:

- **Cloze procedure:** Technique to build comprehension and language skills by supplying a passage with missing elements.
- **DIBELS:** A measurement system to assess a child's skill levels in phonological awareness, alphabetic principles, and oral reading fluency.
- **Fernald Method:** Uses the visual, auditory, kinesthetic, and tactile senses to teach whole words.
- **Orton-Gillingham Method:** Focuses on the multi-sensory, systematic, and structured language procedures for reading, decoding, and spelling.
- **Reading Recovery:** A reading program designed for young children who have problems learning to read.

Written Language

Through written language, the areas of listening, speaking, and reading, all processes of the language system are integrated. Written language is the most challenging aspect of the language system to learn, especially for students with learning disabilities.

Problems in written language may be evident in difficulties with handwriting, sentence structure, organization of ideas, spelling, and vocabulary usage. Students with learning disabilities who demonstrate problems in reading often have difficulty with writing. Students with written language problems need structured learning periods and specific directions to acquire personal strategies to help them with written language across all subject areas.

Three specific components comprise the written language category. They are written expression, spelling, and handwriting.

- **Written expression:** This involves all of the language processes. The instructional emphasis should be on the process and not the product. Early literacy is critical for the development of this area, as it is focused on the exploration of writing, which creates active and interested learners. The stages of writing include pre-writing, drafting, revising, and sharing.

Following are the strategies for teaching written expression:

Allow students to choose their own topic.

Model the writing process.

Use graphic organizers.

Encourage the use of invented spelling.

Vary the writing tasks.

Teach the process.

Promote ownership and control of the assignment.

Provide frequent and clear input.

Schedule opportunities to write.

Use computers and word processors.

- **Spelling:** This is a difficult area, as the English language does not follow specific patterns. Children must learn to apply a variety of phonics and structural analysis to spell a word and retrieve it from memory without the help of visual cues. Strategies include:

Develop auditory perception of letter sounds.

Promote a visual memory of words.

Utilize multi-sensory methods.

Teach word families.

Analyze new words.

Conduct informal testing.

Play sound-word games.

- **Handwriting:** The more concrete of the communication skills, it also depends on other skills. It requires the perception of accurate symbols, visual and motor skills, hand-eye coordination, and visual and kinesthetic memory. Manuscript writing is easier, as it is the connection of circles and straight lines, but cursive writing and keyboarding are also important. **Dysgraphia** is the condition of poor handwriting ability. Strategies to teach handwriting are:

Use prewriting practice.

Include fine motor activities and tools—use stencils, templates, color-coded paper.

Conduct training periods.

Use verbal cues.

Model letters.

Practice position and pencil holding.

State the parts of the word as it is written.

Mathematics

The National Council of Teachers of Mathematics (NCTM, www.nctm.org) promotes standards and basic principles that guide mathematics instruction for all students. The principles are related to the topics of equity, curriculum, teaching, learning, assessment, and technology. The general education curriculum impacts the education of students with disabilities in inclusive settings, so the knowledge of expectations, standards, and principles are essential to their instructional programs.

Mathematics should be learned across a continuum of skills from concrete (representational stage, symbolic, use of manipulatives) to abstract (using numbers to solve problems), incomplete to complete knowledge, and unsystematic to systematic learning. It should be delivered in a hands-on manner, using manipulatives and providing problems that relate to real life situations. With review and reteaching of math concepts and the on-going diagnosis and assessment of math skills, teachers may adjust the instruction and determine an individual's progress.

Early math skill acquisition is critical. To achieve at the average rate on number sense, children need experiences with manipulating objects, such as counting, sorting, matching, and comparing. Since math is a sequential process, early number learning leads to a better understanding of spatial relationships, visual motor skills, and visual perception skills and the concepts of time and direction. When a child has issues with perceptual skills, attention problems, or motor difficulties, he may not be exposed to activities that promote the knowledge of quantity, space, time, or distance.

There are two areas of mathematics, according to federal special education law, that may interfere with school achievement and, therefore, must be addressed for students with learning disabilities: mathematics calculations and mathematics reasoning. When a student has limited math ability or is identified with a math disability, she generally is poor at visual-motor tasks and may also lack adequate handwriting skills.

Students with learning disabilities in the area of mathematics demonstrate qualitative learning deficits that specifically emerge in poor information processing (attention, memory, auditory processing, visual processing, spatial processing, and motor control), language and reading disorders, cognitive learning strategies delays, and math anxiety. At the secondary level, a math disability may differ, as the tasks are more complicated and require more stringent standards that pertain to high-stakes tests. **Dyscalculia** is a medical term for a severe math disability, and it affects the learning of math concepts and computations based on neurological or central nervous system dysfunction.

Students with disabilities in mathematics need to learn basic facts, gain skills in how to problem solve, develop a positive attitude about math, and gain skills in functional math, estimation, measurement, and word problems. They need to establish reasoning abilities, develop math communication skills, and understand the connection of math to the real world.

Several principles for effective math instruction include the following:

- Teach precursors of math learning.
- Progress from concrete to abstract.
- Provide opportunities for practice and review.
- Teach math vocabulary.
- Teach generalizations of skills to new situations.
- Consider individual strengths and weaknesses.
- Build solid foundations of math concepts and skills.
- Balance instruction of quantitative concepts, number skills, and problem solving skills.

Math instruction should focus on cognitive learning strategies that promote the acquisition of skills to meet the challenges of math and allow students to take control of their own learning. Direct instruction helps students achieve mastery of math skills through explicit, structured, planned instruction, and activities. The steps include targeting a specific math objective and the sub-skills to meet that objective, determining the skills the student already knows and sequencing the steps to achieve the objectives. Strategies that help at the secondary level include providing examples, allowing for practice, and promoting explicit instruction. Integrating math throughout the general education curriculum is highly recommended.

Instructional mathematics activities are critical for maintaining interest and reviewing new concepts. Three categories for focus include the following:

- **Early number skills:** classification, grouping, order, counting, recognition
- **Computation skills:** parts, wholes, fractions, math operations
- **Word story problem skills**

Technology use also helps students with learning disabilities in the area of mathematics, and these tools should be further investigated for individual students: calculators, computers, software programs, and spreadsheets.

Study Skills

The acquisition of study skills is important, but the ability to use proper study skills is invaluable, especially for those with learning disabilities. For these students, instruction in specific study skills acquisition is necessary as they are needed for improving reading, taking notes, using the library, managing time, handling behaviors, listening, writing reports, taking tests, and preparing oral presentations.

For students in secondary settings, a higher level of study skills are necessary since there are more lectures, more writing assignments, and additional complex information to organize in a variety of subject areas. Students must be prepared to read from higher level textbooks and remember the intricate information, using it for more compound assignments. Strategies and activities must be presented so students may obtain the necessary study skills to aid in their learning. Some strategies consist of keeping a daily schedule, asking questions, skimming, using mnemonics, and paraphrasing.

Self-Management

Taking responsibility for one's own learning and one's own behavior is called **self-management.** Having this ability helps students complete academic tasks and reduce undesired and inappropriate actions. Whether addressing academic learning or behaviors, students should identify the expectations, set goals, and consider the desired actions, so they learn to self-record, self-monitor, self-reinforce, and self-evaluate.

Placement Options

An IDEIA provision regarding the placement of a student with a disability to receive necessary services is called the **continuum of services or continuum of alternative educational placement** options. This mandate specifies a variety of educational options that must be available for students to obtain special education services, related services, and access to the general curriculum. When the IEP team determines the appropriate placement for a student with a learning disability, this continuum must be carefully considered.

The least restrictive environment, LRE, for students with learning disabilities is the same as the placement for all children, the general education classroom. The more restrictive options (homebound or hospital setting) are far more limiting regarding the access to general education and activities, yet mandated to include those opportunities. LRE continuum options include least to most restrictive: general education classrooms (inclusive model), resource rooms (integrated model), self-contained programs (separate, segregated model), separate schools (private setting), a residential facilities, homebound placements, and hospital settings.

Inclusion

Since the early 1990s, **inclusion** has been a trend in the field of education for students with disabilities or exceptional needs. Its implementation was promoted to reduce the number of restrictive and segregated placements for these students, while making more placements into the general education programs. It is a compelling philosophy and highly recommended practice for students with learning disabilities due to their strong cognitive abilities. They are capable of quality academic achievement with proper focus, attention and support to their strengths and abilities.

Since students with learning disabilities demonstrate such diversity, their placement into the general education classroom can result in challenges for regular education teachers. Due to these different needs, these students require adaptations, modifications, and accommodations of the general education curriculum to become successful. They may require drill, practice, feedback, and extra time, which may appear to slow the pace of instruction. Special education teachers, trained to work with learning disabilities can provide assistance to general education teachers by informing them of the student's needs, helping to access supports and resources, and providing professional development opportunities.

Technology

Computer programs and systems will continue to emerge and evolve in order to aid students with learning disabilities in accessing their environments and completing daily tasks. Students may now use e-mail, the Internet, and CD-ROM technology to find information and communicate with others. Word processing programs, voice recognition devices, text readers, and other computer application programs all offer assistance to students with learning disabilities so they may overcome barriers to learning at school and throughout their life.

Developing Educational Plans

Developing education plans for students with disabilities is mandated under the law, and the best way to create these plans is to base the decisions on the comprehensive assessments conducted and the evaluation materials gathered on each student.

Three types of plans are required under the law: an **individual education plan,** an **individual transition plan,** and an **individual family service plan.** The participants who must be included on these planning teams include the parents, a regular education teacher, a special education teacher, a school representative, the evaluator, the student (as appropriate), and others with knowledge or expertise pertaining to the student.

Individual Education Plan-IEP

According to IDEIA, Part B, the purpose of an Individual Education Plan (IEP) is to ensure services and develop a written education plan to manage a student's overall program when placed in special education, 3 through 21 years. An IEP is designed to support the educational needs of a student with a disability and outlines the services the student will receive. An IEP addresses the student's specific and unique needs by creating goals and implementing the selected, appropriate services.

For the majority of students with learning disabilities, educational services are delivered in the general education environments that include accommodations. The general education teacher becomes a key team member and a highly valued service provider. Her role is to monitor student progress and to ensure the delivery of services, the implementation of accommodations, and the accountability for the educational program, alongside the special education teacher.

An IEP is constructed after a comprehensive assessment is conducted and the student's eligibility for special education is determined. A team of professionals (therapists, teachers, and specialists) along with the parents work together throughout the special education process, including the development of the IEP. Each member represents an area of expertise necessary to the student's programming, and parents help make decisions about goals, services, and placement.

Required IEP components include present levels of educational performance (based on strengths and weaknesses), specific annual goals, related services, and placement options. In general, special education teachers manage the plan and the entire team; however, some states may identify a case manager for students with disabilities.

Individual Family Service Plan

An Individual Family Service Plan, IFSP, is a legal document required under special education law, IDEIA, as a provision of Part C for infants and toddlers, birth through 2 years. The purpose of an IFSP is to focus on and support the entire family of an infant who exhibits developmental delays, and outlines goals, the service providers, and specific services to be received.

Family members are considered team members who provide input about their child's development, identify an appropriate environment for services, and share goals to support the child's program. The family's resources, concerns, and needs are evaluated by other team members to create a plan that details the preferred outcomes for the child and the family.

Since the family is considered the primary service provider, a service coordinator is selected from the early intervention agency to assist and support the family through the implementation of the IFSP services. Every six months, the family has the option to accept or decline continued services.

Transition services are required under an IFSP when a child transitions into a public preschool program from an early intervention program. The child may be re-evaluated, the IFSP reviewed, and an IEP created to align with the current educational needs. The law allows for an IFSP to be used for preschool-aged children or an IEP for children aged 2 who will transition in one year to a preschool program; however, this is not a common practice.

Differences of IEP and IFSP

The primary differences are in the age groups and programs these support. An IEP is used for school populations, ages 3 through 21, and an IFSP is used for children birth through 3 in state early intervention programs. Although both an IEP and an IFSP require a written present level of the child's functioning, there are specific differences in these two statements. An IFSP provides an overall statement of functioning across all developmental abilities, while the IEP must focus on the present levels of educational performance pertaining to the specific disability. An IFSP is reviewed by the team every six months, while an IEP has an annual review providing regular progress reports throughout the year. Both require goals to be written, but the differences are in the focus of these goals; an IEP focuses on detailed goals related to the student's specific educational needs, and an IFSP produces general goals primary to the family needs and the child's needs.

Individual Transition Plan-ITP

The majority of students with learning disabilities are quite capable of living and working independently as adults given the proper training and early supports, yet they have the highest drop-out rates. In order to become a successful adult, a student with a learning disability needs assistance and training prior to graduation and this has been mandated under IDEIA. An individual transition plan is required for all students, age 16 and over. A student's needs and preferences must be addressed through non-biased instruments and procedures. The student, the parents, the teachers, and appropriate community partners are involved in the assessment process, program development, resource identification, and service implementation.

An individual transition plan is an addition to an IEP and must include all of the functioning areas related to adult involvement in the community, which prepares the student for the transition. These areas include employment, continued education, daily living, health, leisure, communication, and self-determination/advocacy.

Classroom Management

Effective classroom management is a direct reflection of the management of student behaviors. When an educator addresses the instructional needs of the all students, achievement increases, and behavior problems lessen. A practical and appropriate classroom environment has a powerful influence on positive behavior management.

With a variety of exceptional learners in classrooms today, effective classroom management is very important, and it requires educator knowledge, skills, and practice. It requires that educators be aware of the physical space, how it impacts learning, and how it delivers more responsive learners. Teachers must have plans for daily schedules, the location of materials, homework guidelines, student motivation techniques, and peer involvement. Educators should incorporate data from current research about the learning variables, such as the general environment, strategies, and materials to use the classroom setting as a powerful tool toward educating exceptional students.

Social Competence

Most typical children learn social skills by observing others and by participating in daily activities. Children use these social skills so they may perform with proper social competence, but for children with learning disabilities, learning social skills may be a difficult task. These students can be impulsive, using improper language and actions in social situations. They often need to be taught the appropriate social skills, practice these skills, and learn to apply these skills through specific instructional techniques. These students need to understand which actions are appropriate when interfacing with others in different settings. A variety of strategies and methods are available to instill a sense of social competence in children with learning disorders.

A student with the potential for a learning disability or one already identified should be assessed in the social-emotional domain so professionals and adults who support this student will be knowledgeable about the needs for social competence. During the instructional phase, emphasis should be placed on the following topics: self-perception, sensitivity to others, emotional awareness, social maturity, and ethical judgments.

Just as learning strategies instruction is important to students with learning disabilities when they acquire academic skills, learning strategies are invaluable for social skill development. Students may learn the appropriate responses to social situations and may think more carefully about their social behaviors after they learn strategies. These strategies include thinking before responding, rehearsing verbal patterns to social responses, visualizing the effect of their actions, and planning the use of social behaviors.

Promoting the development of social skills in the classroom may occur in the general education classroom informally, as well as in a special education setting with a one-to-one focus. Teachers can ask students to examine the behaviors of characters in stories, use pictures that depict social situations, and teach conversation and friendship skills. Many published programs focus on the social skills areas. Additional information about this subject may be found through the websites listed in the "Resources" section of this guide.

Behavior Modifications

Students with learning disabilities not only exhibit academic or learning deficits but may utilize inappropriate behaviors in daily situations. Feeling frustrated or misunderstood, they may begin to develop a poor self-concept and lack of self-esteem. Some students with learning disabilities demonstrate feelings of anxiety, depression, loneliness, and oversensitivity. Because of these emotional influences, these students begin to develop learned helplessness and lose the intrinsic motivation that is critical to learning.

Students with learning problems need to learn behavior management strategies that will help throughout their lifetimes. The IEP teams should determine the behaviors that need to be corrected and be sure that they are observable and measurable. To successfully manage behaviors, a behavior analysis should be conducted. This analysis consists of the identification and definitions of antecedents, target behavior, and consequent events that will then support the development of a behavior management plan.

A systematic process of behavior management will aid the students in becoming independent in self-monitoring and management of these behaviors. Several methods that aid in promoting desired behaviors and actions are reinforcement (positive and negative), contingency contracts (an agreement of change), shaping behaviors, token reinforcements, and time-out (removal from activities to isolation). As with other instructional methods, the coordination of efforts between home and school is critical. When all persons who are in contact with the student are consistent, then the student will improve.

Classroom management is a key to behavior management. Strategies that help students with learning disabilities regarding their behavior issues in general education classrooms are specific seating arrangements, daily schedules, concise directions, structured routines, a variety of activities, and consistent feedback.

Physical-Social Environments

Organizing a classroom requires an educator to establish expectations and set criteria for several areas: setting the class tone, establishing classroom rules, engaging the learners, organizing the instruction, and using accommodations. Involving the students in creating the specific guidelines may help them accept, own, and perform appropriately in the environment.

Establishing a positive classroom tone reflects an educator's attitudes about learning and about the learners. Teacher behavior impacts student behavior, as does the teacher's attention to the environment, support to students, and implementation of expectations. Instituting classroom rules and procedures is a structural and social component of effective classroom management and organization. Setting rules affects student behaviors and allows students to work more productively.

Preparing the physical space is of great value in promoting learning, and it should reflect the teaching style of the educator, while addressing student educational needs. Studies have shown that a classroom arrangement influences the amount of time students spend as active learners. An appropriate classroom allows students and teacher to move easily, access materials without barriers, and work in various group arrangements.

Facilitate Transitions

Students with learning disabilities need a variety of instructional activities with the structure of a daily schedule and school routine to benefit from their learning. Determining the alertness and motivational levels of students are critical factors when preparing academic schedules and delivering educational information.

Transitioning between activities is a difficult period of time, especially for those students with learning disabilities. During the school day, there must be a balance of teacher-directed activities and student-guided activities. Giving warnings prior to schedule changes are especially important for those with attention problems and processing difficulties as they need time to think about the change and finalize their work.

Methods used to move from one activity to the next include outlining the goals of each lesson, summarizing the concepts learned, introducing the next activity, providing reinforcement for attention, monitoring progress, and providing feedback. Students may become more active learners when they are given the opportunity to be involved in creating the learning activities and participating in the schedule planning. Involving the students in carefully planning transitions between activities, lessons, projects, or classes will help in maintaining class control.

Mild to Moderate Disabilities (0542)

Introduction

Understanding federal legislation and the mandates for students with disabilities will be the basis for developing further knowledge on how to plan programs and implement practices for students in the mild to moderate categories. The federal laws include but are not limited to

- Individuals with Disabilities Education Improvement Act (IDEIA)
- No Child Left Behind (NCLB)
- Rehabilitation Act-Section 504
- Family Education Rights and Privacy Act (FERPA)

Being knowledgeable about federal laws for students with disabilities helps examinees in understanding student and parent rights, the definitions of disabilities as well as the components of individual programs and assessments. For specific information about these and other laws, refer to the "Core Content Knowledge" portion of this guide.

The Mild to Moderate Disabilities (0542) exam is designed to assess an individual's application of special education topics in given instructional situations. With three content categories, examinees should be prepared to answer five constructed-response questions within a one-hour period. The practice exam allows each examinee the chance to see examples of the questions in the format found on the actual exam, and the opportunity to self-pace in preparation for exam 0542.

This exam about exceptional students is intended for individuals planning to teach students with mild to moderate disabilities at any grade level from preschool through grade 12 in a special education program. The actual exam presents teaching situations in which the examinee must apply the principles of special education with regard to students with mild to moderate disability conditions. The three content categories are Assessment (1 to 2 questions, 25 to 42 percent), Curriculum and Instruction (1 to 2 questions, 25 to 42 percent), and Structuring and Managing the Learning Environment (1 to 2 questions, 25 to 42 percent).

Studying for a Praxis II exam is critical to obtaining teacher certification. The following study information and practice test should help an examinee prepare for this particular examination. Since most of the information about students with disabilities, the causes, the educational practices, and the instructional methods have been provided in college coursework, this study guide should be used as a review to determine the areas of study for which an examinee should focus his time. If additional information is needed, reference other resources, such as textbooks, the Internet, or practitioners. Suggested websites are also provided under the "Resources" section.

Examinees should prepare for this particular examination by focusing on the different types of disabilities, the information about student services, the development and implementation of an IEP and an ITP, the preferred classroom strategies and methods, the required assessments, and the overall practices regarding curriculum and instruction. More detailed information about disabilities and specific practices are found in the "Core Content Knowledge" portion of this guide.

Use the questions in the practice exam and the content in the appendices to study for this exam. Practice writing IEP goals and present levels of education performance statements, as well as behavior intervention plans and transition plans.

Another Praxis II study guide is available if examinees must prepare for other special education tests required for certification in certain states. *CliffsTestPrep Praxis II: Special Education (0351, 0352, 0690, 0371, 0381, 0321)*, developed by the same author and published by Wiley, Inc., contains another section on core knowledge and one on the application of core knowledge, which may be helpful in preparing for special education exams.

Content Clusters

The following set of 10 questions is presented so examinees can check their basic knowledge as it relates to exceptional students with **mild to moderate disabilities.** Study these concepts and the content of each broad topic as these will aid you in test preparation. Through thoughtful and careful review of these topics, examinees should be better prepared for the Education of Exceptional Students: Mild to Moderate Disabilities, Praxis II (0542) exam. Writing detailed answers on a separate sheet of paper will help examinees concentrate on the constructed-response question responses and the pacing for the actual exam. Answers to these questions are found throughout the study guide and these broad questions are only provided as a guide to studying for the Praxis II exam, as they are based on the criteria that is imbedded in the test.

1. Describe the components and the process of developing an IEP that specifically focuses on students with mild to moderate disabilities with emphasis on an inclusion setting. Include a PLEP and written goals.

2. Discuss the causes and various characteristics of students with mild to moderate disabilities.

3. Identify the cultural and linguistic diversity issues and how education may be addressed in these two areas, specifically for students with mild to moderate disabilities.

4. Explain the various assessment approaches and measurement tools for use with students who have mild to moderate disabilities.

5. Outline the required components on an ITP and explain the process of developing one for a high school student with mild to moderate disabilities.

6. Demonstrate an understanding of the process of planning and developing a unit, a lesson plan, and other educational activities for students with mild to moderate disabilities.

7. Reflect on the use of accommodations, modifications, adaptations, equipment, and assistive technology devices and services for students with mild to moderate disabilities.

8. Describe the various needs for students with mild to moderate disabilities in the areas of social skills and study skills.

9. Explain the process of conducting a Functional Behavior Assessment and its relationship to developing a Behavior Intervention Plan. Include the components of each and practice writing target behavior statements, behavior goals, and interventions.

10. List the methods used to collaborate with parents during the IEP process and during a student's placement in special education programs.

Constructed-Response Questions

The following includes examples of the constructed-response questions that are intended for use on this Praxis II exam. The examinee must develop answers written either as a short-answer narrative or an essay. It is critical that examinees understand what they are being asked in the question before proceeding to answer it, especially when taking the actual exam. The answers for the constructed response questions on the actual exam are scored by examination readers who use an established and standardized scoring rubric or guide.

A brief explanation of the scoring guide follows:

3	Demonstrates thorough understanding of subject covered
2	Demonstrates a basic understanding of subject covered
1	Demonstrates a lack of understanding of the subject covered
0	Inaccurate, limited, or no response

Read the following question and then read the given task, carefully planning and then writing a constructed response.

Scenario

An elementary student, Kyle, is 9 years old. According to a recent evaluation, his IQ is 110. He is a verbal child who enjoys speaking with both peers and adults about a number of topics. His average intelligence and solid understanding of spoken language are positive aspects of his social development. His written language, however, shows a performance level comparable to a 6 year old. Although he can read words and knows letters, he demonstrates difficulty in motor planning and writing the actual letters and words. He sometimes forgets how to begin the task, and his handwriting is illegible. He also has problems in mathematics, as it requires a certain amount of writing numbers and story problems. His memory, attention, and motor areas are also affected, which places him two grade levels below his peers in his academic performance. This highly verbal child struggles daily and has begun to use behaviors that are undesirable. He refuses to complete his math and spelling work when he is highly frustrated, and on occasion he will use inappropriate gestures and words. He has been known to throw his writing instrument and drop his papers on the floor. The team must reconsider his placement and his IEP goals.

Task

1. Identify how Kyle's academic performance and his behavior problems will influence the team's decisions regarding his least restrictive environment and his IEP goals.

Response

1. Kyle's needs are changing, and they may no longer be represented in his IEP goals. As Kyle ages and the academic tasks become more complicated, his frustrations will build unless he has the support and the tools to use specific strategies. With his high verbal abilities, it may cause Kyle to feel that neither math nor writing is very important to complete. He needs to be made aware of the reasons for the difficulties he actually has with writing and math. In order to meet Kyle's current needs, regarding his newly exhibited behaviors and his increasing frustrations, the LRE may need to be changed, even for a short period of time. Kyle may be better placed in a resource setting for a small amount of time each day to help him with his writing and math work and to learn how to focus on his tasks with strategies that meet his apparent learning disability. He may also need the assistance of occupational therapy to address his motor delays (handwriting and motor planning), as well as the addition of accommodations or assistive technology to support his written tasks. It may be wise for the team to re-evaluate Kyle in all academic areas in order to write more appropriate IEP goals, as well as to conduct a functional behavior assessment to address his behaviors. His academic performance and his behavior problems are the cause for additional evaluation and review, so a discussion by the team with effective team decision making will better meet Kyle's needs.

Topic Overview

Students with **mild to moderate conditions** exhibit a variety of characteristics that span academic skills, physical traits, social skills, emotional stability issues, family unit needs, and health status. They may fall under the categories listed in special education of **learning disability, behavior disorder/emotional disturbances, autism, other health impaired,** or **mental retardation.**

The terms **mild** and **moderate** are used to identify the level of difficulties a student with a disability is experiencing. **Mild disabilities** most often include those students with LD or OHI due to the limited academic and behavior barriers. Some students with ED may qualify, and some students with MR also qualify, although they may have serious adaptive delays. Students with mild mental retardation are considered those with an IQ range of 50 to 75, impaired adaptive behaviors, and socialization skills below age. Educators who work with students who exhibit mild disabilities most often use common instructional methods and strategies. **Moderate disabilities** include students with ED, MR, and A as they have greater academic needs and behavior challenges. They often need a greater variety of instructional methods and strategies and more focus on their individual characteristics and needs.

Mild conditions affect students in the development and mastery of skills that can be diagnosed at different age levels as students mature and experience more complex tasks. Young children may have problems with memory, early basic academics, listening, and attention, and older students experience problems with organizing and gaining study skills, developing work skills, managing self, and completing more complicated academic tasks.

Moderate conditions exhibit extensive needs in one or more areas, and the disability affects the student not only during school but in all aspects of life. They can learn and improve with proper supports. Moderate disabilities can affect a student's behavior, social interaction skills, communication, adaptive behavior, attention, motivation, organization, health, physical strength, emotional status, attitude, and self-concept. These students need constant appropriate support and opportunities to gain daily coping skills.

Instruction for students with mild to moderate disabilities must be designed by incorporating all aspects of a student's being. But prior to developing a program, educators must gather information about the student's knowledge of skills and abilities. The use of student assessment as a link to instruction helps the team make quality decisions about individuals with disabilities with regard to teaching practices and instructional delivery. Specifically helpful are assessments that are aligned to the curriculum as a way to further monitor student progress.

Certain national and professional standards outline the skills and knowledge necessary for educators to regulate assessment practices. Teachers must be knowledgeable about the types of assessment, how to use evaluation tools, how to conduct an assessment on individual students and groups of students, how to deliver results to team members, and how to use the information to create or measure learning.

For more information on the various types and about the specific characteristics of students with disabilities, refer to the "Core Content Knowledge" portion of this guide.

Assessment

Special education services require that students be evaluated to determine their needs for support through specialized programs and services. It is recommended that multi-factored methods of assessing students be used to identify the exceptionality and various needs. Assessments are used for identification, placement, and program decisions.

Assessments are used to

- Evaluate skills, habits, and talents.
- Link information to assessment.
- Measure progress in achievement.
- Improve behaviors.

An assessment can determine the specific needs of each student and help a team decide which instructional strategies and methods will deliver the most benefit to the student. Assessment results should lead to the development of an **individual education plan.**

Policies and Steps

Assessment requirements follow the same basic principles for all special education students (see "Core Content Knowledge"). The following steps outline the special education process.

1. **Pre-Referral:** A student exhibiting problems in the general education classroom is provided interventions to determine any benefit from them.
2. **Screening:** Professionals gather additional information that may detect individuals in need of a more comprehensive evaluation.
3. **Referral:** Professionals use information from several sources and conduct an observation to study classroom performance and behaviors.
4. **Evaluation and identification:** A comprehensive evaluation is conducted to determine the student's disability and possible eligibility for special education services.
5. **Instructional program planning:** Assessment information is used to create goals, determine placement, and make plans for instructional delivery.
6. **Placement:** Decisions about **least restrictive environment** and services are made.
7. **Review and evaluation:** Monitor the student's progress and overall program.

Instruments and Measures

Appropriate assessment procedures are required under the law: use of a variety of assessment tools and strategies; administered in the student's primary language; and free from racial or cultural bias. The assessment tools used must be the most appropriate for the student so functional, developmental, and academic information may be gathered to determine the educational needs of the student.

Assessments are used throughout the special education process to develop, review, revise, or evaluate a student's individual educational program. Several types of measurement tools are available for a comprehensive evaluation or for an evaluation of student progress. Following are some of the common assessment types that may be administered.

- **Criterion-referenced:** A formal measure that evaluates a student on specific content domain and is used to provide students with feedback and teachers with information on progress.
- **Curriculum-based:** Evaluates student progress and performance of skills based on the curriculum or student behaviors, which helps teachers decide how to assist the student.
- **Norm-referenced:** A formal tool used to compare the performance of one student to other peers in the same age group.
- **Performance-based:** An informal measure used by teachers to assess a student's knowledge, skills, and abilities.
- **Standards-based:** Formal evaluation that measures progress toward meeting goals or standards as previously established by the district or state.

Additional information on types of assessment may be found in the "Core Content Knowledge" section of this guide.

Linking Assessment to Instruction

A key to planning instruction for students with disabilities is to establish a beginning point by linking instruction through assessment. Then the team can plan the instruction, implement the accommodations, integrate assistive technology, and manage behavior. Therefore, it is imperative that teachers have assessment data available on their students before planning instruction (characteristics of learner, skills levels, abilities). Not only should educators use the individual assessment information, but they must consider the content standards and performance indicators. Setting up the instructional environment and providing access to meaningful instruction and learning activities will then smoothly follow.

A comprehensive assessment should examine all aspects of a student's development. The results may be used to help an IEP team make decisions about a student's educational program. The results may be transformed into a statement of present levels of educational performance, which is used to build upon a set of measurable goals. Then the expected learning outcomes will determine the materials, methods, and strategies best suited to the student.

Instruction for a student with a disability is based on the present levels of educational performance, which identifies the student's strengths and needs. A team conducts an assessment, gathers evaluation information, shares past records and performance, shares current class work, and conducts an observation to develop the PLEP. Team members also share information about the student, both strengths and concerns. From this statement of current functioning, the team can link the assessment to the appropriate instruction to meet the student's individual needs. Specifically designed instruction is used to meet an individual student's needs and includes special methods, certain instructional strategies, implementation of chosen accommodations/modifications, and necessary materials, equipment, and learning resources.

Also from the instruction, the team is able to identify the most appropriate accommodations and modifications that are intended for use in the general education classes, special education programs, and in testing situations. Some accommodations include allowing extra time to take the test, providing an alternate format (oral, open book), allowing a scribe to write answers, and use of computers for testing.

For more information about assessment and PLEPs, refer to the "Core Content Knowledge" portion of this guide and the appendices.

Curriculum and Instruction

Most students categorized with mild disabilities are those who can be educated and served in the general education classrooms, as they do not have serious problems that affect their learning. Students with learning disabilities, mental retardation, and behavioral disorders, as well as speech/language disorders are considered students with mild disabilities. These students have characteristics similar to one another, and therefore, may be instructed in similar ways by use of common instructional practices.

Students with moderate disabilities require some different teaching methods and different placements. These students often demonstrate a lack of motivation and interest in school. Generally, the special education teachers who support their programs are certified in one specific and separate category of special education. They may use common instructional practices, such as cooperative learning and peer tutoring, but may also need to address specific strategies to support students with mild-moderate disabilities. These students may be placed in general education programs but may also benefit from time in special education programs.

Inclusion programs offer the best selection of options for students with mild-moderate disabilities, as they require the collaboration of special education and general education teachers. Students with mild-moderate disabilities often do well in the inclusive general education classes as they have strong models of language, behaviors, and academics. Critical to the instruction of these students are the choice of the curriculum; the focus of the instruction; the selection of methods, strategies, and techniques; and the materials used.

Knowledge of Curriculum Materials

Research has found that students with mild disabilities are very similar to students who are underachievers or at-risk. Their instructional levels, styles of learning, and the rates at which they learn are most comparable. Therefore, the instructional formats, strategies, and methods should follow best teaching practices. This is sound advice because most students with mild to moderate disabilities are placed in inclusion settings of the general education programs, and when they receive the same instruction in the same manner (with accommodations) as their peers, they perform quite well.

Selecting the appropriate materials can be a complex task when teachers must consider the diversity of learners in a general education setting. They not only must base their decisions on the general education students, the special education students, the at-risk population, and other exceptional individuals, but also make considerations for cultural and linguistic diversity, genders, ages, abilities, interests, and subject matter. Materials selected must be age appropriate, with a logical set of objectives, adaptable to varying learning styles, have measurable outcomes, and have reinforcement activities.

Some materials require accommodations or modifications, which may include any of the following:

- Alter the amount or task required.
- Change response mode of questions.
- Use peer tutoring system.
- Utilize Cloze procedures.
- Establish learning centers.
- Vary auditory and visual activities.
- Break tasks into smaller units.
- Highlight information.
- Use tape recorded text.
- Use advance organizers or daily schedules.
- Provide directions in multiple formats.

Use of Resources

A variety of resources are available to educators that will help in developing and enriching student programs. Educators must be savvy about the resources available, and it takes some time to research these helpful tools. Acknowledging the presence of a resource is only the first step toward using it. An educator must decide how each resource best enhances her classroom program and her individual student programs. The following lists some suggested areas to search for outside classroom assistance.

- National professional organizations
- National professional journals
- National parent support groups
- State and district workshops
- State academic standards
- District learning competencies
- Course goals and objectives
- Local community agencies
- Other professionals
- Peer teachers
- Parents

Some of the professional organizations that may help with regard to curriculum standards include the following:

- National Science Teachers Association (NSTA)
- National Council for Geography Education (NCGE)
- National Council for Teachers of English (NCTE)
- National Council for Teachers of Mathematics (NCTM)
- National Council for Social Studies (NCSS)

Instructional Strategies

When educators are seeking the appropriate strategies for use in classrooms for students with mild to moderate disabilities, they must be concerned with what will maximize each student's learning. Using a variety of instructional strategies to meet the needs of diverse learners is called **differentiated instruction.** This means that the strategies meet the needs of various individuals and their varying degrees and levels of strengths and weaknesses. This method of instruction incorporates accommodations, options, and flexibility into the teaching day. Some examples include multiple assessment approaches, various groupings of students, engaging all learners at their level, and effective classroom management.

An **instructional strategy** is defined as a teaching routine or method in which the steps, techniques, or activities are grouped in a logical manner to promote and reinforce academic achievement. Examples of instructional strategies include the following:

- **Coaching:** Helps students by giving them hints or suggestions to enhance learning by performing a task or gaining a skill.
- **Cooperative learning:** Students work together to gain knowledge and enhance social skills.
- **Cueing:** This is a stimulus or reminder for the student to perform the correct response.
- **Graphic organizer:** Helps students acquire and retain information through a visual format.
- **Guided practice:** Activities related to goals in which students can practice the concepts and skills under the supervision of the teacher, through homework, or with a small group of students. Guided practice may include review, organizing information, rehearsing, summarizing, comparing, and so on.
- **Incidental teaching:** A strategy that teaches a skill or concept during an event or situation in which it is presently occurring.
- **Modeling:** A more skilled person performs the task, activity, or project for a person less skilled so that person may learn to perform the same.
- **Monitoring:** The teacher is constantly involved in the student's work to observe the progress and identify areas of concern.
- **Peer tutoring or peer instruction:** Students skilled in certain concepts, tasks, or behaviors help less skilled students learn the information.
- **Preteaching:** Helps students recall prior knowledge and background information as well as previous experiences about a topic. It prepares them through the introduction of vocabulary and concepts when presenting a new subject. Ways to utilize this strategy is through field trips, videos, experiments, and so on.
- **Reciprocal learning:** Helps students learn skills, concepts, information, and new ideas by completing a task after viewing the modeling of the teacher or other students. The teacher may then provide coaching, cueing, or scaffolding as the student engages in the activity.
- **Scaffolding:** These are strategies that support a student as he acquires knowledge, skills, or gains concepts.
- **Sequencing:** A task is broken into segments or steps and the student completes the activity by completing one step at a time until the entire task is done.
- **Shaping:** This is the beginning stage of task completion, as it is an approximation of the targeted behavior. The student is rewarded when repeatedly attempting the mastery of the task.

One reason to select proper strategies for students with mild to moderate disabilities is for the strategies to help instill functional skills, so these students may connect academics to real life. Educators should focus instruction on high expectations for these students and use the special strategies to teach them the general education curriculum. It is the responsibility of the educators to know the various strategies that are available so they may make wise decisions in using them for diverse learners. Using the appropriate strategies will demonstrate effective professionalism and respect for learners.

IEP Goals

Writing goals for a student's IEP requires knowledge about the student, which is gathered through a non-bias and appropriate assessment. The goals must be based on the student's needs in the disability areas and be both measurable and attainable during the program year. They must clearly state the expectations for the student. In most states, goals are related to the state academic standards for the general education curriculum. Related service providers are involved in the process, since some of the goals are related to the provision of services through their disciplines.

IEP goals have a required format, which is adjusted across states. The goals are to include components that resemble the following: condition, performance, criteria, assessment, and standard. These goals are reviewed annually, with periodic progress checks, but can be adjusted or changed through team consensus any time a team member believes there is a need.

Some professionals recommend the use of curriculum-based IEP goals for students with mild to moderate disabilities. Data is gathered based on performance through various assessment methods, but primarily through the use of curriculum materials. The conditions and behavior components of the goal are specified in relation to the level of the curriculum. The criterion set for success in the goal is based on the curriculum standards.

Note: Refer to the appendices for more information on developing IEP goals.

Planning Instruction

The IEP process allows team members to offer information about a student regarding his strengths and concerns. The information that is gathered becomes the inspiration for team members to jointly produce and write a clear and concise **present levels of educational performance statement** (PLEP). This statement will provide an overall summary of the student's abilities and disabilities, as well as outline what the student requires to become successful in school.

At this point, the team members address the instructional needs of the student. The team reviews the concerns and areas of needs and makes decisions about any specially designed methods, strategies, or techniques to deliver instruction and services. This includes classroom necessities, such as materials, equipment, assistive technology, supplementary aids, and services and accommodations or modifications, as well as resources to support the individual student's program. This is the process of linking assessment to instruction.

Team members may link assessments to instruction in all areas of academics and in the area of behavior. Team members look at the specific concerns about a student's academic performance, identify the skill levels, and may develop IEP goals and programming that address those needs. The same is possible for the behavioral component. As the team conducts assessments, each member may gather information about the student's behavioral abilities, and the team may also conduct a functional behavior assessment providing linkable information to developing the IEP.

After the individual program is developed, educators must consider the types of programs that would most benefit a student's performance. Some examples of instructional models and methods include the following:

- **Brain-compatible instruction:** Use of brain research and the suggested techniques.
- **Direct instruction:** Includes a set of designed instructional steps with demonstration, guided practice, and feedback essential.
- **Functional curriculum approach:** Teaching basic life skills in a meaningful and practical manner.
- **Learning strategies method:** Giving students a set of methods to help them improve their own ability to learn.
- **Multisensory instruction:** Including all the senses to make learning more effective.
- **Precision teaching:** When the teacher or learner records responses on a standardized chart.
- **Student-centered learning:** Focus on student's developmental needs related to learning and her whole self.
- **Task analysis approach:** Breaking down tasks into smaller parts and teaching each as a separate skill.

Note: See the appendices for more information on writing an appropriate PLEP.

Structuring and Managing the Learning Environment

Research on the use of effective instruction demonstrates that it is the very basis for positive and successful classroom management. When students are exposed to a well-structured and planned environment, it is bound to increase preferred behaviors and lead to successful individual education programs. Classroom management builds upon academic success, but the leading contributor toward student success is the exposure to constructive and well-designed teaching.

The classroom organization should reflect the essential teaching practices and involve the students in the learning process. With the diversity of learners, creating a positive environment presents educators with an enormous task, especially in inclusion settings. Setting up a classroom requires the establishment of expectations, the class tone, and classroom rules, as well as designing techniques to engage learners, organize instruction, and use accommodations.

For effective student achievement to occur, a learning environment must be focused on the needs of individual students. In classroom settings, teachers must include curriculum content, specific learning strategies for certain students, and specific methods for meeting all students' needs. Some recommended ways to enhance the learning environment and student achievement for those with mild to moderate disabilities are as follows:

- Outline student expectations.
- Keep transitions well organized.
- Use appropriately paced instruction for all learners.
- Use multi-age classrooms.
- Implement innovative practices.
- Consider the use of looping.
- Maintain inclusive settings.
- Use cooperative learning activities.
- Integrate the curriculum.
- Vary the activities.
- Teach conflict resolution.
- Address student motivation.
- Embed IEP goals into the curriculum.
- Use individual and small group instruction.
- Select age-appropriate content and a variety of organized materials.
- Allow students to have choices in learning situations.
- Collaborate efforts of general education teachers and special education teachers.
- Implement accommodations/modifications.
- Use corrective feedback.
- Utilize the information from the evaluation of the students and environments.

For more information on structuring and managing the learning environment, refer to the "Core Content Knowledge" portion of this study guide.

Behavior Management

It is the role and responsibility of the IEP team to assist in determining the needs of students with mild to moderate disabilities for positive behavioral interventions and strategies. A student's behaviors must be under control, as her actions impact learning and academic achievement. Some behaviors affect the student using them, and some affect other students in close proximity. Students who have difficult behaviors often lack social skills.

Behavior management is a designed program that integrates the needs of the individual student with the environment. Students in special education are provided behavior management tools through the use of the following:

- **Functional Behavior Assessment (FBA):** The process of observation and discussion to gather information about a student's problem behaviors and used to determine the need for behavior interventions and a behavior plan.
- **Behavior Intervention Plan (BIP):** An individual program designed by using the information from an FBA and structured to help a student learn to manage her behaviors.

The FBA will identify the behavioral areas of concern for the team, who then reviews the information to develop a BIP. For the BIP, the targeted behaviors must be selected. The BIP is based on the hypothesis that is developed after the behaviors are explained.

Note: Both of these items are further explained and defined with examples of document preparation in the appendices of this guide.

Behavior modification is a method of teaching prosocial behaviors to students with mild to moderate disabilities. Examples include contingency contracts, token economies, timeouts, and cognitive-behavior interventions. Both **nonverbal** and **verbal** techniques are used.

The **nonverbal** techniques are preferred as they are nonintrusive. These actions help manage inappropriate behaviors while not drawing attention or reinforcing the exhibited behaviors. They include the use of body language, gestures, signal interference, and planned ignoring.

The **verbal** techniques can be used in combination with nonverbal or instead of if the nonverbal technique does not work. These include the use of messages, praise, restructuring, humor, and smooth transition actions.

Preventive discipline is another method that aids in managing behaviors. This is the use of teacher actions that decrease disruptions and emphasize student self-control. Knowing one's own teaching style and the learning styles and needs of the students is a step forward in the use of this pre-emptive measure.

Additional terms useful for further study of behavior interventions and management for exceptional students may be found in the "Core Content Knowledge" section of the study guide.

- **Charting:** A method to record behaviors over a specific period of time.
- **Duration recording:** When conducting an observation of behaviors, this method allows the observer to measure the length of time for the behavior.
- **Event recording:** When conducting an observation, the behavior is recorded each time it occurs.
- **Hypothesis:** A description of the predicted function and analysis of the behavior.
- **Interval recording:** During an observation, this is the measurement of whether a behavior occurs in a specified period.
- **Latency recording:** During an observation, it is the measure of the amount of time between a request and a behavior.
- **Observation:** The act of watching and recording a student's behaviors in a variety of settings to determine the factors associated with the behaviors.
- **Recording:** Documenting behaviors.
- **Replacement behaviors:** Those that must be substituted for the undesirable behaviors.
- **Self-discipline:** Students learn how to control their own actions and take responsibility for their behaviors.
- **Setting events:** An occurrence that influences a student's behavior and may alter the established IEP or BIP programs.
- **Supports:** People, tools, or modifications that help the student in the general education program.
- **Structured interviews:** Asking a set of predesigned questions to adults in the student's environment to gain further information about the student's behaviors.

Self-control is an essential skill for students with mild to moderate disabilities, especially since most of their day is spent in inclusive settings. Also known as **self-regulation,** it identifies the ability of an individual to manage her own behavior in a given situation. As a student gains maturity in her area of behavior, she may be better able to use her past experiences and learned skills when faced with a new situation. Self-control is especially necessary for students identified with behavior disorders/emotional disturbance and learning disabilities. These students are best instructed in self-control techniques through direct instruction and use of instructional strategies such as constructive feedback, prompting, reinforcements, coaching, and modeling.

The use of a **learning strategy** is an effective way to aid these students in using appropriate social skills and maintaining self-control. The Center for Research and Learning has identified eight steps to teaching a learning strategy to students with disabilities.

1. Pretest student on tasks to identify strengths and challenges.
2. Separate the strategies into parts and discuss with student.
3. Model the new, expected steps in the strategy.

4. Suggest student rehearse each step until it is absorbed.

5. Develop a controlled situation for the student to practice using the strategy, giving feedback.

6. Attempt the use of strategies in real situations.

7. Post test student, providing feedback.

8. Support student in generalizing strategy and monitor progress.

Approaches that are found to be most effective in enhancing academic success are the following:

- Students with disabilities work cooperatively with peers and receive feedback from them.
- Teachers use direct instruction and strategy instruction to promote skill development.

Problem Solving and Conflict Resolution

Instructing students with disabilities on how to problem solve will improve their abilities to resolve issues and address problems throughout their lives. When educators model problem solving, show students how to analyze problems, allow them to practice problem solving in different settings, and help them identify metacognitive strategies, students gain the necessary skills to face problems and deal with them appropriately.

Social problem solving is a skill most children need to develop, but it is essential that students with disabilities learn how to approach problems and acquire the skills to generalize these skills to other situations. A method that works well for students with mild to moderate conditions, both in inclusive general education settings and in special education programs, is for teachers to focus on actual classroom situations. Teachers may use these as examples and discuss them with all of the students in the class or at the very least, with those involved in the situation. A teacher should state the problem and list the facts related to the issue. Students are then asked to figure out what should be done to settle the issue or conflict as members of a group. The teacher must acknowledge each member's ideas, model respect for the other members, affirm member perspectives and help them brainstorm solutions. The teacher should refrain from solving the problem for the students and act only as a group facilitator. When students participate in real-life situations, the social problem-solving skills have more meaning and are more readily mastered and retained.

The instruction of problem-solving skills for students with disabilities needs to be consistent and planned. It is important that students work both independently and in small groups to figure out how to solve problems. For students who exhibit particular difficulty with problem solving and for those with behavior disorders, establishing a plan best suited to the student's needs may be the best option for success. A suggested outline is given here, and it resembles the components in a behavior intervention plan.

1. Discuss outcomes: What the team expects the student to do by the end of the year.

2. Identify the student's strengths/talents and needs/challenges.

3. Describe the special problems: What precipitates the problem and when it occurs.

4. Develop goals and objectives.

5. Plan the program and interventions.

6. Implement the program and interventions.

If the age and ability are appropriate, including the student in the planning process will help the student focus on success. The student will be more knowledgeable and more accepting of the program and interventions to impact his problem-solving skills. Two group techniques used to help solve problems are as follows:

- **Group strategies:** A nominal group technique is a decision-making process in which each member is allowed equal status. All ideas are acceptable, and the group priority ranks them together.
- **Brainstorming:** Members share information and ideas. They discuss the possibility until a solution or implementation is agreed upon.

Integrating Related Services

Just as related services are provided for all students with disabilities who need them, they are available to students with mild to moderate disabilities. These services are identified for individual students based on their special needs through team decisions at the IEP meeting. These services must assist a student with a disability to benefit from special education and cover a range of services such as speech-language therapy, occupational therapy, transportation, health services, counseling, and audiology to name a few.

When students with disabilities are placed in the primary LRE of general education, the team may determine that related services should also be provided in that same natural setting. Services offered in a **reach-in model** are those that are brought into the general education classroom where students with disabilities have access to appropriate materials and peer models. It allows these students with mild to moderate disabilities to master skills in their natural environment, and they learn to generalize skills in meaningful settings.

Collaborating with Others

The process of collaboration is a recommended best practice in special education. Working with exceptional students requires the thoughtful sharing of ideas, expertise, and instruction. Professionals and parents have skills and knowledge that will aid in the development of an appropriate educational program, solving problems related to the student's needs/services, and sharing responsibilities for implementation of services.

Collaborative teaming occurs when two or more people work together to enhance a student's education program. They may discuss issues, resolve problems, assess the student, develop plans, and implement programs. To be an effective team, members must support one another, develop trust and respect, communicate effectively, understand roles, and justify decisions.

Parents should be considered members of school teams, according to federal law. They should be utilized in building the educational plan, implementing interventions, and assessing student progress.

Educators who work with exceptional students should be cognizant of the available community resources. Effective teachers help students and families access services, connect them with community resources, and work collaboratively with agencies on school programs and transitions in the adult programs.

Self-advocacy is another area that offers a behavioral support technique and a form of collaboration. Students with mild to moderate disabilities, especially those with LD and BD/ED, need to have opportunities in which they can learn to advocate. It is an ongoing process from elementary (where they learn about self and the disability) through high school (where they develop transition plans and prepare for the future). Through direct instruction, peer interaction, research on disabilities, and gaining self-management or self-control skills, students learn to support themselves in a variety of settings. This allows them to become a member in the collaborative efforts to enhance their success.

Developing collaborative partnerships has a lasting effect when school personnel, families, outside therapists, medical providers, community agencies, and the student work together to promote the student's program and enhance his success in education. One prime example of collaborative partnering is the IEP process and how the team members should most effectively participate.

Other examples of collaboration include co-teaching, consultation, using paraprofessionals, and including parents, which are all further explained topics under the "Core Content Knowledge" portion of this guide.

Severe to Profound Disabilities (0544)

Introduction

Special education programs are guided by the mandates of federal legislation. It is through these provisions that educators learn how to plan programs and implement services for students with severe to profound conditions. Educators who understand the perimeters of the federal laws for students with disabilities gain knowledge about student and parental rights, definitions of disabilities, components of individual programs, and assessment procedures. The primary federal law is the Individuals with Disabilities Education Improvement Act (IDEIA). For specific information about laws, refer to the "Core Content Knowledge" section of this guide.

The **Education of Exceptional Students: Severe to Profound Disabilities (0544)** is a 1-hour exam designed to assess an individual's application of special education topics in given instructional situations. Examinees should be prepared to answer five constructed-response questions based on the three content categories. A practice exam at the end of the guide allows examinees the opportunity to self-pace and prepare for exam 0544.

The exam about exceptional students with severe to profound disabilities is designed for individuals who plan to teach students with severe to profound disabilities at any grade level from preschool through grade 12. The actual Praxis II exam illustrates teaching situations and student scenarios in which the examinee must apply the principles of special education regarding students with severe to profound disabilities. The three content categories are Assessment (1 to 2 questions, 25 to 42 percent), Curriculum and Instruction (1 to 2 questions, 25 to 42 percent), and Structuring and Managing the Learning Environment (1 to 2 questions, 25 to 42 percent).

Obtaining a passing score on the Praxis II exam is essential to securing teacher certification or licensure. Examinees should have comprehensive knowledge about students with severe to profound disabilities, the etiologies, the assessments, the educational practices, and the instructional methods from college coursework, so this study guide should be considered a review of those areas. If additional information is needed, reference other resources, such as textbooks, the Internet, or field practitioners. Suggested websites are also provided in the "Resources" section.

Examinees should focus their studies on the characteristics of disabilities, the information about delivery of services, the development and implementation of an IEP and an ITP, the preferred classroom strategies and methods, the required assessments, and the overall practices regarding curriculum and instruction. More detailed information about disabilities and specific practices are found in the "Core Content Knowledge" portion of this guide. Also available as an aid to studies is the content in the appendices. Since the exam is comprised of constructed-response questions, examinees may want to practice writing present levels of educational performance statements, IEP goals, behavior plans, and transition plans.

Some states require additional exams for certification. Another Praxis II study guide is available if examinees must prepare for other exams. *CliffsTestPrep Praxis II: Special Education (0351, 0352, 0690, 0371, 0381, 0321)*, developed by the same author and published by Wiley, Inc., contains a section on core knowledge and one on the application of core knowledge, which may be helpful in preparing for additional exams in the special education field.

Content Clusters

This set of 10 questions is provided for examinees to determine their knowledge as it pertains to exceptional students with **severe to profound disabilities.** Examinees should study these concepts and the content of each broad topic for test preparation. These questions will help examines study for the Education of Exceptional Students: Severe to Profound Disabilities, Praxis II (0544) exam. Using a separate sheet of paper to write the answers will help examinees plan for the constructed-response question responses and pacing for the actual exam.

1. Identify the various psychological and social-emotional characteristics of students with severe to profound disabilities.

2. Discuss the etiologies and medical conditions that affect students with severe to profound disabilities.

3. Describe the various types of assessments and techniques used with students who have severe to profound disabilities.

4. Explain how assessment information may be used to develop a program of instruction for students with severe to profound disabilities.

5. Define some of the specialized health care techniques that must be managed in schools (catheterization, tube feeding, seizure management, and so on).

6. Define the term **collaboration** as it relates to students with disabilities and then identify ways that professionals and parents may collaborate for the best interests of the student with a severe or profound condition.

7. Describe the use of accommodations, modifications, adaptations, equipment, and assistive technology devices and services for students with severe to profound disabilities.

8. Explain how related services should be integrated into instructional settings and how community resources may assist with programming.

9. Describe the components and the process of developing an IEP, an ITP, and a BIP that specifically focuses on students with severe to profound disabilities.

10. Explain how teachers should select and develop curriculum materials for students with severe and profound disabilities.

Constructed-Response Questions

The Praxis II exam for students with severe to profound disabilities utilizes constructed-response questions. Written answers in the form of a short answer narrative or an essay must be concisely developed by the examinee during the actual exam. To best answer the questions, examinees need to clearly understand what they are being asked and think carefully about the answer before proceeding to write it. The answers on the Praxis II exam are scored by examination readers who use an established and standardized scoring rubric or guide, which is briefly explained here:

3	Demonstrates thorough understanding of subject covered
2	Demonstrates a basic understanding of subject covered
1	Demonstrates a lack of understanding of the subject covered
0	Inaccurate, limited, or no response

Read the following question and then the given task. Carefully plan the written constructed response.

Scenario

Sharlene is a 12-year-old elementary student who has a developmental disability and has just transferred to another school. She is nonverbal and must communicate using signs and gestures. Her team has discussed the use of an assistive technology tool to help her, but the assessment has not yet been conducted. Sharlene has been in foster care for 9 years and changed placements 5 times. She was not well cared for in two of the placements and demonstrates problems with grooming. She is confined to a wheelchair due to her severe motor difficulties, so self-care in the area of toileting and feeding are significant problems. She is working on her academics under a functional curriculum and performs at about a 3-year-old level.

Task

1. Identify how the related services personnel should integrate their services into the classroom and other instructional settings to benefit this student.

Response

1. It appears that Sharlene's needs could best be addressed through a team approach by the special education teacher, the foster parent, the general education teacher, the occupational therapist, the physical therapist, and the speech-language pathologist. With regards to the related services she could use support with her self-care skills in the areas of toileting and feeding. The related services personnel, OT, PT, and SLP should conduct co-treatment sessions as she is attempting to perform a task related to self-care. They should structure the task using the method of sequencing the tasks so she can learn the steps required to complete the task. The related service providers should work together with Sharlene as she tries to feed herself. The SLP and OT would work on the feeding activity, and the PT would work on the positioning. They should collaborate and co-treat Sharlene in her toileting attempts as well. The team should also be present for the assistive technology assessment and conduct portions of it together, as they address her needs according to their areas of expertise. Working together, they may share their observations and techniques to better address her needs and support her skill acquisition.

Topic Overview

Students with **severe to profound disabilities** exhibit a wide range of conditions and individual needs. Many demonstrate multiple disabilities and limited academic achievements. It is, therefore, important to carefully analyze the student's needs to determine the areas of instruction and to promote appropriate skills acquisition.

Many students with severe to profound disabilities participate less in general education inclusive settings than the segregated or self-contained settings. This placement is due in part to the extreme needs of these students and the difficulties of the general education teachers to support their needs. It is often necessary to provide a functional or community-based curriculum approach to meet their needs. These students perform best when provided with instruction related to real life and when learning skills while performing daily tasks.

Students with **severe to profound conditions** possess a multiplicity of traits that extend into academics, physical problems, social-emotional issues, and health concerns. They may be identified under categories listed in special education as **behavior disorder/emotional disturbances, autism, mental retardation,** or **developmental disability.**

The national organization, the Association for Persons with Severe Handicaps (TASH), has developed a definition to describe persons with **severe disabilities.** It is summarized as including individuals who need ongoing, intensive support in one or more areas of major life functions so they may participate in community activities and enjoy some quality of life. They may need help with communication, self-care, mobility, and learning in order to pursue employment and independent living.

The federal definition for **developmental disability** is considered a chronic disability that stems from a mental or physical impairment, or both. It manifests prior to age 22 and appears to be a permanent condition. The individual may require specialized services and supports for extended periods and exhibit limitations in one or more of the following areas: language, learning, self-care, mobility, independence, and employment.

Characteristics of Learners

Students who have severe or profound disabilities are a diverse and complex group of individuals. They often need the support of others to effectively maneuver their environment and function independently. These students with severe or profound conditions are usually categorized more specifically with mental retardation, developmental disabilities, or as having autism. They may have multiple disabilities that include a hearing impairment, a vision impairment, a physical disability, a social-emotional disturbance, or other medical conditions.

Students with severe to profound disabilities demonstrate problems with memory, attention, language, and generalizing skills across settings. They have problems understanding presented information, retaining knowledge, and using learned skills.

Etiologies of Conditions

Known causes for the conditions related to severe and profound disabilities include disease, genetics, environmental affects, and birth defects. Yet, sometimes the cause is considered *unknown*.

Students with severe and profound conditions may have multiple influences for multiple problems. Children may be exposed to illness, trauma, accident, or injury that would result in a permanent and severe condition. They may also be affected by heredity, biochemical imbalances, neurobiological conditions, brain disorders, and prematurity-related problems that result in a more profound disability.

Causes known for specific disabilities are listed in the "Core Content Knowledge" portion of this guide.

Psychological and Social-Emotional Characteristics

Students with severe to profound disabilities, particularly those with mental retardation or cognitive impairments have demonstrated higher rates of psychopathology or mental illness than the general population. Some of the more commonly diagnosed disorders include bipolar disorder, schizophrenia, depression, obsessive-compulsive, anxiety, and hyperactivity disorders.

Students with severe to profound conditions have problems relating to their environment. They have difficulty with problem solving, making decisions, and dealing with daily stressors. These problems contribute to their psychological state and social-emotional status.

Medical Complications/Implications

Medical issues and health conditions are greater for students with severe to profound disabilities than the general population. In addition to the educational disability, these students often present with health or medical conditions such as epilepsy, cerebral palsy, orthopedic problems, vision or hearing impairments, and health impairments.

The most common movement disability is **cerebral palsy (CP),** which is caused by a central nervous system disorder. There are three types of CP: spastic/hypertonic (high muscle tone), hypotonic (low muscle tone), and fluctuating tone (mixed tones in the body). Students with cerebral palsy often have other medical conditions (deformities, appetite issues, toileting problems, seizures) or additional disabilities (mental retardation, vision impairment, hearing impairment, speech-language problems). These students generally develop abnormal movement patterns, use improper positions or incorrect posture, and have a restricted range of motion.

Students with severe to profound disabilities can experience a **hearing impairment** with a demonstrated loss that ranges from mild to profound (hard of hearing to deaf). There are three types of losses: sensori-neural, conductive, and mixed.

A **vision impairment** can also range from mild to severe. This impairment can include a problem with acuity that may be corrected by glasses to a more severe loss, which is considered legal blindness. A student with legal blindness may have a constricted visual field, but still have use of some residual sight.

Assessment

All special education students participate in assessments for various reasons. Whether identifying a student for services or determining a level of progress, assessments provide valuable information to the examiner and the team who work with the student. The requirements for assessment protocol for all special education students can be found in the "Core Content Knowledge" section of this study guide.

The steps outlined for the special education process include various assessments: pre-referral; screening; referral; evaluation and identification; instructional program planning; placement and review; and evaluation. The assessments conducted throughout these stages provide information that will determine the student's program, placement, and instructional design.

Under the amendments of IDEA in 1997, students with severe to profound disabilities were included in the educational accountability reform. According to this reform, they are to participate in the high-stakes testing according to their IEP and may qualify for the alternate form of assessment; however, standardizing those assessments can be a difficult task. Due to the needs of these students, they rarely participate in the same general education curriculum and primarily focus their studies on functional outcomes. These functional life skills are difficult to examine through a paper and pencil assessment, as they require real materials and activities. And these students seldom do well with paper and pencil tasks, so attempting a standardized exam may result in failure as it is inappropriate to their needs. Many states have developed alternate versions of the standardized tests for use with this type of student.

The preferred methods of assessing students with severe to profound disabilities is to observe them performing their activities and tasks, document their generalizations of skills, conduct an interview with other service personnel and parents, and review progress reports and behavior records.

Instruments and Methods

Assessment procedures required under law include using a variety of evaluation tools and strategies; administering tests in the student's primary language; and ensuring the tools are free from racial or cultural bias. Because functional, developmental, and academic information may be gathered to determine the educational needs of the student, the tools and procedures must also be appropriate to the student's levels and abilities. Being flexible, patient, and knowledgeable provides positive assessment results and makes a more pleasant experience for the student.

From the many types of assessments available, one should be selected based on the purpose of the evaluation and the student's abilities. Educators and examiners should know the typical developmental sequences because selecting instruments and methods must be based on the student's developmental or functional age, rather than chronological age. Using baseline data or performance-based data will help in making this decision. These tools are used to determine progress, develop new goals, review pertinent data, or to revise a student's program. The primary types of assessment tools include criterion-referenced, curriculum-based, norm-referenced, performance-based, and standards-based.

A description of these types of assessments may be found in both the "Core Content Knowledge" and the "Mild to Moderate Disabilities (0542)" sections of this study guide.

Educators should observe and become familiar with all areas of the student's performance and development so the assessment tools and procedures may be refined and changed to accommodate the student's severe to profound needs. They must determine whether the student is nonverbal, has limited motor skills, or has other impairments that require support (hearing, vision). These students often demonstrate splinter skills that can be misleading when confirming abilities. A **splinter skill** is one that is observed or considered to be more advanced or unusual to the determined ability level of the student, so evaluations should not be based on this skill.

Areas other than the learning domains to consider for evaluation include the instructional domains of domestic, leisure, community, vocational, and school. The information to be obtained will be valuable because students with severe to profound needs are generally instructed in these areas as the skills are incorporated in the functional or community-based curriculum. The environment and setting for these instructional domains and the activities to be addressed should all be considered when conducting the evaluation.

Adaptations and Modifications

The same provisions made for instruction on a student's IEP should also be acceptable for assessments. If a student needs an adaptation, a modification, or an accommodation during instructional periods, those should be considered and allowed for an examination period. The team makes the final determination regarding what a student needs to take an assessment.

Students with limited mobility and motor control or those with severely impaired language may need very specific adaptations to the equipment and materials used in the assessment process. Evaluators should be aware of a student's limitations that may require certain modifications and accommodations throughout the testing period. Communicating with parents and the teachers will help to determine how the student should be accommodated.

Procedures for Assessment and Reports

Assessments may be used for the identification and placement of a student in a special education program as well as to make specific individual program decisions. An assessment can determine the specific needs of a student and help the team decide the instructional strategies and methods that will provide the most benefit to the student. Assessment results should lead to the development of an **individual education plan** (IEP). Assessments are also utilized as an on-going classroom tool to gauge progress and amend programs and goals.

The main purposes of an assessment for a student with severe to profound disabilities are as follows:

- Evaluate existing skills.
- Link the collected information to instruction.
- Measure progress in achievement.
- Improve behaviors.
- Analyze instruction.
- Identify support services and strategies.

Developing a comprehensive report and delivering findings are part of the team work that must occur to create an appropriate individualized education program. Parents should be involved in the discussion of the results and assist in programmatic design.

Utilizing Assessment Information

When the formal assessment phase is complete, the team reviews findings and uses this information to create the instructional plan. A team that works collaboratively with a person-centered focus will best address the educational needs of that individual. The team should prioritize the needs and areas of instruction according to developmental age, functional needs, individuals' interests, and parents' preferences. Linking instruction through the assessment generates a statement of present levels of educational performance (PLEP) and the goals necessary for the IEP, while also helping to select the competencies, content standards, performance indicators, and strategies best suited to each student.

Informal assessments are essential for teachers, as they provide performance-based and authentic information about skill development at any given moment in the educational program. Teachers can utilize this information to make immediate changes in instructional delivery and to determine the level of mastery on certain skills. With the students who have severe to profound needs, continual informal assessments are vital in determining regular needs. These students may lose their mastery of skills if these skills are not practiced or used so teachers must continue to assess for proficiency levels.

Applying the assessment information to the design of instruction includes determining the methods, the instructional strategies, the accommodations/modifications, the materials, the equipment, the resources, and the technology. Examiners may gather data on the student's motivation level, communication needs, and supervision concerns as related to classroom, vocational, and community instruction.

Annual assessments are conducted to determine the progress that has been made on the selected goals and learning criteria, as well as to form the goals for the next school year. The assessments will deliver information on the areas of progress as well as the areas where progress did not occur. These non-progress areas would be the topic of discussion for teams in selecting the areas and establishing goals for future programming.

Note: Significant information about assessment in the special education process is available in the "Core Content Knowledge" portion of this study guide. Also refer to the appendices for information on writing PLEPs, IEP goals, behavior plans, and transition plans.

Curriculum and Instruction

Curricular development is a difficult area for teachers of students with severe and profound disabilities. As proposed through the special education movement, it is important to begin with the typical or general education curricula for students with disabilities, but the individual's needs must still be addressed. They should participate in activities and instruction suited to their same-age peers as much as possible.

Students with severe and profound conditions often need adapted curricula. They may genuinely need a functional curriculum with integrated vocational and life skills instruction. Utilizing the concepts of general education curriculum and applying them to a student's daily life are critical for students with severe and profound needs. The use of an applied curriculum and authentic assessment provides a means to obtaining essential information on student progress and on-going needs.

Using an **applied curriculum** provides students with authentic activities that apply to regular and real-world occurrences, making learning more meaningful. Teachers can observe the student's skills acquisition and identify progress in a more direct manner. The competencies pertain to practical experiences and information that may be used in other settings. Specific models of applied curriculum include school-to-work programs, vocational education programs, community-based instruction, apprenticeship programs, and career education programs.

Inclusion programs should be considered and available to all students with severe to profound disabilities, and if utilized, they should require strong collaboration of the special education and general education teachers, as well as related service providers, to support the student. Students placed in inclusive settings may need the support of a paraprofessional or peer tutor. The curriculum, the instruction, the methods, the strategies, and the materials must all be appropriate to the student's needs.

The curriculum for students with severe and profound needs is an important factor in their overall education. The selection of materials is essential to their ability to achieve academic standards and educational success.

Curriculum Materials

Instructional formats, teaching strategies and methods, and educational materials are best selected by determining the needs of the students who will be using them. Because students who are severe to profound are so significantly diverse in their abilities and needs, this decision becomes most complicated.

Although the ability levels of students with severe to profound disabilities may be limited and reflect a much younger age level, the selected materials must still be age appropriate, with reasonable objectives, and measurable outcomes.

They must be flexible to various settings and adaptable to varying learning styles. Some of the materials may also require accommodations, modifications, or adaptations to suit the individual students.

Teachers should add supports as necessary to aid students in the retention of material and improve their concept development. This may include the use of pictures, cue cards, enlarged print, various material positions, manipulatives, color coding, learning centers, or demonstrations and models.

Integrating Related Services

A major portion of the program for a student with severe to profound needs may be the time spent with therapists and related service providers. Related services are mandated as a component of the IEP and, therefore, should be identified for individual students based on their special needs through team decisions. These services must be selected so the student may gain benefit from special education. Related services may include but are not limited to speech-language therapy, occupational therapy, transportation, health services, counseling, behavior specialist, audiologist, vision specialist, and the school nurse.

Students with severe to profound disabilities may be placed in general education programs so the team should decide what related services will support the student in that setting. Services that may be offered in a **reach-in model** are those that are brought into the general education classroom where students with disabilities have access to appropriate materials and peer examples. This program model allows students with severe to profound disabilities the opportunities to master skills in their environment, while also learning to generalize skills in meaningful situations.

For many students with severe to profound disabilities, the **integration of related services** occurs in self-contained or segregated settings, but nevertheless has tremendous value and a positive impact on their access to an education. Related services personnel who work with the student to meet the educational needs (OT, PT, SLP, and so on) provide the services in the classroom during the daily schedule, implementing interventions and supporting skill development in a meaningful way. Students with severe to profound disabilities gain skills by interacting with their environment and practicing in the normal daily situations. These students are better able to generalize when given the opportunity to work in natural settings with typical events.

Providing **integrated therapy** in the classroom setting offers several very positive aspects. One is that the staff, both educators and paraprofessionals, are able to observe the sessions and learn how to reinforce the therapeutic measures. The second is that students who need behavior support or plan interventions will have an entire team working on the same program. Third is that therapists learn how to support one another's program for the individual student. Fourth is that more adult support is available for services in a classroom with intricately challenged students. All adults working with these students may then collaborate for the benefit of each individual.

Community Resources

Community resources will be invaluable to students with severe to profound disabilities as they become adults. These students must be prepared during their high school years for community life later so they are more effectively integrated. This preparation may be accomplished through the development of an Individual Transition Plan and involving the various community agencies who will maintain continued support to the individual once they leave school. Agency staff can demonstrate their support to the student and family by participating in the development of the transition program.

The goal for the student is to reach a level of independence best suited to her needs and to improve overall function in community living. Educators should work with the family and the various community agencies to select the most appropriate services and resources. The types of services and their availability differ among communities and across states, so educators must be familiar with their area and the needs of their students.

IEP Goals

An individual education plan, mandated under federal law, has a series of components that are required. One required component is the creation of clearly stated annual goals. The goals are determined by the IEP team according to the non-bias assessment, and they are based on the student's needs. They must be both measurable and attainable. Expectations are set in the goals according to state criteria, which may include the conditions, performance, criteria, assessment, and state standard reference.

The annual goals focus on specific skill areas that the individual student needs to learn or acquire by the end of a predetermined time period (most often a year). Periodic informal progress checks are made, and regular formal annual progress reports are written and provided to parents. Should a problem occur with the student's program, changes may be made through a team meeting. For more information on IEP goals refer to the appendixes.

Planning and Implementing Instruction

Since students with severe to profound disabilities demonstrate such a variety of needs, educators must gather information about each student through assessments, past performances, and other team members to adequately plan and implement instruction.

These assessments provide a link to instruction that helps the team make appropriate decisions about the teaching practices and instructional delivery. The assessment information can be summarized in the **present levels of educational performance statement** (PLEP) on the IEP, which distinguishes the specific areas needing focus and interventions. Determining the least restrictive environment for service delivery will also make a difference in implementing instruction. Linking assessment to instruction is essential for students with severe to profound needs.

Students with severe to profound disabilities need basic functional academic instruction as well as a curriculum designed to deliver instruction in the areas of self-management, choice making, decision making, problem solving, and self-advocacy. These students will work toward independent functioning. They need the instruction and modeling of independent daily living skills, such as self-care skills (grooming, feeding, dressing), language and communication skills (including assistive technology needs), employment skills (responsibilities, expectations, and job-related skills), and social skills (conversational skills, interactions with peers). Implementing a peer buddy program can help students with more severe problems learn from someone their own age.

Functional reading includes the following:

- Daily use of sight words: food preparation, household work, and so on
- Community sight words: stores, restaurants, and so on
- Safety/survival sight words: transportation and daily activities
- Functional vocabulary: foods, clothing, days of the week, and so on

Functional math includes the following:

- Money management skills
- Time and date management

Methods for implementing instruction include modifying directions and instructions; scaffolding instruction; using auditory, visual, and tactile cues; structuring the lesson to suit the learners; and using computers, calculators, and tape recorders. Some students may need leveled instruction or leveled assignments that may alter the content.

For students with cerebral palsy, the goal of intervention and treatment is to provide support and instruction so they develop appropriate controls. The preferred method is during normal daily patterns, routines, and activities. Strategies for working with these children include establishing a team, working collaboratively with occupational and physical therapists, as well as a speech-language therapist, assessing assistive technology needs, using adaptive equipment, providing support for the use of appropriate posturing and proper positioning, watching for abnormal reflexes, and maintaining seizure control.

For students with hearing losses, knowing the type, the cause, and the range of the loss are important in establishing a program and identifying the service providers. Students may need support from a hearing specialist or an audiologist as well as amplification equipment to access their education. Students with hearing losses may require support for care and maintenance of hearing aids, training in speech and in how to use residual hearing. These students may also need a communication system such as sign language, environmental accommodations, or an interpreter.

Students with severe to profound needs frequently have vision impairments. Through an assessment, if the student is found to be impaired in the severe range, a vision specialist should be involved in the instructional program and treatment. The student may need vision support, special materials, and equipment, orientation and mobility training, and direct services. Students with vision impairments use visual aids and a multisensory approach and may need environmental accommodations.

Planning and Implementing Transitions

Students with severe to profound disabilities need the support of a transition team when they are approaching age 16. Many of them will need continued services as adults, and making plans for the transition of services better prepares the student. An individualized transition plan should be carefully developed to meet the needs, interests, and preferences of the student while planning for a more independent life.

Transition services should be based on a functional vocational evaluation and should identify the areas to be addressed by the team. Involving the appropriate community agencies is necessary in order to develop a relationship between the student and the personnel who will support the student in the adult years. The team will incorporate goals that focus on future needs in instruction, related services, community experiences, employment, and other post-school adult living activities.

Note: See the appendices for information on the content and writing of an appropriate ITP.

Collaborating with Others

Collaboration is an effective method of teaming for students with multiple severe to profound disabilities. Due to their special needs, these students require services and expertise from a variety of disciplines and trained personnel. Collaboration is considered a best practice strategy in special education that enhances individual student programs.

A **collaborative team** is comprised of two or more members who work toward successful outcomes for individual student's according to the IEP goals. Effective and ongoing communications, as well as meaningful interactions are the keys to the positive collaboration of team members. Collaborative efforts must be a continual and flexible process.

Collaborating with colleagues, specialists, parents, community agencies, administrators, family members, and students requires that roles be defined, trust and respect developed, regular communications established, expertise accepted, conflict resolution methods determined, common goals and outcomes created, and responsibilities shared. Team members may convey ideas and recommendations for instruction and interventions. Decisions by the team should occur when all members have gained the information they need to make informed and justified conclusions.

Under federal law, parents and family members are considered partners on student teams. They may assist in program plan development, intervention design and implementation, and in evaluating student achievement. Include parents in the special education process by inviting them to all meetings, asking their opinions, and seeking their input on instructional strategies and individual goals. Communicate with families and provide them with ongoing information and progress reports.

Three team models are suggested for the implementation of the special education process. These are the **multidisciplinary team,** the **interdisciplinary team,** and the **transdisciplinary team.** The transdisciplinary team is regarded as being the most effective.

Community resources are available through agencies to assist students and parents. Connecting families to these resources will help in the development of programming and transitions into the adult programs. Involving the community resources early to assist in developing a transition plan helps both the student and the family be more knowledgeable about the options for the future.

Structuring and Managing the Learning Environment

The learning environment is influential to the successful outcomes for students with disabilities. A structured and user-friendly environment should involve the student in the learning process and engage them in their education. An effective learning environment should be based on student needs and abilities. The use of curriculum, the materials, and the strategies all contribute to the learning environment.

For more information on structuring and managing the learning environment, refer to the "Core Content Knowledge" or "Mild to Moderate Disabilities (0542)" portions of this study guide.

Behavior Management Plans

Federal law, IDEIA, includes a provision for behavioral intervention in which a Functional Behavior Assessment and Behavior Intervention Plan may be used to support a student in her educational program. Behavior management can be a complex task for students with severe to profound disabilities, and it is the responsibility of the IEP team to use these tools to identify the problematic behaviors and develop a plan to address them with positive behavioral interventions and strategies.

- **Functional Behavior Assessment (FBA):** The process of gathering information about a student's problem behaviors to determine the need for behavior interventions and a behavior plan.
- **Behavior Intervention Plan (BIP):** An individual program designed by using the information from an FBA to structured interventions that help a student learn to manage his behaviors.

To properly determine the behaviors that must be changed, team members should conduct observations. Through these observations, they should identify the occurrence, the frequency, the circumstances, and the environment. Methods used to document observations and record behaviors include the following:

- **Anecdotal recordings:** Taking notes on the activity, the student's behaviors, the reactions of others, and the setting
- **ABC analysis:** Determining the antecedent, behavior, and consequence of a behavior, as well as its function
- **Durational recordings:** Accounting for the amount of time a person engages in a behavior
- **Frequency recordings:** Documents how often the behavior occurs
- **Permanent product recordings:** Identifying the tangible items or behavior outcomes

For students with severe to profound disabilities, the function of the behavior may be the major key to determining the interventions. A behavior can imply more than one function, and the environment will be a critical factor in making that determination. Some of the more common functions for students with multiple severe to profound disabilities include gaining attention, seeking tangible items, attempting communication, avoiding a task, and seeking sensory input.

Strategies used to increase desired behaviors for students with severe to profound disabilities are to teach desired replacement behaviors, adjust the environment, adapt instructional materials, change the instructional strategies, and use of reinforcements.

Both an FBA and a BIP are further explained along with examples of documents in the appendices section of this guide.

Problem Solving/Conflict Resolution/Crisis Management

Students with special conditions depend on others to meet their needs, yet the goal is for the individual to reach independence at the highest level possible. For students with severe to profound disabilities, the ability to be less dependent is difficult but important to their self-concept and self-determination. A primary outcome to seek is to limit the experiences that end in failure and build upon those opportunities that provide success and offer feedback on achievement for these students.

One way to help students reach levels of self-management and increase independence is to instruct them on **problem solving.** Gaining these skills requires direct teaching, modeling, and the integration of training into daily activities. It is from systematic training that students with severe to profound disabilities acquire confidence in their individual ability to solve daily problems. The use of actual problems as they are occurring is one of the best teaching tools in this area for these significantly disabled students. Help students by identifying the problem presented, pinpointing various consequences and alternatives to solutions, and being flexible and patient as the student chooses a solution. After the exercise is completed, aid the student in analyzing and evaluating the outcome to the best of his ability.

Generalizing the problem-solving skills can be a challenge for the more involved and disabled students, but quite necessary to their survival. Even students with minimal cognitive and language abilities can learn some problem-solving skills with continued instruction and training as they need these lifelong skills.

Crisis management is another aspect of caring for and educating students with severe to profound disabilities. Certainly, educators should have a plan in their classroom for handling students when a crisis occurs. Most schools and districts have a written plan, with policies and procedures, and provide training to all staff in case of emergencies. It is a key component to IEPs for students with severe to profound needs to have an individualized plan that pertains specifically to the student's on-going medical needs. In a crisis, the team must know exactly what should happen to support the student and receive the care needed.

Crisis management also refers to behavior interventions when a behavior has escalated beyond the behavior plan interventions. These possibilities may already have been indicated by the student's previous behaviors, so if the team believes the student may be a danger to self or others, a behavior plan should provide a written plan for a pending crisis. Some schools have crisis teams who are prepared and knowledgeable about implementing support in a variety of difficult and dangerous situations.

Some schools and districts allow the restraint of students when the situation warrants the need. This is determined through a series of training sessions and gaining the knowledge to handle very serious and complicated emergency situations. Educators learn how to remain calm in order to address the student's needs and the needs of others involved. Restraint is a last resort and should never be used unless the person implementing it has been carefully trained.

Specialized Health Care

Just as the educators, staff, and parents must be aware of the educational needs of individual students, they must also be aware and understand the physical and/or medical conditions, the pertinent provision of services, and the methods of proper care. Students who range in the severe to profound category generally have medical complications that need to be addressed during the school day. Educators should seek assistance in designing a specialized health care program from parents, therapists, primary care physicians, or other medical practitioners.

First Aid

All professionals who work with students who have exceptional needs should obtain the basic first-aid certifications. But it is particularly vital to have first-aid knowledge when working with students who have severe to profound needs. Due to their sometimes precarious health status, they seem to have a higher rate of injuries, health needs, and perhaps life-threatening incidences that require attention and quick thinking from staff. Educators and paraprofessionals, in addition to the related service personnel, should be trained in first aid by certified trainers. Education staff working with these types of students must also recognize the first signs of implementing emergency procedures and contacting outside assistance.

Positioning and Management

Positioning for seating, standing, feeding, accessing educational materials/activities, and other physically related events are critical to students with severe to profound needs. Those students with orthopedic difficulties do not always use the proper positions so many are treated by an OT or PT with ongoing daily support from the education team. Positioning is essential for students to access educational programs and materials. Students with physical difficulties, vision impairments, hearing impairments, and other medical conditions need adaptations that may include assistive technology tools, changes in the environment, use of specialized equipment, and provisions for modifications of the materials.

Seizure Management

Seizure activity, its cause, the type, and the treatment must be diagnosed by a medical practitioner. Seizures may occur more often in students with severe and profound conditions. There are two types of seizures: partial (involuntary movements or altered consciousness with repetitive motor movement) and generalized (grand mal or tonic-clonic).

Teachers must clearly understand the impact and treatment of a seizure disorder for an individual student and must monitor and document the activity: date, time, associated behaviors, and antecedent. They need to care for the student's health, comfort, and safety and be fully aware of the procedures and policies for notifying parents, medical personnel, and emergency assistance. Commonly, students are treated for seizures through the administration of medications, which also require strict adherence to policies and procedures and staff who understand the importance of the medical treatments.

Tube Feeding

Nasogastric tube feeding and **gastronomy tube** feeding are options when a student is unable to take food or liquids orally. A nasogastric tube is used to feed an individual through the mouth or nose. A tube placed in the stomach, a gastronomy tube, is more permanent. Educators need training in conducting tube feedings and knowledge about the care and sanitation that is required. The school nurse and the family should be involved in establishing a plan for training and on-going care.

Catheterization

A procedure used in a school setting to aid some individuals to empty their bladders through tube insertion is **catheterization.** Known as **Clean Intermittent Catheterization (CIC),** this method requires that the person managing the procedure and care be trained by a school nurse or medical practitioner. Communication between the special education teacher and the child's family care taker is essential.

Tracheostomy Tube Care

A **tracheostomy tube** is used to help open the airway for students with difficulty breathing on their own and is inserted directly into the trachea. These tubes need intermittent care, so educators need training from a medical provider or school nurse to properly support the use of this type of medical equipment.

Educators must be cognizant of the specific needs of the child, so communicating with the parents is essential. Working with the parents on the child's specific signals and listening to the child's breathing patterns will help alert staff to the need for suctioning. Certain procedures for eating and drinking will be necessary, and critical attention is required depending on the severity of the child's involvement. The speech-language pathologist will also be helpful in establishing the method of communication, whether that is through assistive technology equipment or the manual use of sign language. A physical therapist or occupational therapist may also be involved in programming with regard to positioning and other motor activities.

Administration of Medications

Students with severe to profound disabilities have high rates of health impairments, and some require medications. The conditions that may need medication treatment include epilepsy, seizure disorder, urinary tract problems, digestive problems, breathing complications, and behavior or emotional problems. Educators need to seek assistance from health professionals such as the student's primary care physician or the school nurse.

The policies and procedures for working with students who have significant health issues and for those who take medications vary from state to state and district to district. Some schools have health plans that become an addendum to an IEP so the procedures and people responsible are clearly outlined.

The more common types of medications taken by this exceptional population include anticonvulsants, antipsychotics, antianxiety drugs, antidepressants, and stimulants. Educators need to know the types and purposes of the medications their students are taking, as well as the side effects in case of an emergency. Communicating with the caregiver about doses and medication changes will support the student.

Final Thoughts and Tips

Test completion day is on the horizon. Taking the preparatory steps regarding registration and completing quality study periods will ensure satisfactory success on these exams.

This section provides important information about preparing for the exams. All test-takers should review and address these issues prior to taking any of the tests.

Registration

Some examinees are required to complete more than one Praxis II exam for teaching exceptional students. This obligation depends on the examinee's preferred and specific field of study and the various state departments of education requirements for teacher certification or licensure. Examinees should be sure to determine which exams are needed in the state where they plan to teach. If an exam regarding exceptional students or special education is compulsory, but not found in this study guide, check *CliffsTestPrep Praxis II: Special Education (0321, 0351, 0352, 0371, 0381, 0690),* also published by Wiley Publishing, Inc., which has a series of other educational study guides for the Praxis II exams that might be helpful.

If more than one exam is a requisite, it is recommended that the examinee take only one test per day to optimize specific study periods and to achieve success on each exam. The exceptional student and special education exams can be complicated, fast-paced, and tiresome. Examinees should consider individual learning and studying styles so goals for adequate performance may be reached.

Review of registration guidelines:

- Check test dates and test locations online at http://www.ets.org.
- Speak with a college or university financial aid officer to determine whether the fee(s) for the exam(s) may be waived.
- Check the online application process prior to completing registration if you think you might qualify for test accommodations due to a disability.
- Register at least one month ahead of the test date to secure a seat and location. (Many examinees find online registration to be the easiest, fastest, and cheapest.)
- Bring proof of registration to the testing center on the day of the exam.

Study Time Tips

Examinees will self-impose personal methods for exam study since all individuals learn in different ways. Studying early and preparing over the long term (1 to 3 months) for each exam required is recommended, as there is a tremendous amount of information covered within the topic of educating exceptional students.

Practice tests are available in this guide to help examinees understand the types of questions and learn how to pace their answers in preparation for the actual exams. Reading this study guide should provide adequate information, but for examinees who seek additional information a resource section of websites is available at the end of this book.

Following are some recommended study tips:

- Review the Table of Contents to determine the topics that are covered on the exam.
- Assess individual strengths and needs regarding the exam content.
- Read the information about the exam format to become familiar with the multiple-choice questions, constructed-response questions, and the case history samples.

- Review and answer the narrative-style questions found in the introduction sections of each of the four topics about educating exceptional students found in this study guide. Examine these broad areas to determine any need for more in-depth study.

- Read and answer the sample multiple-choice questions at the beginning of each chapter, while practicing pacing.

- Develop an individualized plan for study based on the recognized individual strengths and needs. Use a calendar, a PDA, or a daily schedule to help stay on the planned course of study. Studying should be an enjoyable and motivational task, and the environment used should be comfortable with study materials easily accessible (paper, pencils, study guide, computer, and so on). Some options that enhance studying include occasionally changing locations, seeking a study partner, utilizing background music, and enjoying a favorite beverage or snack.

- Study each and every day prior to the exam. Review the information studied the day before prior to studying the new material. Use an outline of information, flash cards, or vocabulary lists to support memorization of important facts and concepts. The outcome of this examination is very important for certification.

- Take the sample practice exam(s) for the specific exceptional student topic either before or after using the study guide materials. Some examinees take the practice exam first to assess abilities and knowledge. Use the answer explanations as a component of study since additional information about exceptional students is included.

- Use the most effective individualized methods and strategies to study and prepare for the Praxis II exams.

Test Day Prep

The day before the exam, do the following:

- Participate in activities that do not distract from the materials studied for the Praxis II exam. The effects of partying and other strenuous activities may be felt on test day, so avoiding these is recommended.

- Eat well and drink adequate water.

- Set out the items needed (proof of registration, identification, pencils, pens, comfortable clothing, and so on).

- Access the directions for the location of the testing center and determine the time necessary for travel.

- Don't stay up late to cram for the exam.

- Get a good evening of rest and sleep.

The day of the exam, do the following:

- Awake early to get ready and avoid rushing around.

- Eat a healthy breakfast that includes protein, water, and/or juice.

- Remember to take the important items needed for the exam.

- Arrive 15 to 30 minutes early to the exam location.

PART II

PRACTICE TESTS WITH ANSWER EXPLANATIONS

Core Content Knowledge (0353)

Learning Disabilities (0382)

Mild to Moderate Disabilities (0542)

Severe to Profound Disabilities (0544)

Read each of the following multiple-choice questions and select the answer that is best suited to complete the concept. Mark the answer on the score sheet.

1. Which of the following theorists contributed to the understanding of human social-emotional development by constructing the Behavioral Theory?

   A. Freud
   B. Piaget
   C. Skinner
   D. Maslow

2. Bandura's Sociological Theory promotes the idea that students learn best through

   A. observation.
   B. repeated trials.
   C. peer interactions.
   D. collaborative providers.

3. When a student lacks the ability to understand the functional use of language or engage in typical conversations, he may be identified with a delay in

   A. syntax.
   B. phonics.
   C. semantics.
   D. pragmatics.

4. A serious and on-going issue regarding program supports for students with exceptional needs is the area of

   A. early intervening.
   B. mnemonic strategies.
   C. assistive technology.
   D. mainstream programs.

5. A student who receives services from the speech-language therapist lacks the ability to understand and comprehend information that is presented. This type of language problem refers to

   A. explicit literacy.
   B. implicit literacy.
   C. receptive language.
   D. expressive language.

6. The parents of a 2-year-old child with mental retardation are concerned about the future. They know about the NCLB requirements of standards based learning, state testing, and increased accountability measures, but wonder how their child might meet those demands. Their child is currently served in an early intervention program, and they are anxious about next year's program. Which of the following is the key component that will help this family?

   A. an increase in services
   B. meet with another family
   C. an effective transition plan
   D. study the rules and guidelines

7. A 5-year-old is having problems remembering the names of colors and can only count to three. He is an active child who enjoys the outdoors, but stumbles often. He speaks in three-word sentences and is able to make his needs known, but still has some difficulty dressing and toileting independently. Parents are concerned that he is not developing as his peers in the neighborhood and have asked the school to help. Based on this information, which is the most likely domain for a potential developmental delay?

   A. motor
   B. adaptive
   C. language
   D. cognitive

8. Team work is essential to the academic success of exceptional students. A team that shares goals, utilizes on-going communication, and shares responsibilities for the student's program is called a

   A. cooperative team.
   B. coordinated team.
   C. consultative team.
   D. collaborative team.

GO ON TO THE NEXT PAGE

9. Physical skill development includes fine motor, gross motor, perceptual motor, and

    A. sensory integration.

    B. affective behaviors.

    C. metacognitive skills.

    D. semantic development.

10. A student with multiple disabilities just enrolled in the middle school. No previous school records are available, so the special education director gathered the group of professionals to begin the process of placement. The team conducted independent assessments in their disciplines and met to share information and developed a plan for the student with interventions and strategies defined. They agreed to implement their specific component of the program and meet periodically to discuss progress. What kind of team is this an example of?

    A. intradisciplinary team

    B. interdisciplinary team

    C. transdisciplinary team

    D. multidisciplinary team

11. Which of the following exceptional student categories is most affected by the lack of adaptive skills?

    A. gifted/talented

    B. mental retardation

    C. learning disability

    D. emotional disturbance

12. During the IEP team meeting, members must discuss where the student will receive her special education services, what the related services must be, and how she will access her general education. This discussion leads to a decision about placement, which is based on the provision of the law referred to as the

    A. supplementary services.

    B. procedural safeguards plan.

    C. continuum of services option.

    D. appropriate education program.

13. Characteristics of an exceptionality condition that are related to genetics or trauma are defined under the major category of _____ causes.

    A. medical

    B. behavioral

    C. educational

    D. psychological

14. Using the **least restrictive environment** scale, the term **self-contained program** is synonymous with the _____ model.

    A. inclusive

    B. integrated

    C. segregated

    D. consultative

15. A student who fails to achieve age-appropriate developmental skills and exhibits a delay in adaptive behaviors may qualify for special education services as a student with

    A. mental retardation.

    B. a learning disability.

    C. an emotional disability.

    D. an orthopedic impairment.

16. According to IDEIA, students with disabilities are entitled to individualized services to meet their educational needs. Which of the following are considered related services under the law?

    A. occupational therapy and physical education

    B. interpreter and special state assessments

    C. speech therapy and transportation

    D. nursing care and reading instruction

17. Confidentiality of exceptional children is protected under the law, and these rights should be explained to the parents according to the

    A. causal hearing.

    B. procedural safeguards.

    C. special education handbook.

    D. manifestation determination.

18. A kindergarten child has been demonstrating difficulty with developing social relationships and has multiple language deficits. When given time in the classroom to interact with others and play with the toys, he seeks the same object each day. Parents have been concerned about his lack of interest in playing with his brother, as well as his reactions to certain foods and clothing, but they thought he was a difficult child since birth. The school psychologist was contacted to conduct an observation, and the school has now referred the child for further testing. Which of the following conditions seem to match the child's characteristics?

   A. autism
   B. learning disability
   C. mental retardation
   D. language impairment

19. Special education is designed as an educational intervention for students with exceptional needs. The three different types of interventions used through special education services are identified as

   A. applicable, remedial, and repetitive.
   B. remedial, compensatory, and applicable.
   C. preventative, remedial, and compensatory.
   D. repetitive, preventive, and compensatory.

20. Which of the following statements is the MOST likely reason that some culturally diverse school age populations are over-represented in special education programs?

   A. Linguistic skills lack support.
   B. Assessment process and tools are inaccurate.
   C. Teachers believe they cannot learn like peers.
   D. Parents with limited skills do not understand the process.

21. An IEP is a written plan for a student with a disability that describes

   A. levels of performance, annual goals, and related services.
   B. learning strategies, test modifications, and supplementary aids.
   C. specific state standards, individual methods, and grade guidelines.
   D. description of course content, related services, and accommodations.

22. A first-grade student continually fails to use the expected age-appropriate speech sounds and is demonstrating difficulty with pronunciations of certain letters and words. She will probably receive services for an

   A. anomia disorder.
   B. apraxia disorder.
   C. articulation disorder.
   D. autism spectrum disorder.

23. Certain components are required in an IEP and IFSP, which are highly similar. Which of the following is the significant difference in these processes overall?

   A. the focus on family and child
   B. lessons and materials to be used
   C. program modifications and adaptations
   D. the involvement of related service providers

24. Professionals believe that in addition to intelligence, the factor of _____ is most essential in the definition of *giftedness*.

   A. literacy
   B. initiative
   C. creativity
   D. academics

25. A fourth-grade teacher instructing a group of exceptional students is working on vocabulary development. She has considered the developmental delays of the students so she is focusing on target words related to the activities of daily living and community settings. This method is called

   A. guided practice.
   B. direct instruction.
   C. authentic learning.
   D. cooperative education.

26. Professionals who work with exceptional children should include the parents in decisions about programming because it

   A. helps the child.
   B. prevents lawsuits.
   C. is required under law.
   D. is the right thing to do.

GO ON TO THE NEXT PAGE

27. Students with superior cognitive abilities or who are highly talented, identifying them as "gifted and talented students", are estimated at _____ percent of the school-age population.

A. 1 to 3
B. 10 to 15
C. 3 to 5
D. 20 to 25

28. When an educator develops a class program based on the concept that everything in the environment and in the learning activities are accessible to all learners, she is implementing a approach called

A. universal design.
B. Cloze procedures.
C. authentic learning.
D. prescriptive methods.

29. The cause of giftedness is considered to be a combination of which of the following two factors?

A. genetics and the environment
B. genetics and socioeconomic status
C. environment and parents' education
D. parents' education and socioeconomic status

30. Students with learning disabilities demonstrate problems with memory ability, word retrieval, and sequential tasks. A strategy that is widely used to accommodate a student with these problem areas is the use of

A. prompting.
B. scaffolding.
C. mnemonics.
D. remediation.

31. It is estimated that about _____ percent of the students receiving special education services also receive services for an identified speech or language impairment.

A. 30
B. 50
C. 60
D. 80

32. Adaptive behaviors are MOST often delivered to students using the method of

A. active learning.
B. guided practice.
C. cues and prompts.
D. chained response.

33. A student with traumatic brain injury periodically hits her head on the table at meal times. The staff are conducting a functional behavior assessment to determine the reasons for this continued and increasing problem. One area that they must focus on during their observations is documenting the degree to which the behavior is repeated. Which of the following behavior terms fits this description?

A. duration
B. intensity
C. frequency
D. extinction

34. A strategy used with exceptional students for the purpose of acceleration is

A. skill drill.
B. time trials.
C. tiered lesson.
D. response cards.

35. Which of the following exceptional conditions has the most probability of being corrected through the delivery of appropriate special education services and will not have an enduring lifelong effect on an individual?

A. visual impairment
B. learning disability
C. speech articulation
D. traumatic brain injury

36. A curriculum that emphasizes skills necessary to performing adequately in the community is the

A. behavior curriculum.
B. cognitive curriculum.
C. functional curriculum.
D. social skills curriculum.

37. An elementary student just diagnosed with an attention deficit disorder, was evaluated by the team for possible special education placement, but the student did not qualify for services under any of the categories. However, this student has difficulty in the classroom, and the team believes the student would benefit from special interventions. Which of the following federal laws would best support this student in school?

A. Section 504 of the Rehabilitation Act
B. Mental Health Coalition Act of 1975
C. Exceptional Children's Education Act
D. Elementary and Secondary School Act

38. A provision in the federal law explicitly states that discrimination is prohibited during the assessment of a student for possible special education services. Which of the following is required to ensure that the evaluation procedures are appropriate?

A. test student with a parent present
B. conduct group test of same cultures
C. administer in student's native language
D. eliminate questions of a sensitive nature

39. In 1988, federal funds were approved specifically for students considered economically disadvantaged, who demonstrated limited English proficiency or had a disability while also being identified as gifted or talented. What federal law allowed this to occur?

A. Gifted Education Consolidation Act
B. Elementary and Secondary Education Act
C. Gifted and Talented Children's Education Act
D. Jacob K. Javits Gifted and Talented Student Education Act

40. A provision in the law supports "early intervening services" whose purpose is to

A. define the numbers of at-risk children.
B. decrease the amount of reading instruction.
C. identify exceptional children prior to age 3 years.
D. reduce the number of referrals to special education.

41. When the high school drama teacher worked with the student advertising committee on the play program, they told her they wanted to include biographies and school information about all of the students who worked on the play. She explained that they would need approval due to a certain federal law, called

A. ADA.
B. FAPE.
C. NCLB.
D. FERPA.

42. A high school teacher needs to gather information about a student with autism who is placed in a general education classroom the majority of the day. This student has been demonstrating some problems during academic periods, and the team will meet to discuss possible changes in the program. They want to know how the student performs during different times of the day in varying activities. Which of the following types of informal assessments would **best** provide this teacher with pertinent information to share with the team and make wise decisions about the student's program?

A. portfolio assessment
B. curriculum assessment
C. ecological assessment
D. behavioral assessment

43. Which of the following laws promoted greater accountability in the schools, options for parents in their child's education, and more highly qualified teachers?

A. ADA
B. NCLB
C. IDEIA
D. FERPA

44. A particular test that is used to measure specific areas of cognitive ability and can offer a prediction of a student's school achievement abilities is an

A. aptitude test.
B. achievement test.
C. authentic assessment.
D. articulation assessment.

GO ON TO THE NEXT PAGE

45. A law that schools must comply with in providing services to students with disabilities that prohibits discrimination, apart from IDEIA, is called

   A. Section 504.
   B. Civil Rights Bill.
   C. Exceptionalities Enactment.
   D. Americans with Disabilities Act.

46. A resource teacher, preparing for a student's IEP meeting will help the team decide on the appropriate program and instructional strategies. These decisions are based on a statement that summarizes how the student performs in specific academic areas, which is called the

   A. continuum of placement.
   B. least restrictive environment.
   C. accommodations and modifications.
   D. present levels of educational performance.

47. Which of the following legal cases supported the rights of children with disabilities to receive individualized special education services?

   A. *Honig v. Doe*
   B. *Larry P. v. Riles*
   C. *Cedar Rapids v. Garrett F.*
   D. *Board of Education v. Rowley*

48. During the second semester, a fifth-grade general education teacher received several students with exceptional needs, some who have learning delays, some with emotional difficulties, and others who are gifted. In addition to the typical students in the class, with such a diverse group, managing the classroom can become a challenge. What is the most effective method this teacher can use in developing a set of classroom rules?

   A. Create a booklet with details that explain each rule.
   B. Copy the rules from the other fifth-grade classrooms.
   C. Involve all the students in the development of the rules.
   D. Use a template of guidelines with simple do's and don'ts.

49. In 1993 a landmark decision was made regarding students with mental retardation being educated in a general education classroom setting. This case involved the _____ family against the Board of Education.

   A. Tatro
   B. Oberti
   C. Zobrest
   D. Rowley

50. Learning strategies implemented in general education and special education classrooms should reflect a _____ approach to address the diversity of students.

   A. kinesthetic
   B. multi-modal
   C. visual-auditory
   D. multiple intelligence

51. It is recommended that _____ become a component of the transition plan for high school students with exceptional needs so they will not only understand their condition, but also their rights.

   A. community life
   B. interagency training
   C. advocacy instruction
   D. vocational workshops

52. A functional behavior assessment is mandated under special education law and is best described as a tool to determine

   A. how the behaviors impact the student's social relationships.
   B. the contrast between typical peer behavior and the student's behavior.
   C. the relationship between the student's behavior and the environment.
   D. how the student will benefit from behavior interventions in school and at home.

53. One of the principles of IDEIA pertains to the child's and the parents' rights regarding the special programs and services available to an exceptional student. This portion of the law refers to

   A. adaptive programs.
   B. exceptional processes.
   C. procedural safeguards.
   D. roles and responsibilities.

54. Research has proven that using _____ and _____ is most effective in promoting desired behaviors.

   A. corrections, rewards
   B. reminders, consequences
   C. feedback, reinforcements
   D. confrontations, consistency

55. Which of the following are the three primary areas of community-based placements for students with disabilities?

   A. medical, educational, social
   B. transportation, family life, work
   C. school, training, skill development
   D. residential, employment, recreation

56. A middle school student who is identified with an emotional disability was found using alcohol in the school locker room. The principal contacted the police, and the student was arrested. Before the student may return to school, the rules for discipline under IDEIA must be followed. Which of the following is the next most important step for the school to take?

   A. Conduct a manifestation hearing.
   B. Arrange a conference with the team.
   C. Suspend the student for the semester.
   D. Place the student in another program.

57. Individual transition plans must be based on a student's individual needs, interests, and preferences. Which of the following identify the major categories on which to focus this plan?

   A. daily living, self-care, functional literacy, behavior
   B. social-emotional, language, cognitive, adaptive skills
   C. education, employment, independent living, recreation
   D. family relationships, student achievement, school, work

58. To ensure a positive working relationship and promote the effective delivery of services to students, what should an educator do to help a paraprofessional in the classroom?

   A. Keep a daily journal and improve skill areas.
   B. Encourage parent contacts and attend meetings.
   C. Establish guidelines and outline responsibilities.
   D. Identify student needs and provide copies of IEPs.

59. Piaget believed that learning is an active process and that children should participate in experiential education, which is a reflection of which theory?

   A. Ecological
   B. Sociological
   C. Psychodynamic
   D. Constructionist

60. After a student graduates from high school and the special education program has been terminated, the student's records may be destroyed.

   A. never
   B. after age 21
   C. within a year
   D. only with permission

113

Core Content Knowledge (0353) Practice Exam Answer Key

1. C	21. A	41. D
2. A	22. C	42. C
3. D	23. A	43. B
4. C	24. C	44. A
5. C	25. C	45. A
6. C	26. C	46. D
7. D	27. B	47. D
8. D	28. A	48. C
9. A	29. A	49. B
10. B	30. C	50. B
11. B	31. B	51. C
12. C	32. D	52. C
13. A	33. B	53. C
14. C	34. C	54. C
15. A	35. C	55. D
16. C	36. C	56. A
17. B	37. A	57. C
18. A	38. C	58. C
19. C	39. D	59. D
20. B	40. D	60. D

Answer Explanations for Core Content Knowledge (0353) Practice Exam

1. **C.** Based on the work of Skinner, the Behavorial Theory reinforces the systematic approach to learning where behaviors may be observed, measured, and documented.

2. **A.** Observation is the primary focus of the Sociological Theory in that gaining knowledge will come through student observation. Students learn from watching others and should be provided with modeling and demonstrations.

3. **D.** Pragmatics is a component of the linguistic system. It is the ability to use functional language, such as that in conversational situations. Examples of two pragmatic skills in using appropriate nonverbal behaviors are taking turns when talking and listening to others. Children diagnosed with pragmatic delays are often categorized as autistic, learning disabled, mentally retarded, or speech/language delayed.

4. **C.** Assistive technology has a significant impact on the programs and lives of exceptional students. However, funding, training, availability, and upkeep of the equipment pose serious problems for schools.

5. **C.** When a child has problems comprehending what another person says, or understanding other environmental input (songs, sounds), it is considered a delay in the receptive language area. Children who are identified with this disability work with speech-language therapists to gain skills to improve this area.

6. **C.** Between early intervention services and early childhood services, families should participate in effective transition planning to move their child from one program to another. This will help to alleviate fears about upcoming programs and also identify the need for assessments and programs changes. Transition planning for this age group is required under the law.

7. **D.** The cognitive domain is the most likely domain that is affected, although the child demonstrates problems in all areas. These other areas are impacted by the development of the cognitive domain, and that is the reason the child is having difficulty in these other areas. It would appear that this child is functioning at 2 to 3 years below same-age peers and may need interventions similar to those for children with mental retardation, particularly because the adaptive behaviors are also delayed.

8. **D.** When professionals all contribute their expertise to implement and support a student's program, it is called a **collaborative team.** In general this practice is used in inclusion models and is most effective when members share goals, use proper on-going communications, practice team decision-making, share the responsibilities, and schedule planning time together.

9. **A.** Sensory-integration is an area of physical skill development important to the use of sensory information such as the tactile sense, the vestibular sense, and the proprioceptive sense. Children who lack skills in this area may seek support from an occupational therapist or a physical therapist.

10. **B.** On an interdisciplinary team, the members conduct separate and independent assessments but meet to share information. They develop an educational plan together based on the assessments, including interventions and strategies. Team members then implement their specific portion of the student's program, while remaining in contact with other members.

11. **B.** Although any child with exceptional needs may have delays or problems with adaptive skill development, it is a primary factor in the identification of students with mental retardation. They have significant difficulties in this domain, and generally interventions are part of an integrated curriculum for this population.

12. **C.** Under IDEIA, a provision related to a range of placement and service options for students with special needs is called the **continuum of services.** This is designed to aid teams in making decisions for the implementation of the educational programs for students with disabilities.

13. **A.** A student diagnosed with an exceptionality caused by a genetic or traumatic condition is considered to have a medical relationship. Medical causes include problems related to diseases, illnesses, trauma, genetics, motor, sensory input, and sensory perception.

14. **C.** The least restrictive environment options are mandated under special education law for students with disabilities. These range from the less limiting setting (inclusion) to a more restrictive placement (such as a hospital). A self-contained program is a setting that is considered separate from the main general education setting, although these students may have mainstream opportunities during the day. It is also referred to as the **segregated model.**

15. **A.** The most common characteristics of a child with mental retardation are the abnormal development of early skills and a delay in adaptive behavior skills. The young child may not crawl or talk at the age-appropriate levels and may exhibit an inability to be toilet trained until a later time. These are key indicators that a cognitive disability may be present.

16. **C.** Speech therapy and transportation are two types of related services considered appropriate for students with disabilities on the IEP. Other examples of related services are physical therapy, occupational therapy, and a sign language interpreter.

17. **B.** The procedural safeguards under the special education law outline the rights of families and their children in accessing special programs for a disability related condition. This provision requires that school personnel explain and provide a copy of the rights to parents at different times throughout the special education process.

18. **A.** Children with autism exhibit a wide range of characteristics, which may develop around 18 months or later around ages 3 to 5. This child seems to have some of the classic signs for the potential of autism, although it could be other special conditions. His communication and language deficits, impaired social relationships, interacting with objects in unusual manners, exhibiting difficult behaviors and atypical reactions to sensory stimuli are all indicators of an autism spectrum disorder.

19. **C.** Interventions are developed by a teacher, a school assistance team, or an IEP team to aid a student in accessing educational opportunities according to his needs. Interventions may focus on the materials, the methods, or the environment, and there are three primary types: preventive, remedial, and compensatory.

20. **B.** Some culturally diverse populations have been found to be identified at higher rates in certain categories and in specific areas of the country. Due to the process of assessment and the tools being used, professionals believe these children should be identified as at-risk youth, but they fall within the range of learning disabled or mentally retarded due to the instruments and process used.

21. **A.** The main components for an individual education plan, IEP, include the present levels of educational performance, measurable annual goals, related services, accommodations, involvement in the general education programs, and participation in state testing as well as the description of specific services.

22. **C.** A student who is having difficulty pronouncing words and letter sounds should be evaluated by a speech-language pathologist who will conduct a formal assessment. An articulation disorder is identified by the inability to use age appropriate speech sounds.

23. **A.** Both an IEP and an IFSP are mandated under the law for children with developmental delays, and they have very similar requirements. The primary difference is in the focus on the family and the child. An IEP aims at programs and services to the child for the areas identified, with the family as a member of the team making decisions. The IFSP places emphasis on the entire family unit and delivers a program and services supported by goals that focus on family and child in all areas of development.

24. **C.** The category of gifted/talented includes students who possess a wide-range of levels, abilities, talents, and traits. Students may also be affected by a cultural, a linguistic, or a disabling condition. Over the years, many professionals in the field have included *creativity* as a significantly central component of the definition

25. **C.** One of the most effective methods for vocabulary instruction for students with developmental delays is to use the words that the student will need and use often. These words are evident in the environment, such as restroom, exit, stop, danger, caution, and so on. Using functional words in an instructional situation and occasionally taking the students into the actual environment is called **authentic learning.**

26. **C.** Under federal law, professionals working with exceptional students are encouraged to include parents and families as "partners" in the education process as it is a better way to function as a team. Including parents is a requirement, but how a school maneuvers this mandate is up to the staff; a partnership based on reciprocal respect and dignity will benefit the child.

27. **B.** Under the exceptional student categories, gifted/talented ranks as the second largest group of students receiving special services in the schools with about 10 to 15 percent of the population identified. Professionals believe this group of students is under identified and underserved.

28. **A.** Universal design is an approach in which the environment is designed so individual students with a range of abilities will have access and participate in the general education curriculum. Teachers who use this will vary the strategies according to the learner and ensure availability of a variety of materials and activities, while respecting all learning styles.

29. **A.** Gifted and talented students are in a range on the continuum that is opposite that of those placed with disabilities, although a student may be identified with both. Students with the attributes of giftedness, creativity, or talent have most likely been raised in rich environments and born of similarly positioned parents. The primary reasons for gifted and talented individuals are based on the environment and genetics.

30. **C.** The implementation of the mnemonic strategy is popular with teachers of learning disabled students, as it is a strategy that enhances memory through the use of key words, acronyms, or acrostics. It may also be helpful for students with autism, traumatic brain injury, and emotional disturbance.

31. **B.** According to reports provided to the federal Office of Special Education Programs (OSEP), the numbers of students receiving services for a speech or language impairment are about 50 percent of the total special education population.

32. **D.** Chained response is the break down of a sequenced task into smaller component parts or steps so a student can more easily complete the task. The student begins with the first step in the sequence and performs each step progressively, linking them toward the more complex end until the entire task is accomplished.

33. **B.** The term **intensity** means the degree to which a behavior is repeated and is important to the development of an IEP, as the goals written will seek to limit the repetition, so a baseline is sought.

34. **C.** A **tiered lesson** allows for extension of the same lesson presented for children who possess differing abilities. Content and assignments can be constructed in levels, so there is a range of basic, medium, and higher level order.

35. **C.** With all probability, speech articulation is the only condition listed that may be corrected and not affect a person during her lifetime. Unless there are medical reasons, such as a hearing impairment, that prevents the person from resolving incorrect pronunciations, articulation has a very high rate of resolution for children with proper therapy and follow through. The other conditions, although they may have some options for "correction," are lifelong conditions that will continue to impact an individual.

36. **C.** The functional curriculum offers students with exceptional conditions the opportunity to learn skills that are necessary to use on a daily basis in the community, after they transition as adults. This curriculum is most often used with students who have mental retardation, autism, and other moderate and severe to profound conditions.

37. **A.** Section 504 of the Rehabilitation Act of 1973 extends civil rights to individuals with disabilities in education, employment, and other community settings. This student may qualify for support under Section 504 according to team recommendations.

38. **C.** Assessments must follow the law with regard to diversity. Professionals must follow procedures to ensure that non-biased evaluations will be given. They must be free from cultural, racial, or linguistic discrimination. Therefore, an assessment must be delivered in the student's native language.

39. **D.** The Jacob K. Javits Gifted and Talented Student Education Act permitted federal funds to students considered economically disadvantaged, who demonstrated limited English proficiency or had a disability while also being identified as gifted or talented.

40. **D.** This provision targets at-risk students in the general education programs by supporting them through the implementation of interventions at various levels. The purpose is to provide basic support services early so the students will not be referred for special education. "Early intervening services" are also referred to by the terms **response to instruction** or **response to intervention** and is different than **early intervention services** under IDEIA.

41. **D.** FERPA is the Family Educational Rights and Privacy Act that affects schools and education programs, as it protects the privacy of all students' educational records. It applies to all schools receiving federal funds.

42. C. All of these informal assessments would deliver information about the student's performance; however, the one that will provide the most and best information of an overall view of the student's achievement, performance, task completion and behavior is the ecological assessment. This involves the use of an informal observation of the student interacting with the environment during a regular school schedule, so the teacher could watch the student throughout the day, gathering information about different time and during different tasks.

43. B. NCLB, No Child Left Behind of 2001 was the Reauthorization of the Elementary and Secondary Education Act with the primary goal for all children to be grade level proficient by 2014. It imposes a requirement for "highly qualified" teachers and key principles regarding stronger accountability, options for parents, flexibility of federal funds, and focus on scientifically researched curriculum.

44. A. An aptitude test is a formal standardized measure that evaluates a student's ability to acquire skills or gain certain knowledge. It is a tool that can provide evidence of a student's potential for achievement.

45. A. Section 504 of the Rehabilitation Act of 1973 extended civil rights to individuals with disabilities by prohibiting discrimination in education, employment, and other community settings.

46. D. The **present levels of educational performance** is a written statement constructed by the team and based on formal and informal assessments of the student during instructional activities across various educational settings. It is one of the required components of an IEP and aids the team in creating an educational program and selecting the proper instructional methods for a student.

47. D. Under the ruling of the *Board of Education v. Rowley*, every children with a disability has the right to receive an individualized education program with supportive services that are deemed appropriate and necessary according to the child's needs.

48. C. Research has shown that when students are involved in developing a set of classroom rules, it is more probable that they will abide by them and reinforce the use of them with their peers. When a new group of students have been added to an existing class of students, the entire tone of the classroom will change, and therefore, it is important to revisit the rules and guidelines with the entire class of students, even if it is the second semester.

49. B. The 1993 *Oberti v. Board of Education* case supported a family's preference to educate their child who had mental retardation in the general education classroom.

50. B. Classroom settings that include exceptional students should provide multi-modal learning strategies so all learners can participate at their own rate and level of learning that matches their learning style. This approach uses teaching methods and strategies that are visual, auditory, tactile, and kinesthetic.

51. C. Students who are aware of their rights and understand their own capabilities develop a more positive self-concept and learn how to meet their own needs. Through advocacy instruction issues and actions about individuals with exceptional needs are addressed. As a component of a transition plan, students can become better prepared to function as adults.

52. C. A functional behavior assessment is used to evaluate a student with a disability in the area of behavior. An observation is conducted on the student to determine the relationship of the undesired behavior to the environmental factors.

53. C. The federal law, IDEIA allows protections to children with exceptional needs and their parents or guardians with respect to the special education process and the implementation of these programs. These rights are explained in the section *procedural safeguards*.

54. C. When students are working toward utilizing appropriate and socially acceptable behaviors, the use of immediate feedback and consistent reinforcements is effective in supporting this performance.

55. D. When a student transitions into a community setting, consideration should be given to the services and resources available and the individual's preferences. Community-based placements include three main areas, which are residential (institutions, group homes), employment (competitive, sheltered, supported), and recreation (hobbies, leisure skills, transportation).

56. A. According to the federal special education law, a manifestation hearing must be conducted to determine the reason for the student's situation and to decide whether there was a relationship of the student's behavior to the action. The team must also review the IEP and establish a behavior plan.

57. C. Adults with disabilities face barriers that may prevent them from becoming independent or successful. Under federal special education law, transition plans for adult services must begin at age 16 and include education, employment, training, independent living, and recreation or–leisure activities.

58. C. Paraprofessionals have improved services in special education programs for years. When they are trained well and work within their boundaries, the benefits to students are endless. An important aspect of ensuring a positive work environment that is appropriate for students is for the educator to first establish clear guidelines and outline the roles and responsibilities of the paraprofessional.

59. D. The Constructionist Theory that was supported by Piaget focuses on engaging students in actively creating things and constructing mental models, which includes experiments and hands-on discovery-based learning opportunities, and often is called experiential education.

60. D. Due to the sensitive nature of the information contained in special education records, there are rules and regulations that govern their destruction. Therefore, permission is required from the special education director, a superintendent, or a state department. Notification must be provided to the student and the parent, in written form, before the destruction is to occur in case they want a copy of the records.

Answer Grid for Learning Disabilities (0382) Practice Exam

CUT HERE

1 Ⓐ Ⓑ Ⓒ Ⓓ
2 Ⓐ Ⓑ Ⓒ Ⓓ
3 Ⓐ Ⓑ Ⓒ Ⓓ
4 Ⓐ Ⓑ Ⓒ Ⓓ
5 Ⓐ Ⓑ Ⓒ Ⓓ
6 Ⓐ Ⓑ Ⓒ Ⓓ
7 Ⓐ Ⓑ Ⓒ Ⓓ
8 Ⓐ Ⓑ Ⓒ Ⓓ
9 Ⓐ Ⓑ Ⓒ Ⓓ
10 Ⓐ Ⓑ Ⓒ Ⓓ
11 Ⓐ Ⓑ Ⓒ Ⓓ
12 Ⓐ Ⓑ Ⓒ Ⓓ
13 Ⓐ Ⓑ Ⓒ Ⓓ
14 Ⓐ Ⓑ Ⓒ Ⓓ
15 Ⓐ Ⓑ Ⓒ Ⓓ
16 Ⓐ Ⓑ Ⓒ Ⓓ
17 Ⓐ Ⓑ Ⓒ Ⓓ
18 Ⓐ Ⓑ Ⓒ Ⓓ
19 Ⓐ Ⓑ Ⓒ Ⓓ
20 Ⓐ Ⓑ Ⓒ Ⓓ
21 Ⓐ Ⓑ Ⓒ Ⓓ
22 Ⓐ Ⓑ Ⓒ Ⓓ
23 Ⓐ Ⓑ Ⓒ Ⓓ
24 Ⓐ Ⓑ Ⓒ Ⓓ
25 Ⓐ Ⓑ Ⓒ Ⓓ
26 Ⓐ Ⓑ Ⓒ Ⓓ
27 Ⓐ Ⓑ Ⓒ Ⓓ
28 Ⓐ Ⓑ Ⓒ Ⓓ
29 Ⓐ Ⓑ Ⓒ Ⓓ
30 Ⓐ Ⓑ Ⓒ Ⓓ

Multiple-Choice Questions

Read each of the following multiple-choice questions and select the answer that is best suited to complete the concept. Mark the answer on the score sheet.

1. A special process known as **response to intervention** (RTI) has been implemented in school programs with a known benefit being that a child may

   A. learn to transfer and generalize skills.
   B. gain knowledge in primary academic areas.
   C. be fully assessed prior to entering kindergarten.
   D. receive assistance before experiencing significant failure.

2. In 1963, the currently used term for neurological problems of learning, a **learning disability,** was coined by whom?

   A. Samuel Kirk
   B. Laura Lehtinen
   C. Newell Kephardt
   D. Marianne Frostig

3. Many philosophers have developed approaches and programs to help students with learning disabilities. Which of the following people is identified with the approach of **direct instruction** for students who have learning problems?

   A. Jean Piaget
   B. B. F. Skinner
   C. Marie Montessori
   D. Madeleine Hunter

4. A vocational assessment has been administered to a group of high school students with learning disabilities. They are preparing to enroll in the auto mechanics course for vocational training. Two of the students demonstrated no interest in any areas on the test. The scores are concerning, so the teacher is seeking the team's assistance to determine

   A. whether the assessment was valid and reliable.
   B. whether the test was too complicated for the students.
   C. whether the students did not pay attention to directions.
   D. what areas of interests the students have and conduct another assessment.

5. The methods of scaffolded instruction, use of graphic organizers, and peer tutoring are all based on the premise of the _____ theory.

   A. cognitive
   B. ecological
   C. behavioral
   D. developmental

6. An elementary child, diagnosed with dyspraxia, needs support in the language arts class. Which of the following accommodations would be appropriate for this child?

   A. Use color-coded paper.
   B. Label materials in the room.
   C. Allow extra time to write assignments.
   D. Provide a tutor to read the long passages.

7. The speech-language therapist working with a preschool child asks the parent to provide interventions in the home to support the child's language development. She has suggested that when the parents are doing an activity they should verbally describe it while the child is completing the task. The parent is using the technique of

   A. self talk.
   B. expansion.
   C. parallel talk.
   D. enhancements.

8. The rate of students with learning disabilities is increasing. Some professionals have related the following to the over-identification of students in this category.

   A. poverty-stricken families with high illiteracy rates
   B. immunizations affecting the central nervous system
   C. lack of early childhood programs to stimulate learners.
   D. use of specific strategies not appropriate to student learning styles

9. The federal definition for a learning disability has mostly focused on the severe discrepancy between

   A. performance and skills
   B. achievement and ability
   C. thinking and processing
   D. comprehension and concepts

10. When a teacher wants to encourage reading skill development, she should use visual cues as they

    A. predict unknown words.
    B. promote word recognition.
    C. reflect word comprehension.
    D. demonstrate knowledge of word order.

11. Several techniques are known to produce effective readers, and some are of great benefit when working with students who have learning disabilities. A common method to build comprehension and language skills used with young children is to supply a passage with missing elements. This is called the

    A. Cloze procedure.
    B. Fernald method.
    C. Reading Recovery Style.
    D. Orton-Gillingham method.

12. A student who is identified with a nonverbal learning disability often demonstrates problems with motor tasks, visual-spatial skills, social relationships, math, and organizational skills; however, they often exhibit strengths in the

    A. verbal domain.
    B. auditory skills.
    C. proprioceptive area.
    D. processing functions.

13. Three specific types of learning disabilities are most prevalent in schools as these conditions emphasize the students' problems in an academic-focused situation. These are

    A. dysnomia, dysphonia, and dyspraxia.
    B. dyslexia, dyscalculia, and dysgraphia.
    C. sensory impairment, motor delays, and behavior disorder.
    D. perceptual delays, social dysfunction, and speech disorder.

14. The process of reading can be divided into two separate components:

    A. word spelling and reading retention
    B. word decoding and instructional phonics
    C. word pronunciation and syntactical structure
    D. word recognition and reading comprehension

15. Developing **fluency** is a critical skill in reading, as it bridges two components necessary to be an effective reader:

    A. phonics to vocabulary
    B. syllables to word meaning
    C. word recognition to reading comprehension
    D. phonological awareness to expressive language

16. A condition called _____, also known as **motor planning,** can cause problems with simple tasks like waving or brushing teeth.

    A. dyspraxia
    B. dysnomia
    C. dysphasia
    D. dysfluency

17. Children with learning disabilities have average to above average intelligence; however, they have problems with reading, writing, spelling, mathematics, and other specific areas. What is the basis for this problem?

    A. It stems from heredity.

    B. There is no known reason.

    C. It is a neurological disorder.

    D. It begins with language delays.

18. There are three primary components of writing, and children with learning disabilities can have difficulties in one or more of these areas:

    A. punctuation, grammar, and spelling

    B. word processing, decoding, and handwriting

    C. spelling, handwriting, and written expression

    D. decoding, written expression, and word processing

19. The stages of writing include pre-writing, _____, revising, and sharing.

    A. drafting

    B. scanning

    C. organizing

    D. describing

20. Difficulties with basic reading and language skills are the most common types of learning disabilities in the schools. It is estimated that around _____ percent of students identified with learning disabilities have reading problems.

    A. 50

    B. 60

    C. 70

    D. 80

21. In addition to the challenges faced in the cognitive domain, students with learning disabilities may also have limitations on their behavior skills and _____ skills.

    A. social

    B. motor

    C. visual

    D. auditory

22. To place a student in special education, a series of steps must be followed. Prior to a referral, the general education teacher must address the student's needs in the classroom and gather important data. Which of the following is an example of a step that occurs during the pre-referral process?

    A. testing conducted

    B. curriculum revised

    C. academic plan developed

    D. interventions implemented

23. An IEP is a valuable tool in the education of exceptional students. Which of the following best describes the primary purpose?

    A. manages student behaviors and includes a method for training staff

    B. defines a student's unique disability and provides parents' with rights

    C. prescribes goals and services for a student and a tool to assess progress

    D. promotes the provisions of the law and guarantees all students an appropriate education

24. A history teacher who has several students with learning disabilities in his class writes key concepts on a **smartboard** while lecturing to the class. This is an example of an accommodation for those who exhibit problems with

    A. receptive language.

    B. auditory processing.

    C. expressive language.

    D. conversational skills.

25. An elementary school student with an identified learning disability has started to exhibit some inappropriate outbursts and uncontrolled behaviors during class periods. The teacher has noticed that after an incident ends, the student becomes quiet, withdrawn, and stares. The teacher should convene an IEP team meeting to

    A. arrange for a temporary mental health facility placement.

    B. amend the plan to include the label of emotional disturbance.

    C. request the family seek the assistance of a medical professional.

    D. conduct a functional behavior assessment and determine the needs.

GO ON TO THE NEXT PAGE

26. The transition team arranged for a high school student with a learning disability to work at the local bakery. The student's deficits are in the areas of auditory perception, memory, oral language, and writing. The student is a very hard worker and socializes well with other employees. However, there are times, even after receiving instructions, when the student seems confused and does not complete the assigned tasks. Which of the following BEST describes what the team must consider to support this student?

   A. Contact the parents to request less work for the student.

   B. Set up a tutor each day before work to review what to do.

   C. Ask the supervisor to write a list of tasks to be completed daily.

   D. Find another employee who can translate the information for the student.

27. According to IDEIA, when a student's behavior interferes with his learning or the learning of other students, the IEP team should consider

   A. identifying a motivational focus.

   B. establishing a set of target reinforcements.

   C. creating an individualized instruction program.

   D. conducting a functional behavior assessment.

28. The American Psychiatric Association suggests that the diagnosis of a student with attention deficit disorder must be made by verifying three symptoms that meet the criteria. These symptoms include which of the following?

   A. age, onset, and severity

   B. severity, onset, and duration

   C. severity, age, and distractibility

   D. onset, distractibility, and duration

29. When creating a classroom environment, the space should reflect the

   A. academic standards in place.

   B. teaching style of the educator.

   C. school's vision about children.

   D. students' preferences for learning.

30. Children with learning disabilities may also be identified with other conditions, called **comorbidity.** Two conditions that are often comorbid with a learning disability are attention deficit disorder and

   A. mental retardation.

   B. hearing impairment.

   C. Asperger's syndrome.

   D. emotional disturbance.

Constructed-Response Questions

Read each of the three scenarios and related constructed-response questions. Some of the questions may have more than one part, so be sure to read them in entirety.

Scenario

A child with developmental delays and her family have been receiving services from the state early intervention program under an IFSP for two years. Upon her third birthday, in 10 months, she will no longer qualify for early intervention services. The child exhibits problems with both expressive and receptive language as well as motor delays. Her speech articulation is delayed, but cognitively she is alert and eager to learn. A year ago, an evaluation ruled out mental retardation and a hearing impairment, but scores reflected the need for services. Neither the parents nor early intervention agency think she is ready for a termination of services and believe she should be served through the local public school programs. The parents have contacted the local school district about the preschool/early childhood services.

Task

1. The school district receiving this child has certain responsibilities under the law, IDEIA. Explain the differences between the provisions of Part B and Part C. Then identify the process of intake for a child from a Part C program to a Part B program, including the roles and responsibilities during the transition of the EI service personnel, the parents, and the EC professionals.

Scenario

A first-grade student suspected of having a learning disability demonstrates difficulty in acquiring reading skills. He does not consistently recognize letters in print and is not able to match words that are similar. He demonstrates the use of an immature vocabulary and has problems identifying rhyming words. The school assistance team has proposed strategies to the teacher, follow-up activities for the parents, and interventions for the child to improve his phonological awareness skills and visual perception skills. The teacher will begin implementation and document the student's success.

Task

2. Both **phonological awareness** and **visual perception** are important pre-reading skill areas. Each has a specific set of competencies that are critical for children in the early literacy stage to become better prepared for developing efficient reading abilities.

   Define the terms *phonological awareness* and *visual perception* and identify the specific components. Then develop two activities for each (phonological awareness and visual perception) that may be used with this child to improve these areas.

Scenario

A high school student with a learning disability in her junior year is becoming anxious about graduation. She wants to become a nurse but has difficulty in math. Her reading and writing skills are average, but she often reverses numbers and cannot remember equations and math concepts. She is passing her math class, but getting increasingly worried about being accepted into the community college nursing program. She lives with her father and two sisters. She works very hard to manage her school life, her part-time job at the coffee shop, and helping around the house. The transition team will be meeting in about a month to outline a plan to help her reach her goal.

Task

3. Identify the areas that should be outlined in her transition plan and create a list of at least five activities that will help this student get prepared for the transition into the community college setting in a nursing program.

Learning Disabilities (0382) Practice Exam Answer Key for Multiple-Choice Questions

1. D	11. A	21. A
2. A	12. A	22. D
3. D	13. B	23. C
4. D	14. D	24. B
5. A	15. C	25. D
6. C	16. A	26. C
7. C	17. C	27. D
8. D	18. C	28. B
9. B	19. A	29. B
10. B	20. D	30. D

Answer Explanations for Learning Disabilities (0382) Practice Exam

Multiple-Choice Questions

1. D. Early screening for all students, placing students having difficulty in research-based early intervention programs, and closely monitoring the progress of identified students to determine whether increasingly intense intervention results in adequate progress are some ways of helping students according to the response to intervention strategy.

2. A. Samuel Kirk coined the term used today to describe individuals who face problems with academic achievement, learning disability. He also published a test called the Illinois Test of Psycholinguistic Abilities (ITPA) to help in the diagnosis of a learning disability.

3. D. Many professionals expound upon the benefits of using direct instruction with students who have learning disabilities. It was Madeline Hunter who provided the instructional theory regarding the role of decision-making in teaching, which is an example of direct instruction.

4. D. Although any of the answers could be a possibility, the primary reason to seek team involvement is to pursue the education of these students. The team should conduct an informal assessment to determine each student's areas of interest, enroll the student in the course, and complete another assessment later.

5. A. The cognitive theory by Piaget reinforces that students need to learn the basic concepts and develop problem-solving skills in all content areas as they move along the general education curriculum, whether they have a disability or not. Since this can be difficult for students with learning disabilities, several methods emerged from this theory and have proven to be beneficial: scaffolded instruction, learning strategies, graphic organizers, concept maps, and peer tutoring.

6. C. Dyspraxia is an inability to coordinate body movements, and a child may be impacted in a language arts class by having a problem with written assignments. This child should be given extra time to complete the work in case uncontrolled movements prevent him from finishing.

7. C. Parallel talk is recommended for young children who are having difficulty with expressive and receptive language development. Parallel talk is the act of orally and actively describing the steps in a task or the process of an activity as a child is doing it. Parallel talk allows the child to hear the words associated with the activity and encourages language development.

8. D. Students are being misdiagnosed with learning disabilities and placed in special education because the student's learning style does not match the imposed instructional strategies and methods and the student fails to achieve at an appropriate rate.

9. B. Although definitions change and debates occur over the wording and the criteria they promote, there has been a focus on the definition for the severe discrepancy between **achievement** and intellectual **ability.** If evident, it would be in one or more of these seven areas: oral expression, listening comprehension, written expression, basic reading skills, reading comprehension, mathematics calculation, and mathematics reasoning.

10. B. A visual cue is a shape or visual configuration of a word or group of words that permits a reader to recognize the word or group of words automatically.

11. A. The Cloze procedure has been used for many years with young children who are learning to read. It has benefit when used with children who have a learning disability.

12. A. Individuals with nonverbal learning disabilities often have specific strengths associated with the verbal domain, which includes acquiring early speech skills, developing a larger vocabulary, gaining early reading and spelling skills, maintaining excellent rote-memory and auditory retention, and using articulate self-expression.

13. B. The three types of learning disabilities are significantly evident in schools: **dyslexia,** a language-based (reading) disability; **dyscalculia,** a mathematical disability; and **dysgraphia,** a writing disability.

14. D. Reading is a process, and there are many skills that are included to develop as an effective reader. Two primary components of reading are word recognition (decoding) and reading comprehension.

15. C. As students begin to read and develop a form of fluency in their reading, they are beginning to move from word recognition to the meaning of the passage, reading comprehension.

16. A. Referred to as problems with motor planning, dyspraxia encompasses a variety of difficulties with motor skills. It can cause problems with single-step tasks such as waving goodbye, or multistep tasks like brushing teeth. It may also include difficulties with establishing spatial relationships.

17. C. A learning disability is a neurological disorder, with some causes known and others considered unknown. There may be hereditary influences or tendencies, and language delays may be also identified in the individual.

18. C. The three components of writing include spelling, handwriting, and written expression.

19. A. The second step in the stages of writing is called drafting.

20. D. About 50 percent of students with learning disabilities face problems with mathematics, and an estimated 80 percent have difficulties with reading.

21. A. Students with learning disabilities have limitations on academic achievement related to reading, written language, and mathematics skills. They may also have issues with social skills development, attention deficits, and behavior problems.

22. D. A general education teacher must implement interventions to address the student's immediate needs and determine whether these are effective for the student. If the student continues to have difficulties, a referral to special education may be made.

23. C. The primary purpose of an individual education plan, IEP, is to implement services for a student with a disability according to a set of prescribed goals and to monitor the student's progress through various assessment techniques.

24. B. A student who can hear what is being said, but does not always understand it, has an auditory processing problem. If a teacher writes key points or concepts, along with specific vocabulary on the board during a lecture lesson, the student may be better able to comprehend.

25. D. A student who has sudden or increased outbursts and exhibits mood changes is exhibiting behaviors that must be addressed with a possible change of IEP. It is appropriate for the teacher to convene a team meeting and to conduct a functional behavior assessment to determine the course of action or to obtain outside assistance for the child and the family.

26. C. Given this information, this student demonstrates problems with memory and oral language, which makes receiving directions a challenging task. The transition team should discuss asking the supervisor to create a written list or a picture list that would be helpful with this student.

27. D. A functional behavior assessment (FBA) is outlined in the federal law for special education. It should be utilized for students whose behavior is inappropriate and needs to be evaluated so a plan may be developed. When a student's behavior affects himself or others, the team should be alerted to the need for an FBA.

28. B. The three symptoms that must be included in a diagnosis of a student with attention deficit disorder (ADD) are severity, onset, and duration. This diagnosis and the on-going care may only be made by a medical practitioner, such as a medical doctor or a psychiatrist.

29. B. Establishing a positive classroom is a reflection of an educator's attitude about learning and demonstrates the teaching style of the educator. The physical space is a tool that affects student learning.

30. D. Emotional disturbances are often comorbid in students with learning disabilities, just as attention deficit disorder may be. These students have difficulty with learning and due to the neurological impact on the brain can develop other conditions that are also neurologically related.

Constructed-Response Questions

1. IDEIA, the special education law, has two main provisions regarding the education of children with disabilities. Part B mandates programs for school-aged children, and Part C provides for children in state programs under school age. The primary differences between these two provisions are outlined here.

Part B focuses on

- students with disabilities ages 3 through age 21
- educational programs in public schools settings
- educators, staff, and other school professionals providing services
- yearly evaluations and an annual review of a student's program
- participation in transition services from Part C
- an IEP that describes the individual student's needs
- an IEP that focuses on the disability and interventions to improve
- follows the main category labels under federal law

Part C focuses on

- students with disabilities ages birth to 3 years
- family and child services in natural environments
- a service or case manager to coordinate the necessary services
- evaluations two times per year with regular reviews
- takes the lead in the transition services to Part B
- an IFSP describes the child's and family's needs
- IFSP focuses on all areas of development, not just the disability.
- child labels are used as *developmentally delayed*

The process for intake into the public school is initiated by the Part C agency on or about 9 months prior to the child's third birthday. They work with the parents to prepare them for the events of transition and contact the Part B program to be prepared for the child and to receive the information. A meeting is schedule by the Part C agency with the parents and Part B personnel. The records are reviewed, and the condition, interventions, and progress are discussed. The Part B agency can then begin to formally work with the family to conduct necessary assessments and develop an IEP prior to the third birthday, so the child may enter the public school at that time.

The roles of the Part C personnel are to initiate the transition process, inform the parents of the process and their rights, introduce the parents to the Part B providers, conduct additional assessments as necessary prior to age 3, deliver records to the Part B program, explain interventions, therapies, and other actions that have supported the child to the receiving staff, as well as to be available as the child enters the new program.

The roles of the parents are to prepare a file of the documents and information used during the EI services, develop a list of questions about the transition, attend meetings of the Part C and Part B programs, help develop goals, share ideas and concerns, and work with the child as carry-over services.

The roles of the Part B providers include attending transition meetings called by Part C program providers, make the parents comfortable by answering questions and providing a tour of the facility, explain the differences between the programs, discuss how an IFSP and IEP are similar, provide information about special education and EC programs, conduct necessary assessments after age 3, and deliver services to the child.

2. **Phonological awareness** is the ability to identify the sounds of language, know how words sound, and how they might be represented in written language.

   Visual perception is the ability to recognize and interpret sensory data presented visually and be able to understand the differences.

   Competency areas for phonological awareness: To become proficient in reading, certain skills must be developed in this area. These skills include

   - word awareness
   - ability to rhyme
   - compare and contrast sounds
   - substitute sounds
   - blend sounds
   - segment sounds
   - identify beginning, middle, and end sounds
   - manipulate phonemes
   - segment phonemes

   Competency areas for visual perception: To become proficient in reading, certain skills must be developed in this area. These skills include:

   - visual discrimination
   - figure-ground discrimination
   - visual memory
   - visual closure
   - letter recognition
   - visual perception and reversals

   Phonological awareness activities:

   To help this child become more proficient in the area of phonological awareness, the teacher may provide an activity of finding and identifying sounds in the environment. Let the child listen to sounds outdoors, play tapes of animal noises, vehicles sounds, and people sounds (laughing, shouting). Play a sound for a child on a tape and ask the child to identify the sound. Use sounds such as a truck horn, a drum, a baby crying, a dog barking, and so on.

   Use a variety of rhymes, songs, and fingerplays during the day and point out the rhyming words. For example: Say the "Twinkle Little Star" rhyme and point out the words that sound the same without using any print words: star, far, high, sky. Listening to songs and singing help a child listen to spoken words.

   Visual perception activities:

   Work on the classification of objects (visual perception) by having the child match objects by shape, colors, and size. Use wooden beads, variety of socks, buttons, trucks, and so on and have the child separate them into cups or boxes according to instructions.

   Help improve memory by asking the child to determine the missing object from a group presented. Let the child see a tray of items familiar to him and then have him close his eyes as the teacher removes one item. When the item is removed, have the child open his eyes, and ask him to tell what object is missing.

3. This student will need several areas addressed on the transition plan: goals based on present levels of performance; information about her interests, preferences, and aptitude; vocational and career education training goals; work or employment setting; independent living arrangements; and recreation/leisure activities.

Activities that will help this student reach her goal include

- Provide access to a mathematics tutor.
- Speak with a school counselor who can help alleviate fears.
- Enlist the father's support in visiting the community college.
- Conduct a vocational assessment to identify skills related to nursing.
- Establish a work study period so she may work temporarily in a clinic or hospital.
- Help her with gaining advocacy skills so she can pursue her career.
- Arrange a contact with an adult agency that will support her in this nursing career.

Mild to Moderate Disabilities (0542) Practice Exam

Constructed-Response Questions

The constructed-response questions included on this Praxis II exam require that the examinee structure an answer that may be written as a short answer or an essay. Examinees must think carefully about the questions and the answers before proceeding to construct the written answer. Outlining the answer or jotting notes as the examinee reads the question may help in creating a concise and complete answer. There will be space in the test answer booklet for examinees to write their answers.

Read each of the five educational situations and related constructed-response questions. Some of the questions may be designed with multiple parts, so be sure to read in entirety.

Scenario

Jake, an only child of professional adults, has no previous formal school experience. At age 5 and now attending kindergarten, his primary caretaker since birth was his maternal grandmother who is a retired teacher. Having worked with Jake for several developmental years, she contacted the school to refer him for screening due to her concerns with his lack of skills in the social area and his aversion to touching certain items. Parents and grandmother deny that there are major problems at home and report that he is well-behaved. His behavior at school has been both physically and verbally aggressive toward other children, and he appears to seek the security of adults when he is upset. He seems to control situations that involve peers during conversations, play, and unstructured periods, often displaying inappropriate interactions that turn to physical altercations. The transportation department has requested assistance for his unruly behaviors. The kindergarten teacher implemented interventions in behavior management, but these were not successful. A special education referral resulted in an arena assessment with the speech therapist, the psychologist, the nurse, and the occupational therapist. There was evidence of delays in receptive vocabulary, social skills, expressive language, sensory integration, and adaptive skills. The team has identified that the child needs special education services as he clearly qualifies according to the definition on the autism spectrum disorder at the higher functioning level. Under the category of autism, the team will develop an IEP and work with the classroom teacher and parents to implement an educational program.

Task

1. The team has declared that this child would be most appropriately placed in the general education kindergarten classroom with supports and services through the special education program and staff. He has many positive aspects of development on which to draw success; however, his needs for improved language skills, social and behavior interventions, and gaining the ability to become more sensitized to the environment will be the main portion of the program. The areas of sensory integration, communication, and behavior management will be the focus of the IEP goals. The meeting with the team will occur in a week, and as the special education teacher, you will need to be prepared for this meeting and manage the involvement of other team members in developing the IEP goals. Identify and explain the five main components of a measurable IEP goal and write two proposed IEP goals for each of the three areas of focus in the proper format.

Scenario

Carlos, who is in second grade, moved into the school district in November. His dad is in the armed services and currently out of the country. Mom is living temporarily in various relative's homes (parents, cousins, sister), moving each three to four months. Carlos is a quiet child who rarely speaks to peers or teachers and has limited eye contact when being spoken to. He does not respond to questions and will try to control a situation at home by doing things his way. He loves to draw and when upset will draw a picture and may tell a story about his artwork. He will speak to others if they first engage him in his drawings. He keeps a book of his favorite sketches in his back pack. New people and new situations make him anxious and at times fearful. The school intervention team suggested that the teacher discover which items in the classroom he favors and use those as a transition to another activity and to allow him to work in small groups for reading instruction with the reading specialist. Screenings and informal inventories identified his academic skills as performing below grade level in reading and math. He has been referred to special education for an evaluation.

Task

2. During the discussion of the school intervention team, the special education teacher on the team asked how the child will respond to new test situations and new people, as she is concerned about the validity of the testing results due to his problems. She has suggested that the members of the assessment team begin implementing assessment accommodations prior to conducting formal evaluations to meet this child's needs. Identify three different accommodations that may be used by each of the following to prepare this child for formal testing.

   - general education teacher
   - special education teacher
   - speech-language therapist
   - psychologist

Scenario

Suzette, a middle school student was born in the United States of a French-speaking mother and bilingual father. She has two siblings, twin 2-year-old boys. Her father is a truck driver and is only home for about five days each month. She has been served in the schools as a speech-language delayed child since the second grade; however, there is no evidence of primary language delay. She was identified in third grade with a learning disability, as the tasks became more complex, moving from concrete to abstract concepts.

Her current IEP provides services for her learning disability with related services in speech-language. She has just entered the middle school where the classes rotate each hour for subject content. She demonstrates difficulties in the science class as the teacher uses a combination of lecture, lab, and small group instructions. She becomes confused by the changes in class structure and during the movement, shows problems with following directions, completing work, and interacting with others. Her reading and writing skills are at the fourth-grade level, and she receives some resource and reach-in services from the special education teacher.

The science teacher has planned a laboratory experiment on the water cycle. The special education teacher and the science teacher are collaborating on how to support Suzette so she may gain the most from this lab period.

Task

3. Identify the three primary elements of instruction. Using these as a format, develop a lesson plan for the class that incorporates Suzette's specific need for reading and writing instruction and include the consideration for any diversity or cultural issues, with any accommodations necessary to access language.

Scenario

Troy is a seventh-grade student in the middle school who is making adequate progress in spite of performing below his peers in all areas. He was identified in third grade with a learning disability in math, and in the fourth grade a psychiatrist diagnosed Attention Deficit Disorder (ADD). His learning disability, which places him one to two grade levels below his age, is well supported with interventions and accommodations, and Troy actually likes math class. The ADD condition, which is exhibited through elevated levels of anxiety, frustration, and aggression, is managed with medication, counseling, and behavioral interventions.

Troy has been in foster care since fourth grade, and in this three-year period, he has had five placements. His current foster parents are concerned about his lack of socialization with peers, his behaviors in the community, and his delays in academics. They are supportive and interested in his progress and are willing to work closely with the school to enhance Troy's chances for success.

It has been reported that Troy's birth parents left him at the Mental Health Clinic one evening when he was about 9 years old. He was placed in temporary custody, and an evaluation showed that he was exposed to high levels of violence and perhaps abuse when living with his birth parents. During his placement, he was easily aggravated, verbally aggressive, and violent. With the counseling and support of the mental health system, he has shown improvement. The team is confident that Troy can learn to be more appropriate with others, as he is bright and wants to improve.

When given academic tasks, Troy works hard if he is interested and capable of the activity. If it is too complicated, he becomes frustrated, and if it is too long, he loses interest and will refuse to finish. He will cuss and throw small objects. He can be noncompliant without regularity, which is confusing to him and the adults. He is unorganized with his academic work and often does not turn in homework.

Troy is interested in art and music and has joined the after-school programs more than one time, but he often is removed after a couple of weeks. He makes inappropriate gestures toward others, exhibits impulsive behaviors, and speaks negatively to others. He can be controlling of certain situations, which pushes away the peers that he may previously have enjoyed.

Troy is in need of additional support in the classroom, after school and at home, in order to improve his behaviors. The adults must work collaboratively to help him with his academic and behavior problems, as they are now adversely impacting his success.

Task

4. Troy is in need of a BIP that will strengthen his skills and help him move toward more independence in less-structured settings, such as after-school programs, home, and community. Select the target behaviors that must be addressed and identify what should be expected of Troy.

Scenario

The teacher who managed the special education resource program moved to another state after five years of working with her students. She was well liked by the school staff and her students. She had developed strong rapport with the students, parents, and families, and there was a sense of mutual respect for the expectations each had. She also had contact on a daily basis with the teachers at different grade levels and the related service providers. She will be missed by the entire school community.

The administration was determined to select another teacher who could step into the role and manage the program as well. They had a group of outstanding candidates, based on resumes, references, and interviews. The area they were unsure of was the development of rapport between the parents and the teacher. This had been a critical need for the students in the program, who will be continuing their placements for another several years. They know how important this portion of the program is for the success of the students at this school.

Task

5. The administrative interview committee has selected you as one of their final three candidates. However, first they want the candidates to complete this task. List the various ways that you, as the teacher, may work toward collaboration with these families to plan an educational program for their child, provide instruction and intervention both at home and school, and arrange for community resources.

Answer Explanations for Mild to Moderate Disabilities (0542) Practice Exam

1. The five main components of an IEP goal are

- conditions (used to present information of when, where, or how)
- performance (specific observable skill the student is expected to accomplish)
- criteria (how well must the skill be done and how often to acquire mastery)
- assessment (how the skill mastery will be measured)
- standards (the reference to the state academic standards)

The basic format of an IEP goal is:

Given a _____ (condition) the child will _____ (performance) with _____ accuracy over a 5-day period (criteria), as measured by _____ (assessment). [PS4.2, O3.1] (standard)

Written examples of proposed goals follow:

sensory integration

During the reading lesson each day, Jake will be provided with a chew device to reduce verbal outbursts from 5 to 3 per period as measured by the teacher and aide, separate observations, and charting over the next 6 months. [P 3.6, O 2]

Each day, Jake will increase his use of standard school supplies (paper, pencil, scissors, and so on) from 10 minutes each lesson to 20 minutes per lesson as measured by teacher observation by February 2009. [P 5, O 4.6]

communication

Jake will increase his use of appropriate verbal interactions by the oral application of one of three phrases (Please stop. I don't like that. I am mad.) by 50 percent in small group periods or with individual peers as measured by informal assessments, teacher observation, SLP recordings, and behavior charts by May 2009. [P 6, O 3]

Jake will improve his receptive and expressive vocabulary by being required to use three attributes to tell about an object upon request, at least 80 percent of the time, as assessed through standardized tools according to an evaluation by the speech and language therapist and observation charting by February 2009. [P 8, O 9]

behavior management

Jake will improve his turning-taking skills, and reduce his aggression related to waiting and personal space issues, by diminishing to 1 of 3 interactions within a 6-month period, as measured by behavior intervention plan recording. [P 1, O 7]

Jake will increase his time on the regular bus by decreasing his verbal insults by 50 percent as measured by bus driver observation, videotape recordings, and parent contacts by February 2009. [P 10, O 4]

2. To prepare Carlos for more formal assessments, the examiners must begin to develop rapport and make him feel more comfortable in their presence and in being asked to perform for them. The three different accommodations that might be used by the examiners include

general education teacher

Ask Carlos to be a helper during an art period in the room.

Determine preferred activities and integrate into informal assessments.

Use a peer in an art activity with Carlos during an informal assessment.

special education teacher

Participate in small group instruction in the general education class.

Act as a co-teacher during a class activity.

Invite Carlos and other classmates to do art in another room.

speech language therapist

Assess the child informally during an observation in the classroom.

Ask the general education teacher to visit the clinician's office with Carlos as a transition.

Collect favorite and preferred objects to have in the clinician's room.

psychologist

Observe the class during various times for several days.

Call a meeting with the family to collect developmental history and invite the child to play in the office setting.

Conduct a home visit with another member of the team.

3. The essential elements of instruction include:

- Anticipatory set presented.
- Objective and purpose explained.
- Input provided (step-by-step instruction).
- Modeling of task used.
- Check for understanding.
- Allow guided practice.
- Give closure.
- Allow independent practice.

The primary three elements include objective or purpose, learning procedures (anticipatory set, step by step instruction, modeling) and the evaluation procedure (check for understanding, independent practice).

For this scenario, the elements are outlined here.

Objective or purpose:

To provide students with an understanding of how the water cycle works and learn about the various ways they can help to protect water resources.

Learning procedures

Examinees should use the types of ideas given in this selection and write a specific plan with the step-by-step procedures:

1. Use vocabulary cards with related words and pictures of the stages of the water cycle (evaporation, precipitation and so on).

2. Utilize charts and posters in the room that show the water cycle and uses of water.

3. Allow students to access video and audio tapes that explain the water cycle.

4. Review the previous day concepts each day before the new concepts are introduced.

5. Incorporate heterogeneous group activities for review of previous day concepts, new concepts, and projects.

6. Provide homework that includes simple review, and meet individually with students who have problems.

7. Demonstrate the many ways that water is used in the world.

8. Show and discuss what can be done to protect the water resource.

9. Construct a bulletin board of ways students protect the resource in their homes.

10. Invite speakers to talk about the aspects of water on the planet and its consumption.

11. Require a group project related to the water cycle or uses of water.

Accommodations: Use of peer reading material, peer tutoring, peer note-taking, audio and visual tapes, graphic organizers of each lesson, notes for review, individual time with teacher to check comprehension, and extra time for assignments and tests.

Evaluation Procedure:

Ask a peer to play the vocabulary card game.

Use a homework chart to show what is being completed each day.

Grade a group project, demonstration, or presentation.

4. Troy is a seventh-grader who is bright and apparently capable of improvement, which is proven by his willingness, his desire, and the observations of adults working with him. Therefore, expectations must be set high, and he should be held accountable to improve his actions. There are several areas to be targeted, and not all of them should be addressed at the same time. Due to his age, the team should be working toward independence, generalization of skills, and outlining his future needs. Soon he will be in high school with higher expectations, more complicated tasks, and the need to prepare for transition. Since he is a capable student and has some interests, it seems he would be a positive contributor to society if given support and instruction now.

The target behaviors that must be addressed and the expectations include the following.

study skills: Troy needs to learn some basic skills for use in the classroom, such as organizing his work, completing tasks, and scheduling time for completing homework. He should be expected to keep a daily schedule of his required work, chart his task completion, and be responsible for his homework.

social skills: Troy's impulsive behaviors and sporadic compliance make it difficult for him and others in his environment. He must learn to speak more positively and appropriately to others, manage himself in different settings for different tasks, and be more appropriate in community settings. Troy is old enough to understand the concepts of using proper skills. He should be expected to maintain himself when frustrated, speak with respect toward others, learn how to act in various situations, and use self-management skills to act accordingly.

behaviors: Troy needs to gain a positive self-concept so he can see he is in control of himself and not focus on controlling others. He must learn coping skills to deal with his frustration, cussing and throwing things. He needs skills to deal with his anxiety, aggression, and non-compliance. Troy must be expected to eliminate his inappropriate behaviors and begin to socialize at an appropriate level for his age.

5. Ways to collaborate with parents and develop rapport include the following:

   - Send a letter of introduction about personal teaching career and a photo, along with expectations and possibilities before school begins.

   - Conduct home visits prior to the school year and throughout the year.

   - Send invitations to visit classroom or attend special function to all parents.

   - Prepare an "All About Me" portion of the room and begin the first week of school about the teacher, and then let each family work on a week with their child.

   - Invite parents to a special open house just prior to school starting or the week after it begins to explain the program and take time for Q & A.

   - Include parents in the development of specific student programs or general class activities.

   - Send notes to the home for individual students.

   - Send e-mails to parents regarding their child.

   - Use daily schedules and behavior charts for individual students.

   - Make phone calls to parents regarding their child.

   - Conduct parent-teacher meetings on individual students.

   - Set up a separate "in-home" intervention for each student.

   - Write class newsletters for all parents.

   - Ask parents to attend trainings or workshops at school.

   - Invite parents to join PTA or other groups that support the school.

   - Send special flyers to parents for information on community events or support groups.

   - Go on field trips to various community places and ask parents to accompany the class.

Constructed-Response Questions

Read each of the following scenarios, which establishes a fictitious educational situation. Then read the task that must be answered in the constructed-response format. Read each question carefully as some are designed with multiple parts.

Scenario

Jordan is a 12-year-old, multiply disabled middle school student who has lived with his maternal grandmother since he was 4 years old. His father left the home at his birth and has never had contact with him. His mother relinquished her parental rights citing the fact that she did not know how to care for or handle him. She only maintains contact with him 1 to 2 times each year, for about 2 to 3 hours each visit. He does not seem to know she is his mother, but rather a family friend. Jordan has three siblings who live with mother, and none exhibit any disability. He does speak about his siblings as "friends" and talks about them, keeping pictures in his wallet, yet he does not understand they are related to him.

Due to family conflicts during his early developmental period, Jordan did not attend school prior to the age of 5. At that time he was evaluated and identified with severe mental retardation, a mild unaided hearing loss, speech-language deficits, and cerebral palsy, causing a mild vision impairment on one side. He has received services in special education programs since he was 5 and most recently was placed in a self-contained program for 100 percent of his day.

Jordan functions at the level of a 6-year-old in most areas. He can count numbers to 20 and can manage money, making change up to $1.00. He works daily in the school coffee shop, and with assistance is the cashier one time per week, which he really enjoys. He loves being in the "store" and having responsibility for money exchange. He has the functional reading vocabulary of a 5-year-old and recognizes symbols that represent familiar places and things (stop sign, restroom, exit). Jordan has an expressive language vocabulary of a first-grader, but is not capable of reading or writing at that level. He must use sign language as the primary means of communication due to his limited verbal skills for his age and his cerebral palsy.

Jordan is easily frustrated when he does not get his way, when others do not give him what he desires, or when he thinks others are in his way. He likes to participate in recreational activities; however, the activities he prefers do not have an academic focus. The teacher has selected a couple of these activities that Jordan may earn for completing tasks. Jordan generally only wants to watch television, play video games, ride his scooter, be with his grandmother, and play with figurines. He also prefers having individual time with the teacher and does not like to work with other students in a group.

Jordan now displays highly inappropriate behaviors that are harmful. He is physically aggressive toward other students, as well as adults. It seems that he directs his anger at whomever is in the immediate proximity. Examples of such irregular behaviors are throwing objects at people, kicking, biting, scratching, punching, and spitting. When Jordan is extremely upset at school, he will urinate or defecate on himself, and he is capable of forcing himself to vomit on others.

Task

1. As the teacher you have called a team meeting to develop a behavior intervention plan, since Jordan's behaviors are impacting his ability to function in school and affecting other students adversely. Write a draft BIP that you plan to present at the team meeting in order to gather additional input from the various members.

Scenario

Eight severe to profound, multiply disabled high school students are provided instruction using a functional curriculum. They are in a self-contained setting with a teacher and two paraprofessionals where they work on skills such as grooming, basic concepts, survival communication skills, and social skills. The students' disabilities span a range of combinations that include mental retardation, physical-motor deficits, hearing and vision disabilities, autism, and communication delays. They have a multitude of behavior issues, but each of them seems to be making progress on their goals according to their behavior intervention plans. They are all involved in transition activities, and some are at the age at which an individualized transition plan is being used.

The teacher has noticed that recently when the group enters the lunch room, inappropriate behaviors have begun to surface. The functional skills the students exhibit in the classroom have diminished in the lunch room. The students are not demonstrating good eating habits and not completing their meals. They have become unruly, and they have difficulty controlling themselves. It takes them a very long time to calm down, but by the time the teacher is able to calm them, it is time for the cafeteria to close.

The teacher has noticed that this problem is prevalent for all the students in the class. She has observed the students becoming anxious as the lunch hour approaches. She noticed that as she walks them down the corridor to the main school cafeteria that the problematic behaviors begin. When inside the lunch area, the noise and the movement seem to over-stimulate the students. They must wait in long lines to get their food, sometimes other students bump into them with their full trays, and sometimes the tables they choose are littered, which is annoying to some of the students.

Task

2. As the teacher you have decided that the lunch period needs to be evaluated and restructured so all of the students may be successful. Develop a routine or plan to help these students cope with this difficult class period, which will also aid them in developing daily living skills, and justify why this plan will be successful.

Scenario

Casey is an 11-year-old elementary school student with severe mental retardation, a severe communication deficit, a motor impairment, a vision and hearing impairment, and diabetes. He is placed in a self-contained special education program almost the entire day. Casey participates in the general education program for music and some vocational activities.

Casey was assessed recently, and these team members conducted a 3-year re-evaluation as he previously received related services from them: the speech-language therapist, an occupational therapist, a hearing specialist, and a vision specialist. Health care and transportation areas were also evaluated. He also required a 1:1 paraprofessional to meet his health and self-care needs during the day. The following data was provided at the review of the assessment team meeting. Another meeting is scheduled to develop the IEP.

Results of comprehensive evaluation: Casey is identified as a student with severe intellectual deficits and a severe communication disorder. He has a seizure disorder that impacts his learning ability in receptive language, motor skills, and comprehension. He is capable of completing tasks, following directions, and understanding basic concepts at a 5- to 6-year-old level. He is partially sighted and has a mild binaural hearing loss. He has receptive language level at a 3- to 4-year-old level, with oral communication and expressive vocabulary around a 2-year-old level. He can use manipulatives to show number concepts to 5, but it is not consistent. His self-help and adaptive skills are at a 3- to 5-year-old level with specific problems in the areas of eating, dressing, and grooming, due to the limited vision and motor control. Casey was an engaged examinee who wanted the attention of the examiner and was upset when his time ended. He enjoyed the tasks and the materials, at times putting them in his mouth or pockets, in hopes to take them home.

Casey is a pleasant student who works hard, responding best when the ratio is less than four students with one adult. He needs to be positioned correctly for each activity presented in order to have optimal performance. Lessons should have a multi-modal approach and repetitions of meaningful instruction are best delivered in a variety of settings. The environment must be modified to meet Casey's needs.

At home Casey has the pleasure of a stay-at-home mother who is constantly willing to meet all of his needs. When the mother is not available, a grandmother or aunt will provide his care. This is an involved and understanding family who wants the best for Casey.

Task

3. As the teacher who manages Casey's team, you are to prepare a list of the areas that must be addressed for his educational program and organize the specific information necessary to develop IEP goals. This list is based on the information discussed at the team meeting, and the team members will need a copy so they may be prepared when the team meets again to construct the goals. Your task is to review the team information gained from the assessments and link that to instruction. Justify why he needs to receive instruction and support in these identified areas.

Scenario

Dijon is a student who is severely multidisabled at an elementary school of primarily caucasian students. He is a fourth-grader of an ethnic minority, and his family is of lower socio-economic status. He is being raised by his grandparents, as his father is in jail and his mother a known drug user. He is a street smart kid, who is very athletic.

Dijon's disabilities include severe mental retardation, motor impairment, and a mild hearing loss (uses hearing aids with positive gains). He was identified when he was 4 years old and has been in a self-contained program since that time. At times, Dijon gives the impression that he performs at a higher level than he actually does. The team believes that the home environment is so unstructured that he is left with neighborhood children and fends for himself, thus gaining vocabulary and gestures that are more representative of a higher functioning child.

Dijon has severe intellectual deficits, difficulties in all academic areas, and 1- to 2-word responses, demonstrating compromised syntax. He has very limited reading skills, in the range of a 2-year-old. Reading periods have consisted of picture stories and requests from the teacher for him to use 1 to 2 words to describe a picture from the story. The speech therapist has provided support to the teacher to use tactile cues and slow the rapid rate of speech, using digital photos on a flip ring for instruction of rules, names of objects, and calendar.

Dijon performs as the class clown, which his peers enjoy, and he gets in trouble on a regular basis. When Dijon does get in trouble, he spews continuous unintelligible streams of utterances. He has a BIP to help with the management of his verbal responses. The team believes that the structure of the self-contained program provides him with the routines, the stability, and organization that he lacks at home. He has demonstrated progress with the appropriate supports in the special education classroom.

Task

4. Dijon is one student placed in a self-contained classroom of 12 other students with severe to profound disabilities. When the school administration team changed last month, they implemented a new school-wide philosophy of full inclusion for all students. Knowing this information about Dijon, identify at least five ways that the team should collaborate with the grandparents to promote learning interventions in the home that will support this change of LRE and then describe at least five ways that the school team may assist in the transition for Dijon from a self-contained setting to a full-inclusion setting.

Scenario

A special education program with severe multiply disabled high school students is focused on the educational programs of students 14 to 16 years old. There are eight students, a certified special education teacher, and two paraprofessionals in the class. The students' disabilities span a range of severe to profound conditions, most with two or more disabilities. Their conditions include mental retardation, severe language deficits, medical issues, autism, traumatic brain injury, hearing impairment, vision impairment, and seizure disorder.

The teacher and parents, along with other team members have developed IEPs and created a functional curriculum that focuses on preparing these students for adult living. By age 16 each student needs an ITP to address individual goals for the future.

Task

5. Identify at least two purposes for the use of the functional curriculum. Then read the following list of instructional areas that are essential for these students and write a class goal for each area and list three instructional activities for each topic.

academic

behavior

independent living

recreation/leisure

employment

Answer Explanations for Severe to Profound Disabilities (0544) Practice Exam

1. There are many different ways a behavior plan might be created for Jordan. The following example utilizes the information from the PLEP to meet Jordan's needs.

Behavior Intervention Plan for Jordan:

Hypothesis statement

By following this plan, Jordan will learn to cope with his frustrations and gain the ability to use some language/communication in place of aggression, thus causing his violent behaviors to decrease.

Behavior(s) of concern

1. aggression toward others

2. aggression toward self

3. manipulation of situations

Behavior(s) defined

throwing objects, kicking, biting, scratching, punching, and spitting (5 to 7 times daily)

urinating, defecating, and vomiting (2 to 3 times per month)

intimidation of others by being aggressive (5 to 7 times daily)

Intervention goal(s)

Jordan will use a simple verbal or other communication intent to display his frustration instead of being aggressive toward others at least 3/5 times.

Jordan will use a picture card of a face showing his emotion indicating to the teacher that he is at his highest frustration level and needs a chance to cool down at least 2 times per month.

Intervention plan

Provide Jordan with word phrases that he may memorize and use when he is frustrated (I am upset; I need a time out.)

Create a set of face cards with various emotions (sad, mad, frustrated) that are easily accessible to Jordan so he may use them when he is considering a self-aggressive behavior.

Instructional strategies

Jordan needs support from the school and from his grandmother in order to make a change in his behavior. Jordan may begin to gain skills through direct instruction in the areas of social skills and language skills by learning the various emotions he feels, and the word phrases that he may need to follow the goals. He should also be re-taught the expectations of the classroom setting through modeling and practice scenarios.

A set of reinforcements may be designed by the team, which are appropriate for Jordan. These include the following:

Token system: When Jordan uses a coping strategy, such as the word phrases or face cards during a frustrating or difficult situation, he earns a token. At the end of the day, he may exchange his tokens for computer time or to get a new figurine. After 4 weeks, the tokens may be saved to exchange on a weekly instead of daily basis.

Teacher contact: If Jordan manages his behaviors so he shows no aggression during the day, he will earn a 15-minute period with his teacher. This time may include additional computer time with the teacher, having lunch with the teacher, or the teacher can read a story or play a game with him.

Earned responsibility: When Jordan is able to eliminate aggressive behaviors for two days in a row, he will be allowed to act as the cashier at the coffee shop for two days.

Intervention data summary:

The team will use charting as the primary mode of evaluation for Jordan. Each time he uses the targeted behavior and each time he uses the desired behavior, the staff will document the location, the time, the people, and the activity. This documentation will provide on-going data regarding his improvement and help the team to reassess the plan periodically.

2. Options that are focused on the individual student needs and designed by incorporating IEP goals that are academic and behavior oriented are to be considered by the teacher. Establishing a lunch program may be completed as a group project for the entire class, while maintaining the individual perspective. The purpose will be to help these students learn the appropriate social skills, behavior skills, and concepts related to having a meal in a public setting, but primarily it is to support their generalization of these skills as they transition into the adult community.

As the educator, it is important to evaluate every student on skill levels, utilizing direct instruction to teach the necessary basic skills, and then practicing to facilitate generalization so each student may be successful in this situation.

The following are options that may be used in the development and establishment of a lunch program. On the exam, one option would be chosen, and a detailed plan presented with justification about why the plan should work. These ideas represent six examples of possible programs:

a. Arrive early to avoid the crowds and have assigned tables. As they become more comfortable in the lunch room, they may become greeters for other classes. *(Explain the steps and justify why this would work for these students.)*

b. Establish a lunch period in the self-contained classroom where students interact with one another to prepare the setting. Make arrangements with the school cafeteria to deliver the food and have students take turns serving the food. *(Explain the steps and justify why this would work for these students.)*

c. Arrange with the school administration and cafeteria to remain open at different times so these students may have lunch as the sole group in this environment. When they are comfortable in the setting, partner with another class to interact and join together for a lunch period, building up to the main period in the cafeteria. *(Explain the steps and justify why this would work for these students.)*

d. Select another space at the school where a functional kitchen area may be set up. Students will learn to cook the food, set up the place settings, serve one another, and clean up after a meal. They may practice restaurant skills, group home setting skills, and home-based skills for eating and sharing a meal with others. Invite other peers or adults to join them as they become more comfortable. Have the students prepare a meal for a group of adults and serve them. *(Explain the steps and justify why this would work for these students.)*

e. Assign each paraprofessional to a smaller group of students and sit in a quieter area of the cafeteria. Preteach and practice the skills needed to obtain food, carry a tray, set up the table setting. and return soiled utensils and so on before beginning. Have the paraprofessional shadow the students as they complete the tasks and work on conversational skills while eating. *(Explain the steps and justify why this would work for these students.)*

f. Assign a volunteer peer to mentor each student (peers must be trained in certain areas before beginning this program). Have the peers come to the classroom to pick up the students with disabilities and walk with them to the lunch room, engaging them on the way. Peers should help them with their cafeteria skill building, modeling in some ways, and sit with them during the period. Teacher and paraprofessionals should be visible and act in a supervisory capacity during this program. *(Explain the steps and justify why this would work for these students.)*

3. There are many areas in which Casey's educational needs may be met, so the following is a simple idea of what type of constructed-response works for this scenario.

Casey has a variety of needs in multiple areas. The assessments completed will help the team link the information to the instruction he needs and develop an IEP that is appropriate for his age and his abilities. He should most likely receive related services in speech-language, occupational therapy, health, vision, and hearing, as well as instruction and training in the home. The following areas should be addressed as goals on his IEP, and the justification is included.

Academics/basic concepts: Casey should be provided with a functional academic curriculum in order to help him improve his core knowledge in the areas of reading, writing, and math. He needs goals that address his math concepts, such as numbers, counting, money, time, and directions. He should learn his colors and basic shapes. In the area of literacy, Casey will benefit from learning functional vocabulary and reading basic survival words. He should learn to write his name and address and learn how to use a menu and cook simple foods.

Language: Casey needs the reinforcement of a consistent communication system. He should participate in a functional language curriculum. He needs goals that relate to improving his vocabulary, using his expressive language, and increasing his receptive abilities. He should improve his pragmatic skills by learning simple conversational techniques, understanding when it is time to end or leave. His goals should focus on language use at home, as well, so all adults supporting his program have the same expectations for Casey regarding his use of language.

Hearing: Goals that focus on the use of residual hearing and understanding environmental sounds will benefit his use of his hearing.

Vision: Goals should be set for Casey to be able to be more aware of his surroundings and learn how to maneuver in new places. Since he is getting older, he should be allowed more independence to prepare for adult living, and therefore, should learn more about the various settings and what can be expected through his vision.

Self-help/adaptive: Casey needs the structure of a functional curriculum with goals that specifically meet his needs for personal care. These goals should be followed by the speech therapist, the occupational therapist, the teacher, the paraprofessionals, and the parents in order for Casey to begin generalizing skills essential for his future living. The team should prepare goals for eating, toileting, dressing, grooming, and using his environment and the tools necessary to complete these tasks.

Health: Since Casey needs the support of care throughout his day to meet his health needs, the team should identify a goal that aids him in beginning to handle a task that meets his own needs. The entire team can work on this skill area, both at school and in the home.

Generalization of skills: In the home, Casey is well cared for, but does not need to use the skills that he learns at school. He has people who will help him dress, toilet, eat, and groom, so he has yet been able to understand the carry over from the classroom. Parents and family members should receive instruction and training in how to help Casey use and improve the skills, following the IEP like the school does. A system of communication, with a record or chart of progress will be helpful to both the family and the school. Goals should be included for the tasks to be completed in the home.

4. The collaboration of the school and home will be essential for Dijon's success. Both will need to support and prepare Dijon for this major change and be sure that they manage his frustrations, his behaviors, and his academic progress. The following lists are some of the many ways that will help Dijon achieve mastery of his goals and be more successful in the inclusive setting.

The team may choose to do the following in order to collaborate with the family:

a. Implement a daily communication log that will provide grandparents with information about his performance each day at school and will let the grandparents share how he manages during evenings and weekends. This will help the team identify whether the plan for transition is working.

b. Select a behavior chart tool to use on a daily or weekly basis on which team members may document Dijon's behaviors. This will provide progress information on the BIP and help the team in adjusting his program.

c. Support the grandparents with academic tools to use at home that are a reflection of the work being done in the school. For example: design a flip ring of pictures that include vocabulary and familiar objects, names, and places.

d. Suggest that they attend parent group meetings or trainings that are pertinent to meeting Dijon's needs.

e. Conduct home visits to help the grandparents understand Dijon's needs, make suggestions for home interventions and model their implementation.

To assist with the transition from a self-contained to a full-inclusion program, the teacher might do any of the following:

a. Set-up activities on disability awareness for the students at the school so they will be able to understand the various abilities of the students in their classes.

b. Invite community members with disabilities to speak with students and visit classes so they may demonstrate the abilities of those with impairments.

c. Speak with the particular class of students about the specific student who will be joining the class. The teacher should get permission from the parents and may even want the parents to be a part of the presentation.

d. Create a reading corner in the classroom with information about famous people with disabilities and about handicaps in general.

e. Begin a social skills series for the entire school where they learn how to interact with people with disabilities with scenarios to practice in the training.

5. Purposes of functional curriculum:

   a. To emphasize skills necessary for adult living so students have the opportunity to develop competencies important for both independent living and employment settings.

   b. To place less stress on typical academics and more on the survival academics necessary to enhance future living.

   c. To develop age-appropriate activities and routines at an appropriate ability level that most enhance the concept of normalization.

Goals and activities

academic: To improve basic concepts that enhance functional skills in reading, math, and writing.

   Work on money concepts.

   Practice time and direction concepts.

   Learn survival vocabulary.

   Write personal information (name, address, phone).

behavior: To increase use of generalized skills that instill appropriate interactions with peers and in adult situations.

   Attend community events.

   Visit restaurants and stores.

   Act out scenarios in the classroom.

   Provide communication skill-building activities.

independent living: To facilitate skill building in all areas of personal adult living.

   Do laundry.

   Learn to prepare simple meals.

   Clean living spaces.

   Create shopping lists and shop.

recreation/leisure: To instill a desire to learn and participate in the various recreation and leisure activities available in the community for adults.

   Learn life sports such as bowling and bicycling.

   Go to movies, concerts, and plays.

   Visit museums, zoos, exhibits.

   Set up an exercise program.

employment: To explore the types of work available to the students and to identify the skills needed to pursue an interest area.

   Develop basic job skills.

   Determine preferences and interests.

   Practice work-related tasks in the classroom.

   Work in part-time positions.

self-help/adaptive: To promote the use of self-care skills on a regular basis and establish proper daily routines.

   grooming

   dressing

   toileting

   eating

Resources

Note: As this book is being written, these Internet sites are current, active, and accurate; however, due to the constant changes in the Internet information, addresses or sites may be altered or become obsolete.

Abuse and Neglect

www.thechildabusehotline.com; National Child Abuse Hotline

www.childabuseprevention.org; Child Abuse Prevention Association (CAPA)

http://child-abuse.com; Child Abuse Prevention Network

www.preventchildabuse.org; Prevent Child Abuse America

Assistive Technology

www.atnet.org; Assistive Technology Network

www.resna.org; Rehabilitative Engineering and Assistive Technology Network of America

Child Development

www.modimes.org; March of Dimes Birth Defects Foundation

www.zerotothree.org; Zero To Three

www.nichd.nih.gov; National Institute of Children's Health and Human Development

www.aap.org/healthtopics/stages.cfm; American Association of Pediatrics

Disabilities

www.ericdigests.org; Educational Resources Information Center

www.nichcy.com; National Information Center for Children and Youth with Disabilities

www.cec.sped.org; Council for Exceptional Children

www.fcsn.org; Federation for Children with Special Needs

www.ncsd.org; National Council for Support of Disability Issues

www.easterseals.com; Easter Seals

Autism

www.NationalAutismAssociation.org; National Autism Association

www.autism.com; Autism Research Institute

Behavior Disorders and Emotional Disturbance

www.ccbd.net; Council for Children with Behavior Disorders

www.nami.org; National Alliance for the Mentally Ill

www.nasoline.org; National Association of School Psychologist

www.nmha.org/children; National Mental Health Association

Learning Disabilities

www.ldonline.org; Learning Disabilities Online

www.ldaamerica.org; Learning Disabilities Association America

www.dldcec.org; Division for Learning Disabilities—Council for Exceptional Children

www.ncld.org; National Center for Learning Disabilities

www.ldinfo.com; Learning Disability Information

www.ldresources.com; Learning Disability Resources

Mental Retardation

www.arc.org; Association of Retarded Citizens

www.councilonmr.org; Council on Mental Retardation

www.aamr.org; American Association on Mental Retardation

www.nads.org; National Association for Down Syndrome

Early Childhood Education

www.naeyc.org; National Association for the Education of Young Children

www.nieer.org; National Institute for Early Education Research

www.udel.edu/bateman/acei; Association for Childhood Education International

www.waece.org; World Association of Early Childhood Education

www.dec-sped.org; The Division for Early Childhood

Education

www.ed.gov/; US Department of Education

www.ed.gov/offices/OSERS/OSEP; Office of Special Education-Washington, D.C.

Family/Parents

www.parentpals.com; Parent Pals, Inc.

www.parentsasteachers.org; National Center of Parents as Teachers

www.parentingresources.ncjs.org; Parenting Resources for the 21st Century

www.familysupportamerica.org; Family Support of America

www.childrensdisabilities.info; Children's Disabilities Information

Gifted/Talented

www.gifted.uconn.edu; National Research Council on Gifted and Talented

www.nagc.org National; Association for Gifted Children

www.ed.gov/programs/javits/; Jacob K. Javits Gifted and Talented Student Education Programs

Research

www.ericdigest.org; Special Education Research

http://ies.ed.gov/ncser/; NCSER: National Center for Special Education Research

www.ed.gov/about/offices/list/osers/nidrr/index.html; OSERS: National Institute on Disabilities and Rehabilitation Research

www.aera.net/; American Educational Research Association-AERA

www.cec.sped.org/dv/; Division of the Council for Exceptional Children

Developing and Using Special Education Components

Individual Education Plan

An **Individual Education Plan** (IEP) is a written agreement, guided by the provisions of federal law, that outlines the services and the placement of services to ensure the appropriate educational program for a student with a disability. This plan is developed by a team, who is knowledgeable about the student, and is based on the information gathered through assessments regarding the student's disability and needs. The IEP is not only mandated to guarantee a student a **free and appropriate public education** (FAPE) in the **least restrictive environment** (LRE), but it is designed to monitor the actual delivery of services and those who are implementing the program.

The team members follow standards in creating this management tool and use team decision-making methods to finalize the program for the student. The IEP is a component of the special education process that basically begins with an initial referral by an individual and is finalized with an agreement of the team for the student's placement and delivery of services. Parents are to be included as active members of the team, and any disagreements may result in mediation or due process. **Parent's rights** or **procedural safeguards** are identified in the law and summarized later in this appendix.

Components of an **IEP** include the following:

- The statement of the student's present levels of educational performance (to include all areas of development, with specification of the student's strengths and areas of need).
- Detailed composition of specific annual goals, which may include short-term instructional objectives or benchmarks and must reflect the state standards for general education (to include accommodations and modifications as discussed later under "Instructional Accommodations").
- A statement of the special and regular education services, related services, and supplementary services necessary to ensure a benefit to the child and identification of the extent to which the student will participate in general education programs and services.
- Information on the specific services to be implemented: initiation dates, anticipated duration, and location.
- A description of the extent to which the student will participate in state and district testing.
- The statement of placement in the least restrictive environment, made at the completion of program development.
- A description of the methods and time frames for which the student and the program will be evaluated on, at least, an annual basis and how progress will be reported to the parents.

According to IDEIA, teams may develop three-year IEPs for students with disabilities. This is not a widely used practice, but when used should be carefully considered for the individual student and situation when used.

Since IEP forms are not required to be in consistent formats across the country, be sure to review the local state and district requirements where you will be teaching. Although the IEP process is mandated under the law, states and districts may interpret this section differently and, therefore, establish guidelines and procedures that are suitable to their institutions.

A sample document may include the following headings:

> Student Demographics
>
> Present Levels of Educational Performance
>
> Annual Goals (possibly with short-term objectives and benchmarks)
>
> Related Services (description, initiation dates, anticipated duration, and location)
>
> Participation (in general education curriculum and programs)

Extent of Participation in State and District Testing

Accommodations and Modifications

Team Members Present

Placement Statement (least restrictive environment)

Evaluation Criteria

Since an IEP contains valuable and detailed information about an individual student with a disability, this document can be quite lengthy (upward of 10 to 20 pages), and the process to discuss and make decisions can take hours. Patience, clear communication, active listening, and proficient reporting all contribute to positive experiences for team members and an effective program for the student.

Present Levels of Educational Performance

The **present levels of educational performance** (PLEP) statement is a narrative description of the student's current functioning in a variety of areas. It delivers general information about the student, as well as the student's past performance and the skills mastered. It also provides information about the student's current needs and areas to be addressed through special education services. The PLEP is a method of describing the student in entirety.

When considering the content of a PLEP, the team must include the functioning levels and individual needs based on the following:

- Results of the most recent evaluation(s)
- Student's demonstrated strengths
- Information gathered from or concerns shared by the parents
- Review of past and present classroom performance
- Communication abilities and needs
- Behavior and social skills

The statement must also describe the effect of the disability on the student's involvement and progress in the general education curriculum. When a student turns 15, information about skills and needs related to the transition from school to post-school services must be included.

A PLEP may describe and identify each of the following areas:

- **Academic:** Measures current reading, written language, math, and subject areas
- **Social-emotional:** Determines social proficiency, attitude, and feelings about school, work, self, peers
- **Adaptive Behavior:** Determines status of self-help skills
- **Functional:** Measures ability to become independent in several different areas
- **Pre-vocational–Vocational:** Indicates interests, preferences, aptitude, and abilities
- **Communication:** Determines the ability to understand and use language, speech, and other non-verbal communication systems
- **Behavior:** Indicates ability to identify and manage self in a variety of situations and places
- **Motor:** Assesses coordination and use of small and large muscles; includes visual and perceptual skills
- **Health/Medical:** Explains current status and historical situations or patterns

Since students vary so greatly, it is not possible to estimate the content or the length of a PLEP for each student. They may be so concise to fill a paragraph or two for a student with mild disabilities, yet cover 2 to 5 pages for a student with multiple or severe to profound conditions.

Samples of PLEP

The four examples here demonstrate the concept of writing a present level of educational performance statement for students with disabilities. Two scenarios focus on students with mild to moderate disabilities, and two emphasize information for students with severe to profound disabilities. At the end of each sample are questions to answer that should aid the examinee in further preparing to take a Praxis II exam for exceptional students. The answers are provided, but attempt to answer these questions in written form prior to reading the given answer. This should help with written practice and pacing for the essay portion of an exam.

Mild to Moderate Example

A second grade student who began services for speech-language delays (moderate receptive and expressive language deficits) at age 3, Tommy continues to need these speech therapy services in both areas. Although he has made progress in the receptive language area, he continues to demonstrate issues with expressive language, specifically in pragmatics (conversations) and his use of syntax. He has problems with word retrieval in situations that require verbal abilities and does not demonstrate the ability to respond with answers when a speaker requests that of him. These problems with language impact Tommy in daily activities and most particularly, as he is beginning to demonstrate significant delays in acquiring reading skills. He has limited phonemic awareness, and his ability to decode is poor when compared to others his age. He lacks a vocabulary commensurate with his maturity level and cannot answer comprehension questions when given a passage to read. On the recent standardized tests conducted by the SLP, in both expressive and receptive language (EOW-PVT and ROW-PVT), he scored at the first-grade level or about one grade level below his age.

Tommy does well in math and is only slightly below his peers, perhaps due to the reading complications, and he is at grade level for science and social studies, although reading can be a critical problem in these subjects. He is provided interventions in the classroom that consist of cooperative learning groups and peer readers for projects. At times, he requires extra time to complete class work. His parents read some of the assignments with him, and his sisters help with homework. He seems to be a bright child, but the language issues complicate his achievement levels.

Tommy rarely answers questions or does any oral participation in class, is reluctant to work with other children during the less structured periods of center time in his classroom, and he is also considered a "loner" on the play ground. Although he does not demonstrate aggressive behaviors, he does not interact well with peers. He tends to stay away from situations that will require his language participation. He does, however, creatively compose his own play.

Tommy comes from a supportive home with two parents, and he has twin sisters who are in the fourth grade and a younger brother who is in preschool. The younger brother has some speech articulation errors, but otherwise none of the other children have demonstrated developmental delays in any areas. Tommy enjoys playing at home with his siblings and seems to interact well, although parents report that he does little talking, especially with two big sisters. The parents have enrolled all of their children very early in music lessons, and they participate in neighborhood sports. Tommy plays the trumpet, which seems to have helped with his early oral motor development, and he is on the soccer team. It seems that neither of these activities requires much conversation or additional expectations for receptive or expressive language skills. Tommy has expressed a desire to join an art club.

The team is concerned about his ability to read and that the skills are not being mastered at the level for which he seems capable. He enjoys school, but is quiet and withdrawn.

> **1.** In what areas do you believe Tommy will need measurable goals and support from the IEP Team? Why did you select those areas?

1. Areas that need measurable goals and support are language, reading, and social skills.

Tommy appears to need assistance with the expressive and receptive language development according to the tests conducted and the recommendation for continued speech therapy. Most likely the SLP has maintained an IEP since his earlier placement and revises goals as he improves skills. Goals should also be developed for generalization into his classroom and on the playground so he may engage with his peers. He also needs assistance in the area of reading for which goals should be developed; however, if he has continued problems with language and reading, he may need further evaluation for a possible learning disability, especially since his ability and his achievement appear to have gaps. It would help Tommy if the team would write goals in the area of social skills development, so he may enjoy the company of peers and improve his interactions with others, particularly in verbal and language related situations.

Mild to Moderate Example

In the fifth grade, Maria is placed in a general education classroom with some accommodations. She needs to improve her ability to read in context, particularly with the fifth-grade reading materials. Her reading scores place her in the lower to mid fourth-grade level. Maria can comprehend short passages and retell a short story in her own words; yet, her vocabulary is sometimes lacking on oral presentation. Sometimes she has difficulty remembering all the details and the sequence of events in longer passages or when others are reading. Maria has a low frustration tolerance when it comes to developing her reading skills. In written expression, Maria is one year below her grade level and lacks manual dexterity. She needs to develop the fine motor skills necessary for writing and improve her penmanship. Maria is at grade level in math and is an average student in science and history.

Maria is extremely verbal and, at times, requires interventions from the teacher when she begins to share personal experiences or to tell stories during academic periods that are unrelated to the topic. She has a poor attention span, so when the material or task becomes more complicated than she can handle, she tends to focus on something she enjoys more, which is talking to others. She can be impulsive when asked to maintain herself and return to task, which can result in discipline referrals. The team recommends that she work with the school counselor on her self-concept.

In spite of Maria's low skills in reading and writing, she performs adequately in these academic areas with support and accommodations. The areas for which she needs the most support are her impulsiveness and fear of failure. These have impacted her ability to progress well in the general education curriculum, to maintain relationships, and to utilize appropriate behaviors in school settings.

---

2. For what areas will Maria need the support of a behavior intervention plan, and who should be involved in addressing these behaviors?

---

2. Areas for behavior support include verbal interruptions, poor attention span, low frustration tolerance, self-concept, impulsiveness, and fear of failure.

Persons to be involved in the behavior intervention plan include Maria, the special education teacher, general education teacher(s), behavior specialist, counselor, psychologist, social worker, and parents.

Severe to Profound Example

Joy is a cheerful and pleasant high school student who, at age 18 years, is placed primarily in a self-contained class with integrated activities outside this program. She has multiple disabilities and requires the primary use of a wheelchair to move about her environment. She occasionally bears weight on her legs but only when transferring to another seat location, using the restroom, or getting into a vehicle. Being confined to the wheelchair causes her difficulty with dressing and toileting. Joy had an unfortunate accident early in life that complicated her existing disabilities, which involved a burn to her upper extremities. Although she manages well and has developed upper body strength, she tires easily and requires periodic hydration since her sweat glands do not function correctly. She needs reminders to drink from her water bottle and to use the restroom at intervals. Managing in the restroom can be difficult for her, and she often requires assistance.

Due to the stroke she suffered *in utero* a month before her birth, Joy is partially sighted in one eye and has a moderate hearing loss in both ears. She does well in compensating for her vision loss and has not required additional services or equipment. Her hearing can be a problem when she is participating in already noisy settings, but she knows that she needs to ask for help if she cannot hear. Sometimes she confuses the information she hears, which is evident to teachers as she gives an incorrect answer (for example, Q: How are you?; A: I am 18.). Joy's speech is clear to most listeners who know her, but new people have difficulty understanding her. Sometimes she speaks in a monotone and mumbles, but the team believes it is her way of cuing herself about upcoming transitions. She works with a speech-language therapist on the functional reading skills and learning the pronunciation of familiar words and survival words. Joy generally can make her needs and wants known, not only at school, but at home, at work, and in the community. She uses gestures and excellent facial expressions to get her point across.

Joy can read some words, and it is estimated that she has a vocabulary at the mid-kindergarten grade level, which allows her to carry on limited conversations and to follow simple directions. She uses 3- to 5-word sentences and knows important information about herself and her family (full name, address, parent's names, town, and phone number). She can write this information when requested and can also write simple common words, like dog, cat, boy, girl, stop, go and so on; however, she needs a special pencil and grip to manage writing tasks. In math, Joy has difficulty with time concepts but is able to count money and purchase items that cost no more than $5. Her parents own the local bakery, and she has helped there since she was a young child. The team believes that being there helped her to understand money exchanges and to listen to the scenarios of making change. Her father bought her a toy cash register when she was 5 that she plays with even today.

Because she now works at the bakery as an employee, she has more responsibilities, with parent supervision. She can maneuver herself easily at the bakery since she grew up in this setting, and her parents want her to remain at the bakery. But the team has concerns about her ability to work and maneuver in a different work situation as she has never had the opportunity. She needs to develop other vocational skills that are based on her interests and preferences in case the bakery is not always in her life.

Socially, she seems immature even though Joy has had opportunities to interact with others through her large family (three brothers and two sisters), her presence at the bakery (most people in her community know her), and at school (she speaks to everyone she meets). Yet the team is concerned that she does not have specific relationships with peers her age. As her siblings move away from the home and her parents age, Joy will need the additional skills to maintain personal and social relationships in adult settings with people with whom she is less familiar.

Joy is well supported in the home and seems to enjoy coming to school each day. She works hard and eagerly tries to learn new concepts and words, although she is challenged in the cognitive area. The team recommends more activities that provide Joy with success and a sense of pride.

---

3. In which main areas does Joy need the support of written goals, and what related services are necessary to maintain and enhance her program?

---

3. Areas to develop written goals include language, speech, written expression, reading, motor skill, social skills, self-help/adaptive, transition-vocational, hearing, functional academics, and recreation/leisure.

Related services include the following:

Speech language therapy (articulation and language)

Occupational therapy (restroom, dressing, monitoring her self-care)

Physical therapy (develop upper body tone and maintain some use of lower extremities)

Hearing specialist (auditory perception and training and use of residual hearing)

Job coach (promote job skills and training)

Transportation (if necessary due to the wheelchair)

Assistive technology: maybe for writing tools, toileting aids, communication

Severe to Profound Example

Trung is a 9-year-old student with multiple disabilities, the most significant being in the cognitive domain. He lives with his mother and two older siblings and occasionally lives with the maternal grandparents on weekends. He had open heart surgery when he was 2 years old, a hernia surgery at age 5, and corrective vision surgery at age 7. His overall health has been sporadically poor with persistent asthma and chronic otitis media. Although tubes were attempted three times, they did not remain in as long as was expected and, therefore, did not offer comfort or correction. His hearing has been compromised, and recently he was diagnosed with a mild loss in one ear and moderate in the other.

Trung is a challenging student. He is difficult to understand verbally, has limited vocabulary, and often does not use more than 1- or 2-word utterances. He has difficulty manipulating objects and maneuvering in the classroom due to gross and fine motor delays. He can respond periodically to one-step directions, but given more than one step fails to comply at all. Trung has problems with receptive and expressive language particularly expressing himself with regards to his needs and wants. He does not take turns and can be physically aggressive—hitting and screaming at others. He is non-compliant with adults if he loses interest or does not completely understand the task.

Trung seems to be confused in different settings, and the team needs to guide and support him through transitions to other activities. He needs a group of peers that he can play with to alleviate his fear and sadness at coming to school.

---

4. Identify some activities in the area of language that should be addressed to aid this student in developing some independent communication and being more appropriate with peers.

---

4. Language is an essential domain and can affect a student's behavior. It is particularly difficult for children with multiple disabilities to self-manage behaviors when they do not have the words or language to function on a daily basis. Trung appears to be one of those children who needs the support of a language system designed to address his disability areas (cognitive delays, hearing problems, speech deficits) that will also help to manage some of the behaviors. By cutting down on the frustration of not being able to express needs and wants by using words, the child should become easier to manage. Then instruction in the other areas may be more effective.

Following are some language-related activities that will help Trung:

- Use a picture exchange communication system.
- Construct board maker pictures and images.
- Teach functional phrases ("No, thank you," "I want that," "Please").
- Instruct using simple sign language (stop, yes, no, come, go, now).
- Practice listening to stories or music to acknowledge residual hearing.
- Work in small groups or with one peer to learn turn-taking skills.
- Set up scenarios to act out with peers, such as how to share a snack or build a tower.

Writing IEP Goals

Annual goals for students with disabilities are based on the compilation of information from a comprehensive evaluation, gathered assessment materials, parent interview and preferences, classroom teacher reports, and student past and current performance or achievement in other settings. After a statement of present levels of educational performance is constructed by the team, based on all the information gathered, the team makes decisions as to the specific areas that need to be improved and prepares to write measurable goals to meet those needs. Goals may be developed with an academic or functional basis or a combination of both, including behavior goals as necessary. They must enable the student to be involved and progress in the general education curriculum and to meet the needs of the student as it pertains to the disability.

Goal Components

The five main components of an IEP goal are listed here and defined with examples:

condition: This portion of the annual goal is used to present specific information about when, where, or how the area of disability or the needed skill will be addressed.

Examples:

- During the reading lesson
- When working in small groups
- At daily language circle time
- While on the bus
- At the end of 12 weeks
- By June 2010

performance: This part of the annual goal is a specific, observable skill the student is expected to improve or accomplish and must be clearly identified according to the curriculum, standards, or teacher-made materials.

Examples:

- Communicate choices without prompts, using gestures, signs, or words.
- Increase reading skills from 1.5 to 2.0 grade.
- Demonstrate improved written language skills including spelling, use of sentences, and correct punctuation and capitalization.
- Use two strategies to aid in appropriate social interactions and conversations with peers.
- Improve study skill acquisition by focusing on organization skills that include a daily schedule, a homework journal, and subject notebook

criteria: This section of the annual goal must identify how well the skill must be completed or how often in order to acquire mastery.

Examples:

- 4 out of 5 trials
- With 80% accuracy
- At least 3 periods each week
- On a weekly basis
- 8 out of 10 times

assessment: This portion of the annual goal will show how the mastery of the skill will be measured and is documented in different ways in separate states.

Examples:

- Through teacher/parent observation
- According to the criterion referenced test
- By the language pathologist on a standardized measure
- By behavior charting and staff reporting
- With the Woodcock-Johnson Test
- On the Basic Brigance Inventory of Skills

standard: This is the properly coded reference of the specific state academic standard in the area for which the goal is written. These are generally identified by the number that represents the standard or objective, but must be done according to the manner in which each state requires it.

Examples:

- Reading (Performance Objective 4.2)
- Language 3.2.9
- MO 6.1, and 6.4
- Sci 2.1, 2.2 and 2.3

Goal Format

The basic format of an IEP goal follows with the components indicated in parentheses:

Given a _____ **(condition),** the child will _____ **(performance)** according to _____ **(criteria),** as measured by _____ **(assessment).** [_____] **(standard)**

Goal Examples

Following are a few written examples of proposed goals.

- At the end of 18 weeks, Sam will perform mathematic problems of two-digit addition (M.O. 1.9) and subtraction (M.O. 2.8) on weekly classroom tests with 80 percent accuracy.
- By May 2010, Chaz will verbally express himself by using three-to-four word sentences to indicate his wants and needs in 8 out of 10 trials as demonstrated by a standardized language assessment and staff observation. (CO 4.2, 4.3)
- By the end of the second semester, during daily concept development periods, Shania will count to five and appropriately respond to a request to show three of five objects with 80 percent accuracy as measured by daily charting and teacher observation.
- Within the first grading period, Lola will write an essay that is based on the seventh-grade literary materials (R.O. 6.4.8) with 80 percent accuracy as measured by the writing rubric.
- By June 2009, Yvette will be able to identify the main characters, define the plot, and describe the conflict of a 4th-grade reading selection (R. 5.1.3, 5.1.4) as assessed by classroom curriculum-based measures and teacher report at a rate of 80 percent accuracy.
- Carly will improve her expressive language by using two to three sentences to describe a daily situation upon request (L 2.9, 2.10), at least 4 out of 5 times as assessed through standardized tools according to an evaluation by the language therapist, staff observation charting, and teacher/parent reporting by May 2009.

- By the end of the fourth grading period, Alec will interact appropriately with same age peers 4 out of 5 times during recess periods as assessed by staff reporting, behavior charting, and self-reporting.

- Provided with adaptive equipment, Chan will acquire three physical skills that promote flexibility and upper body tone and strength by June 2010 and demonstrate the generalization of these three skills at least 50 percent of the time. (PO 6, 5, 4)

- When in a difficult situation where anger begins to build, Tanya will use anger management techniques, and a specific self-management strategy according to the BIP and recognize the need to remove herself from the environment, eliminating referrals to the office and disciplinary notices at least 3 out of 5 times per week by second semester as assessed by behavior charting, office records, and staff observation. (See BIP goals 2 and 3.)

- Boyton will comprehend reading passages that are written at the 7th-grade level with 75 percent accuracy by using decoding and specific reading skills by May 2000 as assessed by the Reading Comprehension Skills Test and teacher observation. (R 2.4, 2.6)

Instructional Accommodations

An **accommodation** is an adjustment to the instruction or environment that is followed in the general education program so the student may gain benefit from the educational services. Appropriate accommodations created by an IEP team can be of significant support to students with disabilities in general education classrooms. Many types of accommodations exist and should be selected, designed, and implemented based on individual student needs.

Accommodations may range from simple to complex and include instructional supports such as note-taking and technology. Teams must be innovative and specifically assess the student's needs so the chosen accommodations deliver the most benefit. Accommodations are generally used to improve organizational and time-management skills, increase attention and memory, develop listening skills, and adapt the subject area curriculum.

Following are examples of the various accommodations:

- Supplementary Aids or Services
  - peer tutoring
  - notetaking support
  - assistive technology device
  - test reader
- Behavior Supports and Services
  - cues or prompts
  - rule reminders
  - frequent breaks
  - defined limits
  - preferential seating
  - communication system or guide
- Use of Materials for Instruction
  - highlighted materials
  - modified assignments
  - study aids
  - manipulatives
  - peer-assisted readings
  - tape recordings
  - visual aids
  - extra time for written assignments or projects
  - assignment notebook or daily schedule

Following are examples of **modifications** that change the instruction or environment:

- Use of Materials for Instruction
  - open book exam
  - preview of test questions
  - translated tests
  - repeated, rephrased instructions
  - shortened instructions
  - modified assignments or tests
  - altered assignments
  - only one task at a time
  - special projects instead of written work

Functional Behavior Assessment

With the passage of the amendments of IDEA in 1997, two additions were made that pertained to classroom management: positive behavioral support and functional behavior assessment. The concept of **positive behavioral support** suggests applying behavior interventions to promote socially appropriate behaviors. The **functional behavior assessment** refers to the process of identifying the undesired behaviors and the events that are related to them.

A Functional Behavior Assessment (FBA) is the process and documentation of observations and input of team members regarding a specific student and her exhibited behaviors. The problematic behavior(s) are identified and defined, and the team determines the action(s) to be taken to develop an appropriate behavioral support system. Most schools have created a step-by-step process and form that team members must follow and use to confer about the student. Generally, an FBA results in the development of a specific and individualized behavior intervention plan (BIP).

The law requires that an FBA be used when a student has violated a code of conduct that adversely affects his performance and results in suspension or expulsion. Many schools also use it for students with complicated or difficult to manage behaviors in order to get them under control so the student may function academically. The purposes of an FBA are as follows:

1. Define the undesired behavior.
2. Describe the environments in which these behaviors occur.
3. Clarify the function of the student's behavior.
4. Gather information about the student's behavior.

The process of an FBA begins with a referral from a team member who either has observed an inappropriate and repeated behavior that interferes with the education of the specific student or those around her or is a result of an infraction of the conduct code at the school. The next step is an observation of the student at various times of the day, in various settings. Team members also gather data from the general education teachers, the special education teachers, the parents, and others who are familiar with the student. Information is also important across various settings and times of the day. A written description of the observation will be useful to team members at the team meeting.

The following demonstrates what may be included in an FBA.

Behavior Description: Justify the reason for the FBA, which is a description of the behavior(s) that has prompted this step. Be specific so the teacher or team member observation may include data on the occurrences of the identified targeted behavior(s).

Problem Behavior: If multiple behaviors are included in the previous description, the team should select one or two behaviors that may be specifically observed and targeted for intervention on the upcoming plan.

Behavior(s):

- **Antecedents:** Defines what actions, situations, tasks, or words may precede the problem behavior(s) and may be concluded by answering these questions.

  When does the behavior occur? (times of day, specific activities/routines)

  Where does the behavior occur? (locations)

  Who may be present when the behavior occurs?

  What other events or conditions immediately precede the exhibition of the problem behavior?

  Is there a time when the behavior does not occur?

- **Consequences:** Indicates what the student might obtain or gain through the action of the undesired behavior and may be determined by answering these questions.

  What does the student gain by demonstrating this behavior?

  What does the student avoid or escape by performing this behavior?

  What has been tried to date to prevent or diminish the behavior?

Function of the Behavior Statement: Explains why the team believes the student is using this behavior. They must clearly state what they think is the function or the need that may be met while the student is exhibiting the behavior. This is a summary statement of the antecedents and the consequences gathered through observation.

For example:

1. When Jane is asked to complete a written assignment, she throws her paper and pencils and sits on the floor with her head in her hands. It seems that she becomes frustrated and wants to avoid the written work, because it is difficult for her to handle, both academically and physically.
2. If Choy is in the hallway, before or after school, and when he is in transition periods, he pushes other students and threatens to fight with them in order to gain attention from others.

Replacement Behavior: Describes what behavior could meet the same function or need for the student without being a problematic behavior. This is an indication of the desired behavior and a reflection of the stated goals.

For example:

1. Rather than throwing things during written work, Jane will learn to ask for help from the teacher and from peers when working in small groups, using the classroom materials in an appropriate manner.
2. Instead of pushing and threatening other students, Choy will learn to walk or stand appropriately in the hallway and during transition periods, using words, and gestures of greetings to indicate a wish to interact and gain attention.

Strategies: This indicates what must be done to accommodate the student in acquiring the desired behavior. The team should ask themselves whether the behavior will improve if any of the following are changed with regard to behavior occurrence: the time, the place, the subject or activity, the people involved, the task, the routine, the expectations, or the equipment and materials.

Instructional Strategies: Identifies the necessary skills determined by the team that must be taught to the student in order for him to be successful and master the plan or goals outlined. This may include adding skills in the areas of communication (teaching words or phrases), social skills (instructing on coping strategies, teaching methods to reduce anxiety), academic skills (teaching certain subjects of base content), and study skills (helping with organization, test-taking techniques). The team should also include how these skills will be taught: modeling, independent practice, group instruction, guided practice, and so on.

Reinforcement: This section describes what the team members may do to increase or improve the desired or replacement behaviors, which therefore eliminates or reduces the targeted behavior. Reinforcement includes identifying the potential reinforcers (computer time, stickers), the criteria (exactly what must be done to earn the reinforcer), and the schedule (frequency of the reinforcer).

Use of Consequence Strategies: This section describes what the team members will specifically do to decrease the problematic behavior. This section may include verbal warnings, redirection, imposed penalties, positive practice, loss of incentive or privilege, or use of a level system.

Delivery System: In this section, the team describes how the student's behavior will be monitored, through the use of a token economy, a point system, a chart or tracking system, group contingency, and so on.

Progress Chart: Some plans include charts or data collection systems specifically designed for the student in order for team members or those implementing the plan to organize and collect on-going and consistent data. Team members can use a daily or weekly tally of behavior data and record the information used for the planned team review or interpret the data regularly to schedule unplanned reviews.

Analysis: When teams interpret the data on the progress of the student, they often describe it in narrative form at the end of the plan, so the behavior progress may be monitored and recorded. This helps in determining whether the implementation procedures are working, whether the problem behavior is increasing or decreasing, and whether the replacement behavior is occurring appropriately. Then the team decides whether the plan may be continued, modified, or adjusted based on this information.

After the team has conducted an FBA, they use the information to move toward the development of an effective and individualized Behavior Intervention Plan (BIP), which is more clearly outlined in the following section.

Behavior Intervention Plan

A **Behavior Intervention Plan** (BIP) is an additional document that accompanies an existing IEP. This record serves as an outline of the proposed positive behavioral support system for an individual student. It is based on the student's needs, the characteristics of the disability, and the Functional Behavior Assessment (FBA) conducted and is completed by the student's individual team members. A review of the observations and information gathered in the assessment process aid the team in making decisions about creating a proper plan to guide the student toward use of desired behaviors.

A typical BIP form includes the following:

Baseline Data Description: A brief overview in narrative format describes the student's present levels of performance pertaining to behaviors. It may include pertinent information about the student's cognitive abilities, communication skills, and social skills and the use of interventions already attempted.

Hypothesis Statement: This is a notation of what is expected of the student as a result of using this intervention. It is a brief narrative of what the team believes will be the outcome for the student by using this plan.

Behavior of Concern: This section discusses a select target behavior that the team has found through the FBA to be particularly troubling and one that has the most impact on the student's overall achievement. It may be one or more than one behavior, but research shows that when attempting to change a student's behavior, limiting the plan to only one or two behaviors is more effective. It takes most students about two weeks to comprehend the components of the proposed change, another two weeks to internalize the changes, and several weeks (2 to 4) to generalize the changes. Expecting too much change at one time can result in failure.

Behavior Defined: This is an explanation of the behavior as it crosses all settings and periods of the day. Identifying the antecedents and including a specific description of how the student performs this behavior will aid in the development of goals.

Intervention Goal: This portion identifies the manner in which the team will aid the student in reaching a goal of improvement or the elimination of this behavior. More than one goal for each behavior identified may be written. Goals must be specific and written in measurable terms that include the format of the progress check.

Intervention Plan: In this section the types of methods, strategies, or techniques that will be utilized to support the preferred behavior are listed. This includes any use of charts, equipment, reinforcements, or other materials that will help the student master the goals.

Instructional Strategies: This section identifies what can be done to support the student in changing or replacing the targeted behavior. This may include clarifying or reteaching expectations, routines, or skills; modifying the tasks, assignments, or environment; or providing additional personnel or equipment. The team may include any support of social skills, communication skills, study skills, or academic skills that will enhance the student's behavior changes.

Intervention Data Summary: In this section the team collects ongoing data of the student's progress in meeting the measurable behavior goals.

Follow-up Information: Any additional essential information is included, as well as an outline of when the plan will be reviewed. It includes the reason for a review and the criteria for reviewing the plan at other nonscheduled times.

Team Member Participants: A list of the team members who constructed the plan and a list of those people who will implement the plan should be included here.

Individual Transition Plan-ITP

Beginning at age 16, or younger if deemed appropriate by the IEP team, students with disabilities should have a designed plan that focuses on the transition from school to the adult community. A statement of the necessary transition services, to include, if appropriate, a statement of the interagency responsibilities, must be joined to the IEP as an Individual Transition Plan (ITP). This is a result-oriented process that drives the component of the student's program to prepare for the future.

An **Individual Transition Plan** is the program designed by the team to ensure that the student is prepared for living in a community. This plan is based on non-bias assessments, and the areas of need are identified while the student is still in school so he may access support and educational services to improve those areas. Appropriate school personnel, family members, and community agencies are included in this plan development, and the student should always be invited as a participating member. This team creates not only the plan for the student, but seeks resource identification and pursues service implementation as they work together to organize and facilitate a smooth transition. The areas addressed on an ITP include employment, continued education, daily living, health, leisure, communication, and self-determination/advocacy.

Any number of highly effective and reliable assessments may be used to identify the student's needs, preferences, and interests. A Functional Vocational Evaluation refers to the assessment designed to target future vocational goals for the student with the disability. This evaluation is conducted by a special education teacher, a school counselor, a vocational instructor, or a community agency staff member in an individualized manner, often in a natural environment. The results shared at an ITP meeting support the team in making efficient and appropriate decisions.

Transition Services

According to federal law, transition services are comprised of a coordinated set of activities for a student with a disability that

- are designed in an outcome-oriented process.
- promote movement from school to post-school activities.
- include post-secondary education, vocational training, integrated employment, adult education, adult services, independent living, or community participation.

These services are

- based on the individual student's needs, preferences, and interests.
- structured by **instruction, related services, community experiences, employment,** and other **post-school adult living** objectives.
- inclusive of the acquisition of daily living skills and a functional vocational evaluation.

Transition services are those required in order for the student to achieve the independent level he is most capable of and to meet the interests and preferences for a satisfying life.

- **instruction:** The school lessons specifically intended to provide a transition service and vocational information or training.
- **related services:** Those services necessary to support the student in the disability areas and to allow the student to benefit from special education services (most often the same as on the IEP).
- **community experiences:** The instructional lessons and actual events that may occur in the community in the most natural environment and allow the student to practice and generalize skills.
- **employment:** Includes actual work experiences, such as part-time work, full-time work in the community, enlisting in a military branch, or seeking vocational training and skills.
- **postschool adult living:** Includes those services that prepare a student for adult responsibilities, such as learning about daily living expenses, monetary budgets, employment, and adult documents.

A transition services form or ITP document may include the following:

- **proposed date:** The planned date of the student's exit from school, which means special education services are terminated and adult services begin.

- **instruction content/goals:** May include study skills, training, self-advocacy training, studies on career planning, job interview skills.

- **community experiences content/goals:** Job shadowing, volunteer experiences, career explorations on the site, organized activities, recreation/sports.

- **employment and post school living content/goals:** Generally adult services, how to prepare/secure employment documents, work experience education, part-time or full-time employment, military involvement.

- **related/instructional services content/goals:** May be reflected in vocational education, language-speech services, adapted physical education, counseling/guidance/mental health.

- **daily living skills content/goals:** May include personal hygiene, domestic skills, money management, recreation, and social interaction.

- **statement of adult lifestyle plan:** To develop the status or desire of the life the student and family hope to achieve, the team should consider any needs for postsecondary education or vocational training, integrated employment issues, participation in adult/continuing education, adult services to support the student, level of expected independence in living skills, and community participation.

- **transition activities:** May be conducted by the student or accomplished by the school, the family, or agency to provide a needed transition service in a specific area, fulfill a goal, or support the student in moving toward a planned lifestyle.

- **agency statement of involvement:** Although agencies may be involved at any level of the plan, there may be a separate statement that defines the participation, but it is not required.

- **Age of Majority:** In some states, the age of majority transfers the rights to the student when he reaches the majority age. The student must be informed of these rights one year prior to the majority age in that state, and it must be documented on the IEP. This is important for ITP preparation, since a majority age student does not need to include his parents in the planning or process, unless he prefers or is unable to perform independently (which must be determined through court action).

Due Process Rights of Parents

According to the federal special education law, schools are to involve parents in their child's education, when the child has a disability, as an equal partner on the team. The team is the decision-making body charged with the task of developing an appropriate program for the child, based on assessment results and evaluation measures and materials. The collaboration of school personnel/professionals with parents is a unique aspect of the education programs for students with disabilities.

Schools are to ensure that parents have a role in the assessment process and any IEP meetings to ensure that all aspects of the student's disability are reviewed and the proper services are in place. Discussing the types of related and supplementary services (speech therapy, transportation, assistive technology) analyzing the suitable placement for services (general education class, resource class, and so on) as well as developing the program (levels of performance, goals, evaluations) are all consistent with the focus of mandates for parent involvement.

A school and parent relationship, based on respect, trust, and clear communication, is very important, as disagreements or failure to comply may result in costly and time-consuming mediations and court proceedings. To guide schools and parents in meeting the regulations regarding the participation of parents is a set of **due process rights,** also referred to as **procedural safeguards.** These rights entitle parents to

1. request or refuse an evaluation for special education.
2. request an individual and independent evaluation at school expense.
3. participate in all IEP (ITP) meetings and decisions.
4. disagree with IEP plan and decisions.
5. appeal all decisions made by the school.
6. review and amend the IEP every year.
7. review and examine all school records on their child.
8. guarantee that the child is educated in the least restrictive environment.
9. cooperative efforts on behalf of the school for all special education issues.